Lecture Notes in Computer Science 6580

Commenced Publication in 1973
Founding and Former Series Editors:
Gerhard Goos, Juris Hartmanis, and Jan van Leeuwen

W0192946

Shmuel Katz   Mira Mezini
Christine Schwanninger   Wouter Joosen (Eds.)

Transactions on Aspect-Oriented Software Development VIII

 Springer

Editors-in-Chief

Shmuel Katz
The Technion
Department of Computer Science
Haifa 32000, Israel
E-mail: katz@cs.technion.ac.il

Mira Mezini
Darmstadt University of Technology
Department of Computer Science
64289 Darmstadt, Germany
E-mail: mezini@informatik.tu-darmstadt.de

Guest Editors

Christine Schwanninger
Siemens AG, Corporate Technology
Software and System Architectures
91050 Erlangen, Germany
E-mail: christa.schwanninger@siemens.com

Wouter Joosen
Katholieke Universiteit Leuven
Department of Computer Science
3001 Heverlee, Belgium
E-mail: wouter.joosen@cs.kuleuven.be

ISSN 0302-9743 (LNCS)   e-ISSN 1611-3349 (LNCS)
ISSN 0302-9743 (TAOSD)   e-ISSN 1611-3349 (TAOSD)
ISBN 978-3-642-22030-2   ISBN 978-3-642-22031-9 (eBook)
DOI 10.1007/978-3-642-22031-9
Springer Heidelberg Dordrecht London New York

Library of Congress Control Number: 2011929866

CR Subject Classification (1998): D.2, F.3, D.3, H.4, I.6, K.6

Typesetting: Camera-ready by author, data conversion by Scientific Publishing Services, Chennai, India

Printed on acid-free paper

Springer is part of Springer Science+Business Media (www.springer.com)

Editorial

Welcome to Volume VIII of the Transactions on Aspect-Oriented Software Development. This volume begins with two papers that were regular submissions.

The first, "A Model-Driven Framework for Aspect Weaver Construction", by Suman Roychoudhury, Jeff Gray, and Frédéric Jouault, uses the principles of Model-Based Engineering to construct language weavers for various programming languages with a language transformation approach. Models are used to capture the concepts of aspect-oriented language constructs and are then transformed to concrete weavers.

The second paper, "A System of Patterns for Reusable Aspect Libraries", by Maarten Bynens, Eddy Truyen, and Wouter Joosen, provides a comprehensive collection of reusable design patterns for aspects. The framework consists of an architectural pattern, four design patterns, and associated programming idioms as well as guidelines for deciding among available options.

These are followed by a special section on Industrial Applications of Aspect Technology with guest editors Christine Schwanninger and Wouter Joosen, under the management of one of the co-editors-in-chief, Shmuel Katz. The background and the approaches of the special section, including the topics of the papers included, are described in the guest editors' foreword. The first paper in this section is an invited introductory paper on the uses of aspects in industry, by Ramnivas Laddad, which is followed by four papers on a variety of applications of aspects in industry, in widely differing commercial contexts. We hope that the insights presented will be of value to potential and existing industrial users, as well as of interest to researchers concerned with overcoming practical obstacles to using aspects. We thank the guest editors for their effort in producing such a high-quality special section.

During 2011 a special section on Modularity Concepts in Programming Languages is scheduled, and will be guest edited by Gary Leavens and Klaus Ostermann. This special section will highlight original and innovative modularity concepts. Of course, we continue to encourage regular submissions on all topics connected to modularity and the development of aspect-oriented software, especially when a single system decomposition does not adequately treat all concerns.

We thank the editorial board for their continued guidance and input on the policies of the journal, the choice of special issues, and associate-editorship of regular submissions. Thanks are also due to the reviewers, who volunteer significant time, despite their busy schedules, to ensure the quality of articles published in the journal. Most importantly, we wish to thank the authors who have submitted papers to the journal so far.

February 2011   Shmuel Katz and Mira Mezini
                                                        Co-Editors-in-Chief

Industrial Applications of Aspect Technology
Guest Editors' Foreword

Technologies for aspect oriented software development (AOSD) have been around for more than a decade now and programming support in particular has been experimented by many, not only by researchers and academic practitioners. In fact, AO has been applied in many research projects, and also in many industrial pilots, trials, and applications. Many of these experiments and applications have remained invisible on the radar of the research community that typically wishes to know more about such activities and aims at sharing a better understanding about what works and what needs further investigation.

Although it is inherently hard – actually impossible – to measures all the activities that assess and illustrate industry adoption, some industry tracks in the AOSD conference program have yielded substantial evidence of real-world applications of AOSD (see e.g. http://aosd.net/2011/past_confer.html) and some recent publications (e.g. Aspect-Oriented Software Development in Practice: tales from AOSD-Europe, IEEE Computer, February 2010, pp 19-26, A Rashid) confirm this observation – although the input remains anecdotal.

In search of more evidence, lessons learned, and especially feedback that can help the community move forward, we issued a call for contributions to this special section on Industrial Applications of Aspect Technology.

The aim was to collect examples, experience reports and success stories of applications of aspect technologies in industry, as well as work inspired by AOSD but not explicitly named as such. We solicited descriptions of successful solutions using, building, extending, or integrating AOSD technologies.

We were looking for papers written from the perspective of applying AOSD in a real-world, industrial environment. Therefore, the criteria for acceptance were fundamentally different from those typically used in academic work. Instead of the novelty of the applied approach and the completeness of the literature survey, we were interested in industrial relevance, lessons learned, and the evaluation of these insights motivated through experience in a real-world setting.

Finally, we can present four articles that each cover different industry-grade applications, including a telecommunication platform, a framework for embedding user assistance in independently developed applications, a platform for digital publishing, and a framework for program code analysis and manipulation.

We received eight submissions, each reviewed by up to five peers. We finally accepted the four that best showed real industrial applications. While the quality of the papers was overall very good, only half of them met our specific goal to prove applicability of AO in industrial settings. In addition we asked Ramnivas Laddad, one of the best known practitioners in the field, to provide his view on aspect orientation.

Like many good ideas, Aspect-Oriented Programming had to go through the well-known Gartner Hype Cycle, and survived! Ramnivas Laddad tells the story of AO's most prominent language in his invited contribution, **A Real-world Perspective of AOP**. He discusses the early market acceptance of AspectJ, the impact of platform support in Spring and how AspectJ made its way from an exciting new hype topic to a valuable technology in enterprise computing.

The regular contributions all describe non-trivial applications of AOSD, and refer to some the most popular aspect-oriented programming languages:

Tackling the Challenges of Integrating 3rdParty Software Using AspectJ by *Uwe Hohenstein and Michael C. Jaeger.* This paper describes the application of aspects in a typical industry project. A system that is not designed for aspects experiences severe architectural challenges that would be expensive or risky to solve with "conventional" technologies. Aspect orientation comes in handy as a powerful tool for the architect to overcome critical situations. In the case described the use of aspect technology has been triggered by the need to deal with performance and stability in a late stage of the development of a service-oriented telecommunication platform at Siemens AG.

Puma: An Aspect-Oriented Code Analysis and Manipulation Framework for C and C++ by *Matthias Urban, Daniel Lohman, and Olaf Spinczyk.* This paper describes a framework for the development of applications that analyze and transform C or C++ source code. The paper not only documents why aspects have proven helpful in the design of this complex system, they also illustrate the maturity of the AspectC++ technology. In addition, and based on their experience, the authors present and motivate useful AspectC++ idioms.

Building a Digital Publishing Platform Using AOSD, Experiences and Lessons Learned by *Dimitri Van Landuyt, Steven Op de beeck, Eddy Truyen, and Pierre Verbaeten.* This paper discusses the development of a platform for publishers who produce digital newspapers alongside traditional broadcast channels and printed press. The authors show how aspect-orientation increases the variability of optional features during the engineering from requirements to run-time. The paper also shows the implementation and deployment of the system using an industry-class aspect-oriented middleware platform, the JBoss application server with JBoss AOP.

An Aspect-Oriented Tool Framework for Developing Process-Sensitive Embedded User Assistance Systems by *Bedir Tekinerdoğan, Serap Bozbey, Yavuz Mester, Erdem Turançiftci, and Levent Alkışlar.* This paper discusses a non-trivial application of integrating context-sensitive user assistance in multiple, independently-developed applications. An aspect-oriented framework combined with dedicated tool support proved to reduce cost not only at development but also at run-time, for both newly-developed and legacy applications. This work has been conducted and validated in the context of the Turkish electronics company Aselsan.

It is not surprising that the majority of the results focus on the use of programming technologies; only one paper reaches out to aspect-oriented software architecture. Programming languages are still the most visible results of AOSD for the industry. The languages covered are AspectJ, AspectC++, and JBoss AOP, and it is those three that still have the most visible impact in industry. The work in other disciplines, like architecture, requirements engineering, and testing, has made its way into industry less obviously, for example in patterns, tools, or methods for handling crosscutting concerns. Many AO-inspired works are no longer attributed to aspect orientation; even though they grew in exactly that spirit. In effect, we feel that the section illustrates the versatility that definitely characterizes the AOSD adoption process.

In retrospect, we have found the creation of this special section a non-trivial exercise, and especially non-standard for the research community. The outcome however, is a representative sample of what has happened "out there", yet probably only a small tip of the iceberg. Indeed, it remains hard and non-trivial to produce the output we are looking for – especially in times when industry is experiencing tough challenges. Academia rarely has access to the real industry applications, while industry folks hardly have the time to write or even review publications on experience with aspect orientation. AO has influenced many disciplines, but has not developed a community of dedicated consultants that takes over the task of publication, like in other disciplines.

Therefore, special thanks must go to both, the authors and to the reviewers of this special section that took the time to share their experience with us. All their efforts have been greatly appreciated.

December 2010   Christine Schwanninger
                                                        Wouter Joosen

Editorial Board

Table of Contents

Special Focus: Industrial Applications of Aspect Technology

A Model-Driven Framework for
Aspect Weaver Construction

Suman Roychoudhury[1], Jeff Gray[2], and Frédéric Jouault[3]

[1] Tata Research Development and Design Center, Pune 411013, India
suman.roychoudhury@tcs.com
[2] University of Alabama, Department of Computer Science
Tuscaloosa, AL 35487, USA
gray@cs.ua.edu
[3] AtlanMod (INRIA & EMN), Nantes, France
frederic.jouault@inria.fr

Abstract. Aspect orientation has been used to improve the modularization of crosscutting concerns that emerge at different levels of software abstraction. Although initial research was focused on imparting aspect-oriented (AO) capabilities to programming languages, the paradigm was later on extended to software artifacts that appear at higher levels of abstraction (e.g., models). In particular, the Model-Driven Engineering (MDE) paradigm has largely benefitted from the inclusion of aspect-oriented techniques. In a converse way, we believe it may also be productive to investigate how MDE techniques can be adopted to benefit the development of aspect-oriented tools. The main objective of this paper is to show how MDE techniques can be used to improve the construction of aspect weavers for General-Purpose Languages (GPLs) through reusable models and transformations. The approach described in the paper uses models to capture the concepts of various Aspect-Oriented Programming (AOP) language constructs at a metamodeling level. These models are then mapped to concrete weavers for GPLs through a combination of higher-order model transformation and program transformation rules. A generic extension to the framework further supports reusability of artifacts among weavers during the construction process. Aspect weavers for FORTRAN and Object Pascal have been constructed using the framework, and their features evaluated against several case study applications.

Keywords: model transformation, program transformation, model engineering, aspect-oriented software development, generative programming.

1 Introduction

The history of software development paradigms suggests that a new paradigm often has its genesis in programming languages and then moves up to design and analysis (e.g., structured programming preceded structured design and analysis, and object-oriented programming predated object-oriented design and modeling). This same pattern can also be observed with respect to aspect orientation. Most of the early work on aspects was heavily concentrated on issues at the coding phase of the software

S. Katz et al. (Eds.): Transactions on AOSD VIII, LNCS 6580, pp. 1–45, 2011.

lifecycle [1], and gradually propagated to other phases (e.g., requirement, design / modeling [2, 3, 4]). Similar to the benefits that aspects can offer to modeling, we believe there are distinct advantages that Model-Driven Engineering (MDE) [5] can provide to impart aspect-oriented capabilities to programming languages. Specifically, we have been constructing aspect weavers for various programming languages using a program transformation approach. From our experience, we have found that MDE provides a capability to isolate the dependence on specific transformation engines and enable the generation of aspect weavers from high-level models. The next subsection outlines the challenges of creating aspect weavers that we have observed from our experience.

1.1 Challenges of Aspect Weaver Construction

As a result of programming language research over the past fifty years, a veritable "Tower of Babel" exists with multiple billions of lines of legacy code maintained in hundreds of different languages [6]. In fact, legacy languages are estimated to account for a large percentage of existing production software [7]. Yet, the majority of Aspect-Oriented Programming (AOP) [1] research is focused on just a few modern languages, such as Java. A generalized approach that brings aspects to legacy software is still missing. A naïve proposal would attempt to migrate legacy code into a modern object-oriented language like Java, such that existing tools (e.g., AspectJ [8]) could be applied. However, such a proposition is often not possible due to technical, cultural, and political concerns within the institution that owns the legacy code [7]. Rather than bringing the code to existing Java-based weavers, an alternative is to take AOP principles to the legacy languages and tool environments. Given the large number of languages in use, a solution that mitigates the effort needed to create each new weaver, is more desirable than an approach that manually recreates a weaver from scratch for each legacy language.

There are several key challenges towards providing an initial methodology that allows usage of aspects in languages other than Java. We have identified four main obstacles toward adoption of aspects for legacy software. The first two challenges (Challenge C1 and C2) are not the primary contribution of this paper and have been addressed in the past with existing technologies. A summary of these challenges are:

- *Challenge C1 - The Parser Construction Problem:* Building a parser for a toy language, or a subset of an existing language, is not difficult. But, designing a parser that is capable of handling millions of lines of production legacy code is an onerous task. As observed by Lämmel and Verhoef [6], the dominant factor in producing a renovation tool, is constructing the parser. Software developers who want to explore modern restructuring capabilities in legacy systems will require industrial-scale parsers to allow them to evaluate the feasibility of adoption within their organization. Incomplete parsers for small research prototypes will not scale and may leave a negative first impression of aspects.

- *Challenge C2 - The Weaver Construction Problem:* When a new program restructuring or modularization idea is conceived (e.g., AOP), it is often desired to impart the idea to older legacy applications. In order to realize such an objective, a capability is needed to perform the underlying transformations and rewrites on a syntax-tree or on an abstract model. This requires considerable effort to provide a sound and scalable infrastructure for program transformation.

Challenge C1 and *Challenge C2* can be addressed by using program transformation techniques [9, 12]. Firstly, full-fledged parsers available in program transformation frameworks can be reused to assist in constructing aspect weavers. Secondly, program transformation engines generally have support for low-level rewriting (i.e., by using term-rewriting or graph-rewriting) that can be used to construct aspect weavers for multiple GPLs.

However, it is often the case that the integration efforts to support a core set of transformations are repeated for each language to which the new idea is applied. Such repetition of effort is unfortunate and strongly suggests the need for further generalization of transformation objectives. Moreover, the abstraction level at which most transformation systems operate is too low for software developers who are familiar with the concepts of AOP, but unaware of the accidental complexities of program transformation. In our previous work [12], we provided initial solutions to the first two challenges related to parsing and weaving for a specific language (i.e., Object Pascal). The main contributions of this paper focus on the two additional challenges that are introduced as follows:

- *Challenge C3 – Accidental Complexity of Transformation Specifications:* An inherent difficulty associated with using program transformation engines is the low-level of abstraction at which a transformation rule is specified. Transformation rules typically quantify over the grammar elements (e.g., terminals, production rules, non-terminals) of a programming language rather than the conceptual elements in the language domain (e.g., objects, methods). Therefore, it is highly desirable to hide the accidental complexities of program transformation systems from AOP end-users and instead provide a conceptual aspect layering on top of an underlying program transformation system.

- *Challenge C4 – Language-Independent Generalization of Transformation Objectives:* Although most program transformation engines provide a general toolkit with pre-existing parsers, the transformation rules that actually perform the desired restructuring are encoded to the productions of a specific concrete syntax (i.e., grammar of base language). Thus, all the effort that is placed into creating the transformations to enable weaving for a given language cannot be reused for another language. A key research contribution of this paper is an approach that adopts an abstract syntax to increase the level of reuse of aspect transformation rules across multiple languages. The contribution uses higher-order transformations to evolve abstract transformations into more specialized versions that are specific to a particular programming language.

In Section 2, *Challenge C3* is addressed by providing an aspect layering on top of a program transformation system. This aspect layering is realized by using model-driven language engineering techniques [21]. In particular, a model-driven front-end is built on top of a program transformation engine that transforms an aspect model to a model that represents the concept of program transformation rules. Such a convenience layer assists in removing the idiosyncrasies of the underlying transformation technology. Section 3 shows how the model-driven front-end is generalized to accommodate a family of related GPLs. This is achieved by using specific techniques like metamodel extension [22]. Within the context of the generalized framework of Section 3, *Challenge C4* is addressed by constructing a library of generic higher-order model transformations that make use of the concrete syntax of the base language to generate lower-order program transformation rules.

We applied our approach by constructing aspect weavers for languages like Object Pascal (a language popularized by Borland's Delphi) and FORTRAN 90. Both weavers share a generic front-end and the core set of aspect weaving transformations was reused during the construction process for each weaver.

Currently, the framework addresses the domain representing the imperative class of languages and is not evaluated against logic based or functional languages like Prolog or ML. From our understanding, the generalization should be restricted within a particular class of languages (e.g., imperative, functional, or logic based) to extract maximum commonality. The results presented in this research are based on the assumption that these languages share a certain degree of commonality and should be regarded as a stepping stone for a more comprehensive solution that requires extensive validation.

1.2 Overview of Paper Contents

The next section of the paper introduces our model-driven framework for constructing aspect weavers. Section 3 discusses generalization of the model-driven weaving framework. In Section 4, a series of case studies demonstrating Aspect Pascal and Aspect FORTRAN illustrate what can be achieved with the approach. A brief comparison of related work is summarized in Section 5, with concluding remarks, lessons learned, and future work appearing in Section 6.

2 Model-Driven Aspect Weaving Framework

This section introduces an extensible and scalable model-driven framework for developing aspect weavers for general-purpose programming languages (GPLs). The framework can be used to construct weavers for object-oriented languages (e.g., C++, Java or Object Pascal) and older legacy languages (e.g., C, FORTRAN or COBOL). Figure 1 represents an overview of the model-driven aspect weaving framework.

The scalability of the framework is provided by using a powerful program transformation engine (PTE); namely, the Design Maintenance System (DMS) [9], which represents the back-end of our framework (*item 3* in *Figure 1*). DMS provides support for mature language tools (e.g., lexers, parsers, and analyzers) for more than a dozen programming languages. It has been used to parse several million lines of code written in any of these languages. The adoption of DMS as a back-end provides a solution to *Challenge C1 (parser construction problem)* through immediate availability of industrial-scale parsers. DMS also provides functionality for transforming a program after it has been parsed. Through transformation rules and a rich API of transformation functions, DMS offers a solution to *Challenge C2 (weaver construction problem)*. Thus, *Challenge C1* and *Challenge C2* as enumerated in Section 1.1 are gratuitously resolved through adoption of a mature program transformation engine into the weaver construction framework [12]. However, the low-level representation of transformation rules introduces new accidental complexities that make it difficult for programmers to specify aspects at this level.

A model-driven front-end (*item 1* in *Figure 1*) raises the level of abstraction and hides the accidental complexities that are generally associated with a program transformation system. The core of the framework is a higher-order transformation rule generator (*item 2* in *Figure 1*) that produces program transformation rules from an aspect program. The aspect code is initially parsed by the front-end and later processed by the program transformation rule generator. The result is a set of generated program transformation rules that accomplish weaving of the source aspect for a specific language. As shown in Figure 1, the program transformation back-end takes the generated transformation rules and the source program as its inputs and weaves aspects into the source program to produce the transformed target program. The model-driven front-end offers a solution to *Challenge 3 (accidental complexity)* because it hides the complexity of using a program transformation system in its native form.

The following subsections discuss each of the key components (shown as items 1, 2, and 3) of this framework in detail, including their primary benefits and internal mechanisms. The subsections also outline the reasons behind choosing each of these components and explain why it is desirable to follow an MDE philosophy to construct aspect weavers for GPLs. The following subsection introduces the technical details of a weaver built from a program transformation engine.

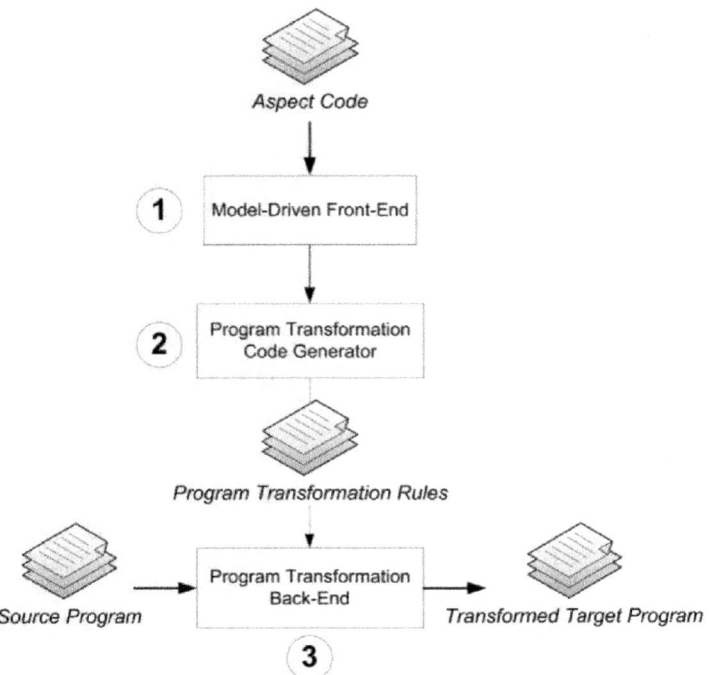

Fig. 1. Overview of our model-driven aspect weaver framework

2.1   Background – Program Transformation Back-End

Fradet and Südholt were among the first to observe that aspect weaving can be performed using a general transformation framework for a specific programming language [10]. Similarly, Aßmann and Ludwig provided an early demonstration of aspect weaving using graph rewriting [11]. Most PTEs support a term-rewriting or graph-rewriting engine such that transformation rules can be constructed that realize the weaving of aspects into a source program. In our previous work, we demonstrated how a PTE can be used to construct an aspect weaver for Object Pascal [12]. Instead of re-inventing a new weaving engine for each new programming language of interest, our objective is to leverage a PTE that provides powerful pattern matching, and term-rewriting capabilities required for aspect weaving.

There are several program transformation engines available with each having their own advantages and disadvantages. In addition to DMS, other popular examples include ASF+SDF [13] and TXL [14]. We chose DMS for the back-end of our framework because of the maturity of the tool (e.g., DMS has been used on several large-scale industrial software renovation projects [15]) and the immediate availability of a large collection of pre-constructed *domains* (i.e., lexers, parsers, and analysis tools) for various programming languages. From our survey of the available transformation tools, DMS was the only tool to supply an Object Pascal and FORTRAN domain that was ready for immediate use to support our experimentation.

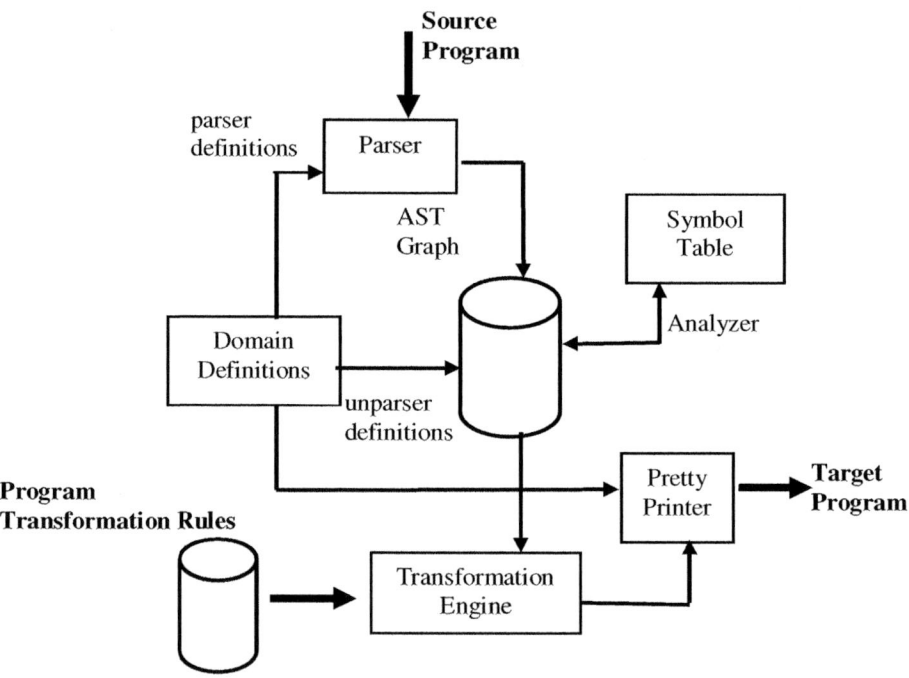

Fig. 2. Overview of back-end transformation process

Figure 2 presents an overview of the back-end transformation process (previously shown as item 3 in Figure 1). The program transformation rule (shown in general in Figure 2 with a specific example in Listing 1) is written in the DMS Rule Specification Language (RSL) and processed by the back-end transformation engine to perform the actual rewriting. RSL provides basic primitives for describing the numerous transformations that are to be performed across the entire code base of an application. An RSL program consists of declarations of patterns, rules, conditions, and rule sets using the external form (i.e., concrete syntax) defined by a language domain.

```
default base domain ObjectPascal.
private rule insert_probe(stmt_list: statement_list):
function_body  →  function_body
= "begin \stmt_list end"  →
   "begin WriteLn(\"Entering Method\"); \stmt_list end".
public ruleset TraceAllFunctions = {insert_probe}
```

Listing 1: A simple example of a program transformation rule that traces function executions

Although term-rewriting has several application domains (e.g., code migration, code refactoring or program refinement), the particular example in Listing 1 highlights an aspect-oriented style. The first line of this transformation rule resolves the *domain* (i.e., language) to which the rule can be applied. In this case, a tracing probe is inserted before the execution of all functions written in Object Pascal. The statement list that appears inside of a function body is passed as a parameter to this rule. Note that a rule is typically used as a rewrite specification that maps from a left-hand side (source) syntax tree expression to a right-hand side (target) syntax tree expression (syntactically denoted by "→" in RSL). The insert_probe rule matches all function body declarations in the source program and adds a WriteLn statement before the execution of the original statement list. Rules can be combined into rule sets that form a transformation strategy by defining a collection of transformations that can be applied to a syntax tree. As shown in Figure 2, these transformations along with the source program are syntactically checked and statically analyzed to ensure the expected weaving behavior. However, RSL rules are typically hardcoded and dependent on the grammar of the base language. For instance, all text highlighted in bold in Listing 1 corresponds either to terminal or to non-terminal symbols in the Object Pascal grammar.

Challenges of Program Transformation Engine Usage

Program transformation engines (PTEs) offer several advantages, especially with respect to reusable parsers and a weaving engine. However, to provide advanced aspect weaving capabilities (e.g., like that of AspectJ), the underlying rewrite rules can become significantly more complex than what is shown in Listing 1. For example, to provide reflective capabilities like thisJoinPoint or to perform signature matching with wildcards, more complicated transformation rules are required. Such rules generally use exit functions to do static analysis on the underlying AST [12]. This requires a thorough understanding of the various term rewriting semantics specific to a particular PTE. Moreover, the rewrite rules are often tied to the grammar of the base language (as highlighted in bold in Listing 1), which impedes reusability when the base language changes. Thus, using a tool like DMS to construct aspect weavers requires knowledge of the base language grammar (concrete syntax), and of the core machinery provided by DMS. However, the design decision to use a transformation engine is particularly useful to *challenge C1* and *C2*. Hence, a suitable solution is desired such that program transformation systems can be used not only by language researchers, but by a larger audience through mainstream software development. In our previous research in constructing an aspect weaver for Object Pascal using DMS [12], we observed these broader challenges and recognized that an appropriate front-end support alongside a systematic code generator was needed to bring program transformation systems closer to mainstream software development. The proper selection of an appropriate front-end and program transformation rule generator can hide the accidental complexity associated with PTEs. Nevertheless, aspect weavers can still leverage the power of PTEs to perform the lower-level complex code transformation. In the following subsection, we introduce our investigation into a model-driven front-end and discuss the primary benefits offered by MDE in the overall context of the framework.

2.2 Model-Driven Front-End

There are many ways to design the front-end of an aspect language. In some examples, the language format is expressed in raw XML [18], but in other cases it is expressed in a more sophisticated declarative language [19]. Through our investigation in the design of various aspect languages, we realized that the declarative nature of expressing aspects (e.g., as popularized by pointcuts in AspectJ) has a common language-independent characteristic. For example, the concepts of join points, pointcuts and advice can be adapted to many aspect language designs within the same paradigm. Metamodels can precisely capture these concepts and their relations.

In addition, a model-driven front-end (item 1 in Figure 1) is well-suited for abstracting the various semantics associated with PTEs. MDE provides an abstraction layer that can be mapped down to lower-level transformation rules. Combining the technical spaces of MDE and PTE offers more possibilities than each considered separately.

Figure 3 shows an excerpt of the abstract syntax of an aspect language in the form of a metamodel represented as a collection of three class diagrams. This metamodel illustrates the specification of Aspect Pascal, which is an aspect language we defined for Object Pascal. An aspect described in this language consists of `Pointcuts` and `Advice`. They together constitute the fundamental elements for defining an aspect-oriented language (influenced by the asymmetric AspectJ style). As evident in Figure 3, an aspect can have multiple `pointcuts` and multiple `advice`.

An `Advice`, defined as an abstract class in the metamodel, can be further categorized as a `BeforeAdvice`, `AfterAdvice` or `AroundAdvice`. An advice can have advice parameters and an advice body (i.e., a list of statements). Every advice parameter has a type and an associated name that is used for passing the context information. Every advice statement conforms to the grammar of the base language. Because the back-end program transformation engine already has the parser/analyzer available for managing the base language, the body of the advice is typically delegated to the back-end for further processing. Such delegation of an advice body reduces the complexity of the metamodel by not including every possible program construct that belongs to the base GPL. These program fragments are referenced in the front-end metamodel as OpaqueStatements (i.e., statements that are not handled by the front-end). In addition to OpaqueStatement, there are other special statements: the loop statement and the proceed statement. The proceed statement is generally used in the bodies of an around advice and the loop statement is a new join point that captures additional weaving operations (e.g., monitoring timing statistics around a FORTRAN "do loop" for performance evaluation). An example of a loop statement is given in Section 4.

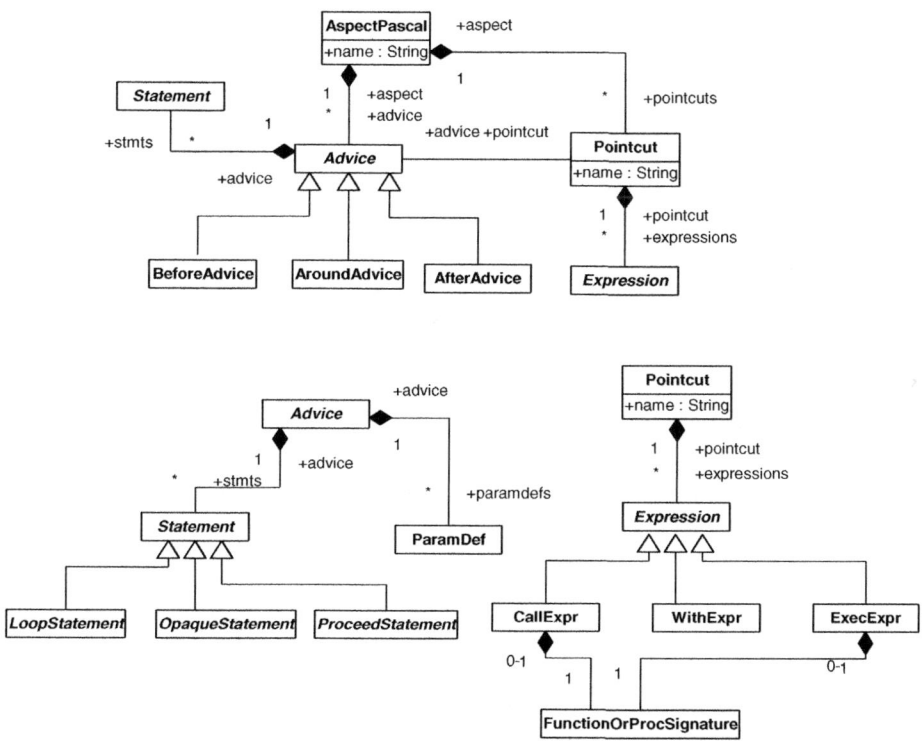

Fig. 3. Subset of Aspect Pascal metamodel represented as a class diagram

Pointcuts consist of pointcut expressions, which can, for instance, be further expressed as *call* expressions, *with* expressions or *execution* expressions. Pointcut expressions form the key for pattern matching in the lower-level transformation rule. All pointcut expressions are derived from the abstract Expression class. As seen in Figure 3, both the call and exec expressions are derived from Expression and both reference the type pattern `FunctionOrProcSignature`, which identifies the prototype declaration (i.e., signature) for a function or procedure defined in Object Pascal. This type pattern is particularly useful for pattern matching. Although `call` and `exec` are the two most common forms of pointcut expressions, new expressions can be experimented with and derived from the base `Expression` class template. For example, Object Pascal allows the definition of `with` expressions that are used to control the execution of code within a specific context. Other pointcut expressions available in the join point model of the base language can be similarly added to the metamodel of the front-end aspect language. *Wildcards* are also allowed and examples are given in Section 4.

The pointcut expressions are translated to RSL patterns or rules that do the actual pattern matching. The front-end AOP layer is simply a façade to the back-end PTE. It helps to hide the accidental complexity associated with PTEs (*Challenge C3*) and also provides a platform to experiment with new AOP language constructs that can be suitably translated to back-end rewrite rules. The translation mechanism that generates the back-end RSL rules from the front-end aspect language is explained in detail in Section 2.3 and Section 3.2.

Implementing the Front-End Aspect Language

The first step in implementing a front-end is to create a metamodel that defines the abstract syntax of the aspect language. The KM3 [20] (Kernel MetaMetaModel) is used for this purpose. Although other MDE tools can be used to define the metamodel, we chose KM3 because it has the added advantage of being independent of the concrete MDE technology (e.g., the Eclipse Modeling Framework or OMG's Meta-Object Facility). The example snippet in Figure 4 demonstrates how KM3 is used to define the Aspect Pascal metamodel.

Figure 4 shows a snippet of the KM3 specification used to implement the metamodel introduced in Figure 3. The `AspectPascal` class contains references to other classes; namely, the core elements `Pointcut` and `Advice`. The `oppositeOf` construct is used to maintain reverse navigational links for efficient traversal purposes required during model transformation (Section 2.3).

In addition to the abstract syntax shown as a metamodel in KM3, the concrete syntax of the aspect language is specified using a grammar-like notation - TCS [23] (Textual Concrete Syntax). Figure 5 illustrates how the concrete syntax of different metamodel elements (e.g., *Aspects*, *Pointcuts,* and *Advice*) is expressed in TCS. In TCS, every class represented in the KM3 specification has its corresponding template definition. It also introduces other terminal tokens like separators, brackets and semicolons that are required to describe the concrete syntax of the aspect language but are not captured in the abstract syntax of the metamodel. Thus, TCS gives the structure of the source aspect language. In addition, context information can also be passed and stored in the symbol table for further analysis. The choice of the particular MDE technology described in this paper (e.g., TCS, KM3, and ATL are part of the overall AMMA platform) is provided only as a proof of concept. Alternative model-driven technologies may be used to implement the aspect metamodel.

```
class AspectPascal extends LocatedElement {
    attribute name : String;
    reference domain container : Domain;
    reference pointcuts[1-*] container : Pointcut oppositeOf aspect;
    reference advice[1-*] container : Advice oppositeOf aspect;
}
class Pointcut extends Element {
    attribute name : String;
    reference aspect : AspectPascal oppositeOf pointcut;
    reference paramdefs[*] container : ParameterDef;
    reference exprs[1-*] container : Expression oppositeOf pointcut;
}
abstract class Advice extends LocatedElement {
    reference aspect : AspectPascal oppositeOf advice;
    reference pointcut : Pointcut;
    reference paramdefs[*] container : ParameterDef;
    reference stmts[1-*] container : Statement;
}
```

Fig. 4. KM3 specification (snippet) for Aspect Pascal

```
template AspectPascal main
        : "aspect" name "{" pointcut advice "}"
        ;
template Pointcut context addToContext
        : "pointcut" name "(" paramdefs{separator = ","} ")"
          ":" exprs {separator = "&&"} ";"
        ;
template Advice abstract;

template BeforeAdvice
        : "before" "(" paramdefs {separator = ","} ")" ":"
          ...
        ;
template AfterAdvice
        : "after"  "(" paramdefs {separator = ","} ")" ":"
          ...
        ;
```

Fig. 5. TCS specification (snippet) for Aspect Pascal

The front-end would be incomplete without appropriate code generators that transform the front-end aspect language to its corresponding target language. In our model-driven framework, the back-end is the transformation language of the PTE; specifically, the DMS RSL in our case. The following section demonstrates how RSL transformation rules are generated from the front-end aspect specification.

2.3 Program Transformation Rule Generator

The program transformation rule generator (shown as item 2 in Figure 1) represents the core of the framework and embodies a higher-order transformation (i.e., a model transformation rule is used to generate program transformation rules). As mentioned earlier, the front-end aspect language is only a façade to the back-end PTE and all pointcut declarations and advice code present in the source aspect language are eventually translated to target RSL code that consists of RSL patterns, external conditions, and rewrite rules. Therefore, the goal of the program transformation rule generator is to synthesize transformation engine specific weaving code (RSL) from the front-end representation defined by a higher-order aspect specification.

Target metamodel for RSL

In order to realize a systematic translation from a higher-order aspect language to a lower-order transformation language, it is necessary to define a metamodel for the back-end program transformation engine. The target RSL metamodel serves two basic purposes: firstly, it allows experimenting with new aspect languages (e.g., Aspect Ruby or Aspect FORTRAN) and new aspect constructs (e.g., loops) without changing the model for the back-end PTE. In this case, the commonalities of different aspect languages for various GPLs can be generalized in a generic aspect metamodel. The differences can be captured using metamodel extensions; however, no change is required for the target metamodel. This helps to improve the generality of the framework.

Secondly, instead of an ad hoc technique, a metamodel allows more sophisticated translations where complex pointcut expressions and join point shadows (areas in the source where join points may emerge) [40] from the front-end aspect language could be mapped correspondingly to patterns and rules in the back-end RSL language. The presence of a target metamodel provides an internal representation of the back-end transformation language (RSL) that can be used to validate the generated lower-order transforms. For future experimental purposes, the presence of a RSL metamodel may also permit bidirectional mappings (currently, the mapping is unidirectional, from Aspect-to-RSL). In such a scenario, given a generated RSL program as input, the corresponding aspect specification for a different GPL may be recovered, provided a mapping exists between RSL and the GPL.

To capture the essential concepts of the DMS RSL, an RSL metamodel has been created in KM3, illustrated by a class diagram in Figure 6. As noted earlier, RSL consists of elements like patterns, rules, conditions, and rule-sets, which are captured in this metamodel. The complete KM3 and TCS specification for the RSL metamodel is available at [30]. It should be noted that the target metamodel defines the essence (i.e., concepts and relations) of a domain without concern for semantics. In our case, the semantics of the various components of the source aspect metamodel is captured in the mapping to RSL defined as an ATL transformation. ATL [24] is the model transformation language of AMMA. The semantics of the aspect language is thus captured in terms of the semantics of RSL, which is in turn processed by DMS. Case studies are presented in Section 4, where complete scenarios describing this model-to-model transformation are explained with concrete examples.

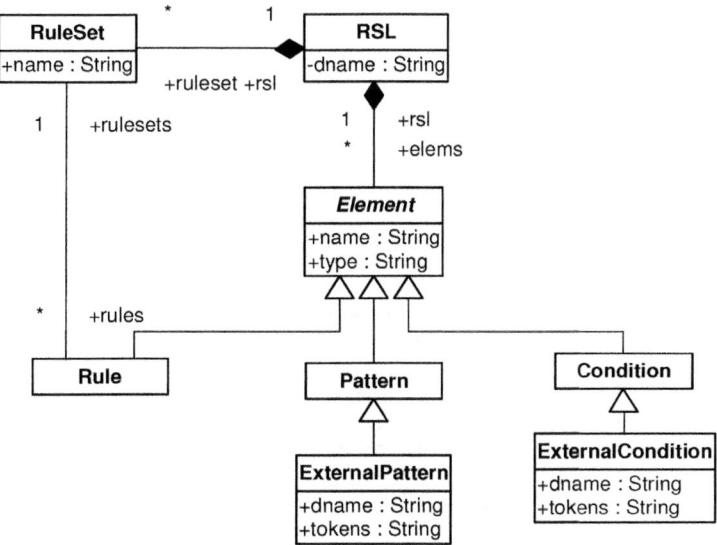

Fig. 6. Subset of the RSL metamodel (as a class diagram)

Model transformation using ATL

Given the definition of the source and target metamodels, it is possible to generate RSL program transformation rules from an aspect program using model transformations. Figure 7 explains the complete model transformation scenario in our framework. In this figure, M1, M2, and M3 are the three modeling levels in the grammarware [28] and MDE technical spaces (TS). From the grammarware TS, the front-end aspect source file is initially injected into a source aspect model using TCS. The aspect model is then transformed into a target RSL model using a model transformation defined in ATL. This ATL transformation forms the core of the program transformation rule generation process. After translation, the generated RSL model belonging to the MDE TS is extracted (using TCS) into the target RSL program in the grammarware TS.

To modularize the RSL generation process, the framework defines a library of ATL transformations with each transformation corresponding to a primitive pointcut specification (e.g., `call`, `execution`). For a given aspect, the corresponding ATL transformation rule is automatically invoked depending on the pointcut specification used in the aspect. The higher-order ATL transformation generates the lower-order RSL transformation that eventually performs the aspect weaving. The collective set of all higher-order model transformations is assembled in a transformation library that implements the semantics of the source aspect language.

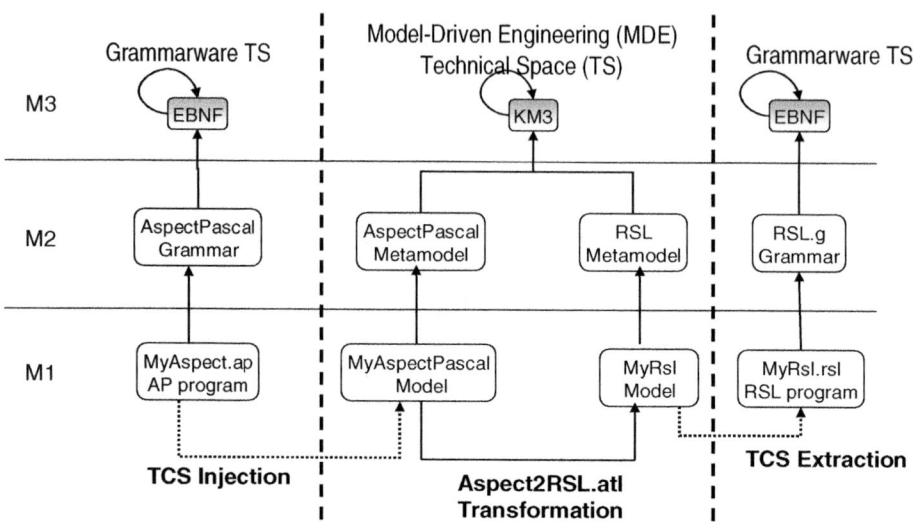

Fig. 7. Model transformation scenario for generating RSL rules from aspects

Figure 8 depicts a snippet of a sample ATL transformation from the core transformation library. This particular transformation evaluates a `call` expression in the source aspect, and generates the corresponding RSL transformation rule. The ATL helper function `EvalCallExpr` is used for this purpose. The transformation maps individual elements from the source aspect metamodel to the target RSL metamodel. For example, Aspect Pascal model elements like advice (Line 10, Figure 8) and pointcuts (Line 11, Figure 8) are mapped to RSL elements like patterns, conditions and rules (i.e., RSL elements in Figure 6). Similarly, *before* advice statements (Line 25, Figure 8) from the source aspect language are mapped to RSL patterns. The relationships between the source aspect model elements to the target RSL model elements can be one-to-one, one-to-many, many-to-one or many-to-many. This depends on the type of pointcut expressions used in the source aspect program.

It should be noted that the source metamodel to describe these pointcut expressions (see Section 2.2) is completely independent of the target RSL language. In addition, it is structurally and semantically similar to a traditional AOP language, like AspectJ. This metamodel captures all the essential concepts of AOP (as influenced by AspectJ) - join points, pointcuts and advice. The actual transformation on the source code is performed using RSL rules that are generated from the higher-order aspect language using ATL. These ATL transformations implement the semantics of the source aspect language and all corresponding mapping information from source to target are embedded in the ATL specifications.

```
 1. module AspectPascal2RSL;
 2. create OUT : RSL from IN : APascal;
 3. rule APascal2RSL {
 4.     from
 5.          s : APascal!APascal
 6.     to
 7.          t : RSL!RSL (
 8.              dname <- 'ObjectPascal',
 9.              elems <- Sequence {
10.                       s.advice,
11.                       s.pointcut->collect(e |
12.                           thisModule.EvalCallExpr(e)
13.                           ),
14.                           ...
15.              },
16.              ruleset <- rs
17.          ),
18.       rs : RSL!RuleSet (
19.              name <- s.name,
20.              rules <- s.pointcut->collect(e|e.name)
21.          )
22. }
23. rule BeforeAdvice2Pattern {
24.     from
25.          s : APascal!BeforeAdvice
26.     to
27.          t : RSL!Pattern (
28.              name <- 'before_advice_stmt_list'
29.              ptype <- 'statement_list',
30.              ptext <-   spt
31.          ),
32.       spt : RSL!SimplePatternText (
33.              ptext <- s.stmts->iterate(...)
34.          )
35. }
-- [original code omitted for brevity]
```

Fig. 8. ATL transformation (snippet) from Aspect Pascal to RSL

The generated RSL is not shown here because it is internal to the framework (i.e., users of the framework do not see any of the intermediate transformation rules); however, interested readers who want to view the generated artifacts may refer to the GenAWeave website [30], which represents the project webpage and includes video demonstrations, papers, and all of the source. In addition to the website reference, the case studies presented in Section 4 also serve as specific examples for describing the complete transformation scenario illustrated in this section.

Benefits of Using a Model-Driven Front-End

There are several advantages of using a model-driven front-end layered on top of a program transformation engine. PTEs typically work at a lower-level of abstraction and are a useful research tool for language researchers. Software developers who are not familiar with PTEs and willing to experiment with AspectJ- like languages will find it increasingly difficult to express aspects in the form of transformation (rewrite) rules. For example if one looks into the generated transformation rules as presented in [12, 30], it is obvious that the complexity of these rules is orders of magnitude higher than the declarative aspect specification that corresponds to the same rewrite rule. Moreover, the transformation rule forces the user to have detailed knowledge of the underlying grammar production rules and the associated parsing techniques. In other words, these minute details are the core accidental complexity that alienates PTEs from mainstream software development. In this research, one of the primary challenges (*Challenge C3*) has been to make PTEs available for general-purpose software maintenance and development. An MDE based approach helped us to realize this goal. By capturing the key concepts associated with AOP as higher-order models (e.g., as expressed in KM3/TCS) and using model transformation rules (ATL) to generate lower-order program transformation rules (RSL), the technique hides the accidental complexities of PTEs, but still leverages the powerful transformation capabilities required to carry out weaving. Thus, the end-user is oblivious to the low-level program transformation machinery and only works at a conceptual level he or she is familiar with. A model-driven front-end helped us to bridge the gap between PTE and AOP.

Remaining Challenges to be Addressed in the Framework

The model-driven weaver generation framework presented in this section offers a solution to the challenge of using a program transformation engine to implement an aspect weaver. The section provided a discussion of the key parts of the framework, including the front-end aspect language, the transformation rule generator and the back-end weaving engine. The context of the discussion was centered on the creation of a weaver for a single base language, such as Object Pascal, to address *Challenge C3 (accidental complexity)* from Section 1.1. However, an additional challenge remains. As mentioned in the beginning of this section, a program written in RSL or any other term-rewriting engine is typically tied to the grammar of the source program (i.e., the RSL example in Listing 1 has Object Pascal grammar productions appearing throughout the transformation rule). Moreover, there are variations in design from one aspect language to another, even if a common generic part is shared. Unless carefully designed, the front-end, the core transformation libraries, and the back-end modules are rendered unusable when constructing a new weaver in another context (i.e., a new aspect language or a new base programming language). The goal of any extensible framework is to not construct a single fixed solution (i.e., constructing each new weaver from scratch) after enough knowledge, time, and effort have been spent. The next section discusses how this framework was made more generic to support reuse in new contexts. Thus, instead of building a new weaver from scratch, the benefit from the experience gained in a previous construction can be reused and applied toward the construction of a new weaver for a programming language even in a different paradigm.

3   Extending to a Generic Framework

Generalizing the framework presented in Section 2 to accommodate a broad range of GPLs is challenging due to the dissimilarities among various programming languages. Yet, many languages in the same paradigm (e.g., structured or object-oriented) may share common concepts at an abstract level such that parts of the framework can be reused. Unfortunately, most aspect weavers are built from scratch with little emphasis on reusing the existing knowledge or framework already available for constructing a weaver for a particular GPL. Previous research towards constructing aspect weavers for multiple languages has been based on the following approaches:

- **Common Intermediate Language:** Weave.NET is a load-time weaver that allows aspects and components to be written in a variety of .Net based languages [18]. It takes an existing .Net binary component as input with crosscutting specifications provided in an XML file. The behavior (i.e., implementation-specific advice code) of an aspect is provided separately in another .Net assembly. Weave.NET recreates the input assembly, but in this regenerated version, join points are bound to behavior in the aspect assembly as specified in the XML aspect file. Because all transformations are done at the intermediate language (IL), it serves as a language-independent weaver. In addition to Weave.NET, Loom.Net [41] is another aspect weaving tool that targets the .Net framework. It uses metadata and reflection mechanisms to weave into the .Net assemblies.

- **Generic Source Model:** SourceWeave.Net uses a generic architecture that is built on top of CodeDOM, which is the .NET standard for representing source code models [17]. Using SourceWeave.NET, a developer can write base and aspect components in standard C#, VB.NET and J#. An XML descriptor file is used to specify the interaction between the aspects and representative components. The technique uses a mapping to identify join point shadows and uses a "pointcut-to-join point binding" to isolate parts of the source.

Comparative Discussion of AOP Frameworks to Support Multiple GPLs

Each of these representative approaches provides a distinguishing set of strengths and weaknesses. For example, Weave.Net offers a strong solution to *Challenge C1 (parser construction problem)* because of the availability of pre-existing industrial scale parsers within the .Net Framework. SourceWeave.Net is weak on *Challenge C1* due to the limited availability of CodeDOM providers beyond a handful of languages (e.g., mainly C#, J#, and VB.Net). However, both approaches are weak on *Challenge C3 (accidental complexity)* because of the reduced expressiveness (or increased verbosity) of raw XML to specify aspects in each of the frameworks.

The representation of the underlying abstract source model also contributes to several differences affecting the solutions to each challenge. Because of its reliance on CodeDOM, SourceWeave.Net has limitations in terms of expressiveness. C# maps reasonably well to CodeDOM, but that is not true for all GPLs. It remains to be determined if either CodeDOM or .Net CLI are applicable to a large class of legacy languages (e.g., COBOL, FORTRAN, C, or Object Pascal) whose language definitions are very different from the expectations of CLI or CodeDOM. Moreover, a considerable engineering effort would be required if all programming languages were forced to conform to a generic source model or compiled to a common IL. Further, such an approach would ignore all of the effort that has already been spent in constructing lexers, parsers, analyzers and other tools for these languages.

Another interesting tool that supports the use of language-independent abstractions of the base program is the Compose* compiler [44]. During compilation, the language-independent model of the base program is generated, which is then processed by the compiler for weaving aspects. The model is finally mapped back to the base program. Although the Compose* compiler does not aim to support multiple language front-ends, the same core can be used for multiple base languages.

While investigating a generic aspect weaving framework, we realized these challenges and discovered a solution whereby the model-driven weaver framework uses the existing parsers of DMS, but extracts the commonalities among these languages. Although such a framework does not automate all the tasks involved in creating an aspect weaver (i.e., making it language-independent), our generalized framework can considerably reduce the weaver construction effort by reusing the shared or common parts among different aspect weavers through abstract models and corresponding model transformations (please see Section 4.3 for a discussion of experimental results).

Moreover, because DMS provides support for 23 different programming languages (including legacy languages like COBOL, FORTRAN, and C), a generic front-end with a reusable code generator that translates our front-end aspect language to DMS RSL can make use of all the parsers and analyzers that are already available within each of the language domains supported by DMS. In addition, we may also consider changing the back-end if another PTE supports other languages that we would like to use. The solution approach introduced in this section addresses the obstacles toward weaver construction enumerated in *Challenge C4 (generalization of transformation objectives)*.

3.1 Support for a Generic Front-End

The first step towards a generalized model-driven weaver framework is to design a generic aspect front-end that can be shared among various GPLs. If the AspectJ definition of an aspect is used as a focus point for discussion, every language that is integrated into the framework must define the meaning of a join point model (JPM), pointcuts, and advice within the language context. Such a notion can be defined abstractly such that each new aspect language inherits and extends this common definition.

Reconsidering the Aspect Pascal metamodel of Figure 3, it can be observed that metamodel elements such as pointcut, advice, abstract expressions, and abstract statements are actually generic in the Aspect Pascal metamodel. Thus, instead of modeling these elements as part of the Aspect Pascal metamodel, they can be extracted to a common generic core. However, there may be differences in the concrete syntax of certain model elements. For example, concrete statements and expressions may vary from one GPL to another. In such cases, the differences can be captured in individual metamodel extensions [22] and commonality can be shared using a general metamodel. To explain this concept, this subsection will summarize the construction of aspect weavers for two different GPLs (i.e., Object Pascal and FORTRAN) using the framework. The example shows how languages across different paradigms can share AOP concepts through metamodel extension.

Figure 9[1] shows the class diagram representing the new Aspect Pascal metamodel that extends the core GAspect (Generic Aspect) metamodel. The latter captures all of the essential concepts that are intrinsic to any aspect-oriented language influenced by the asymmetric AspectJ style. For example, the core model elements such as pointcuts and advice belong to GAspect. There are also abstract placeholders for expressions and statements in GAspect. Although the figure does not show a metamodel for a Join Point Model, a further enhancement in this direction could be made in the future to define different JPMs.

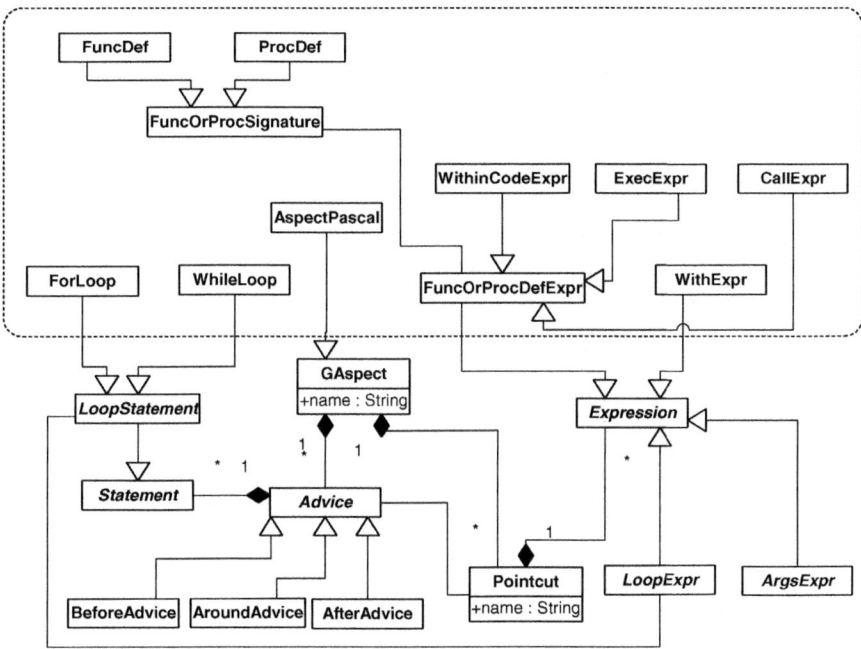

Fig. 9. Class Diagram (snippet) of Aspect Pascal (top) extending from a common Generic Aspect metamodel (bottom)

Every language-specific expression and statement must extend from these abstract definitions. For example, a concrete `execution` expression join point or a `call` expression join point for any aspect-oriented language (AOL) must be derived from the abstract `expression` join point of GAspect. In Figure 9, the `call` expression and `exec` expression of Aspect Pascal inherits from `FuncOrProcDefExpr` (which itself is derived from the abstract `Expression` class) and references the

---

[1] Typically in UML, inheritance is drawn from top to bottom. However, the inheritance relationship for Aspect Pascal is shown in reverse to denote its extension from the generic aspect metamodel and also to accommodate all of the elements in the limited space. However, this does not affect the common understanding of the UML notation used.

`FuncOrProcSignature` type pattern. The type pattern captures the concrete syntax (i.e., signature) for expressing functions or procedures in Object Pascal and is dependent on the grammar of the base language. For every new language, the concrete syntax of type pattern varies. The dotted rectangle in Figure 9 depicts all those points of variability that are specific to Aspect Pascal.

Because most programming languages have some form of support for loops, we have introduced the notion of a loop execution join point in the generic metamodel. Concrete loop statements belonging to the base AOL must be derived from the abstract `LoopStatement` of GAspect. The Aspect Pascal metamodel shows support for `while` loop and `for` loop join points that are extended from the abstract loop execution join point present in GAspect. The concept of a loop execution join point is not present in AspectJ, but has been found to be useful for monitoring high-performance scientific applications [25].

Furthermore, a join point for capturing `with` expressions in Object Pascal is introduced in the Aspect Pascal metamodel. An example of a crosscutting concern based on a `with` expression join point is given in [12]. In a similar way, the entire join point model for an AOL can be constructed by adding concrete extensions from the abstract GAspect metamodel. Moreover, the technique allows experimentation with new features (e.g., `loop` execution join point) to be added to an existing AOL. Such an addition is beneficial if the aspect language evolves. The Aspect Pascal metamodel shown here is only a snippet of the original. The complete KM3 and TCS specifications are available at [30].

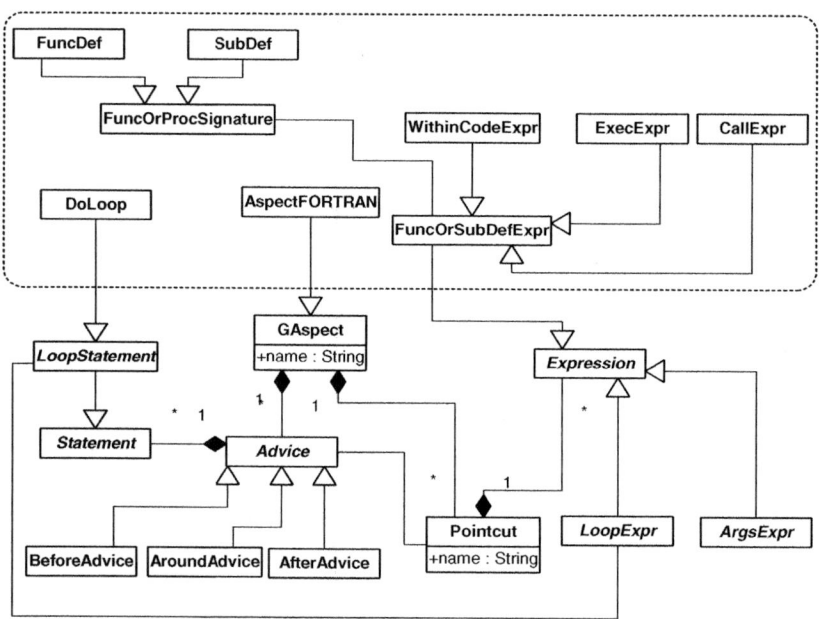

Fig. 10. Metamodel (snippet) of Aspect FORTRAN (top) conforming to a common Generic Aspect metamodel (bottom)

Figure 10 shows the corresponding metamodel for Aspect FORTRAN. Similar to Aspect Pascal, the Aspect FORTRAN metamodel is extended from the generic core GAspect. However, the points of variability (shown by the enclosed dotted rectangle) for this metamodel exist in their concrete syntax. In the case of Aspect FORTRAN, the `call`, `exec` and `withincode` expressions reference subroutine/function definitions unlike the procedure/function definitions in the Aspect Pascal metamodel. Moreover, the concrete function definitions for Aspect FORTRAN and Aspect Pascal are different due to the dissimilarity in their underlying grammar. The TCS specification in Figure 11 shows this variability of concrete syntax for the two metamodels.

```
1. template FuncDef
2. :   "FUNCTION" name "(" paramdefs{separator = ","} ")"
3. ;
4. template SubDef
5. :   "SUBROUTINE" name "(" paramdefs{separator = ","} ")"
6. ;
```
```
1. template FuncDef
2. :   "function" (isDefined(classifier) ? classifier ".")
3.      name "(" paramdefs{separator = ";"} ")"
4. ;
5. template ProcDef
6. :   "procedure" (isDefined(classifier) ? classifier ".")
7.      name "(" paramdefs{separator = ";"} ")"
8. ;
```

Fig. 11. TCS specification showing differences in concrete syntax for Aspect FORTRAN (top) and Aspect Pascal metamodel (bottom)

Figure 11 shows the differences in the concrete syntax of function/subroutine/procedure declarations for Aspect FORTRAN and Aspect Pascal. The upper half represents the TCS specification of Aspect FORTRAN function/subroutine declaration whereas the bottom half shows the corresponding function/procedure declaration for Aspect Pascal. All points of variation between the two metamodels are captured in their corresponding extended metamodel (dotted rectangle) whereas the commonality is captured in the generic aspect metamodel. Generally, the point of variation between two aspect languages will be in their formal syntactic representation.

In addition, GAspect also captures certain program fragments belonging to a GPL that may not be analyzed or parsed by the front-end. Instead, these program fragments are delegated to the back-end PTE for parsing and analysis. Such fragments typically appear in the body of advice code and are referenced as `OpaqueStatements`. This considerably reduces the complexity of the aspect metamodel as several language constructs of the base language need not be parsed or analyzed by the front-end. Instead, the back-end PTE that already has the capability (parser/analyzer) to process the base language (Object Pascal / FORTRAN) can handle such program fragments. An example of using `OpaqueStatement` is shown in the case study of Section 4.

The construction of a generic aspect metamodel helps to generalize the commonalities among distinct aspect languages. Each common concept may be refined using language-specific metamodel extensions. Furthermore, an extension of GAspect may categorize commonalities within a paradigm that can be reused (e.g., a metamodel named Object-Oriented that extends GAspect with common OO concepts, which is then extended by concrete OO languages). This was one of the important lessons learned in using MDE during the course of this research and can significantly improve the genericity of the metamodel. The issue of additional specialization of the GAspect metamodel is further discussed in Section 6.1 as a future enhancement.

3.2 Generalizing the Rule Generator Design

The goal of the program transformation rule generator (item 2 in Figure 1) is to translate a given aspect to a corresponding program transformation rule (e.g., RSL). This role is handled by an assembly of transformation libraries written in ATL. In the context of a generic framework, it is desirable to reuse as much of the transformation library code as possible when constructing an aspect weaver for a new GPL. To realize this objective, the transformation libraries must follow a general guideline (similar to a generic API) that ensures maximum reusability.

   The guideline ensures that every transformation rule that captures the semantics of a particular weaving intent must conform to a generic rule interface. For example, an RSL rule that captures the semantics of a method invocation join point (i.e., to capture a particular method call and trigger advice) should conform to a generic method invocation rule interface that the back-end transformation engine expects. Generally, the back-end rewrite rules are parameterized and expect a set of parameters that would be used during the transformation. Thus, it is important to normalize the parameter structure to a common interface specification. These parameters are determined by the semantics of the joinpoint that is to be encoded in a program transformation rule. By conforming to this generic interface, model transformation libraries written for various GPLs may share a generalized common pattern. For example, to represent a method call join point, the back-end program transformation rule should conform to a generic rule interface called `generic_advice_call`, which accepts the following five named-parameters: `program_root_`, `method_id_`, `proceed_call_`, `before_advice_` and `after_advice_`. The first two named parameters refer to the abstract syntax of the program under consideration, `program_root_` captures the root of the tree and `method_id_` captures the current method being advised. The rest of the named parameters capture the semantics of this join point. Every named parameter has a type associated with it, which is determined by the concrete syntax (grammar) of the base GPL. For example, for a FORTRAN 90 program, this generic function should be encoded as follows:

```
{name  →  type}
generic_advice_call  (
{ program_root_   →  Fortran90_program },
{ method_id_      →  Name},
{ proceed_        →  Name},
{ before_advice_  →  execution_part_construct_list },
{ after_advice_   →  execution_part_construct_list },
) →  Fortran90_program
```

One may note that although the types (shown in *italics*) are concrete, the rule interface is abstract. This generalization is necessary to address *Challenge C4 (language-independent generalization of transformation objectives)* and facilitate the ATL rule generator to program to a common rule interface that can be reused among various GPLs. At this point, one may recollect from Listing 1 how RSLs or any term-rewrite rules are tied to the concrete syntax of the base programming language. The `proceed_` is internally used to determine if the advice is an around advice that makes a call to procced. Similarly, for an Object Pascal program, the `generic_advice_call` is encoded as follows:

```
{name → type}
generic_advice_call  (
{ program_root_   →  ObjectPascal },
{ method_id_      →  IDENTIFIER},
{ proceed_        →  IDENTIFIER},
{ before_advice_  →  statement_list },
{ after_advice_   →  statement_list },
) →  ObjectPascal
```

For every join point in our AOP language model, we have developed a set of formal rule interfaces to which each corresponding ATL transformation must conform (i.e., there is a separate rule interface for method execution or loop execution join point). The generic rule interfaces not only enforce the code generators for different aspect weavers to adhere to a known abstract interface, but also considerably reduce the development time and effort to transfer knowledge from one rule generator to another.

Figure 12 and Figure 13 show comparative snippets of the higher-order model transformation rules (ATL specification) for translating a method call join point written in Aspect Pascal or Aspect FORTRAN to a corresponding lower-order program transformation rule (RSL rewrite specification). Each of the ATL specifications (Figures 12 and 13) consist of several smaller ATL rules that together perform the actual transformation on the metamodel. For example, the rules `AfterAdvice2Pattern`, `BeforeAdvice2Pattern` and `PointCutToExternalPattern` (as shown in Figures 12 and 13) are used to construct the ATL specification for translating a *method call join point*. However, this is only a subset; the complete ATL specification is available at [30]. The individual rules (e.g., `AfterAdvice2Pattern`, `BeforeAdvice2Pattern`) are fired whenever a corresponding model element (e.g., model elements like `BeforeAdvice`, `AfterAdvice` in the Aspect Pascal metamodel) in the source metamodel is reached.

Both of these higher-order transformation rules conform to an abstract structure (generic rule interface) that drives the ATL rule generator. As a direct benefit of forcing the ATL transformations to conform to a common structure or interface, the model transformation rules presented in Figures 12 and 13 appear distinctly similar. For example, all of the three rules (i.e., `AfterAdvice2Pattern`, `BeforeAdvice2Pattern` and `PointCutToExternalPattern`) have the same *left-hand-side (LHS)*, such that the main difference lies in their concrete syntax (i.e., the grammar of the two languages).

```
    rule BeforeAdvice2Pattern {
        from
                s : APascal!BeforeAdvice
        to
                t : RSL!Pattern (
                        phead  <- ph,
                        ptoken <- 'statement_list',
                        ptext  <- spt
                ),
                ph : RSL!PatternHead (
                        name <- 'before_advice_stmt'
                ),
                ...
                )
    }
    rule AfterAdvice2Pattern {
        from
                s : APascal!AfterAdvice
        to
                t : RSL!Pattern (
                        phead  <- ph,
                        ptoken <- 'statement_list',
                        ptext  <- spt
                ),
                ph : RSL!PatternHead (
                        name <- 'after_advice_stmt'
                ),
                ...
    }
    lazy rule PointCutToExternalPattern {
        from
                s : APascal!Pointcut
        to
                t : RSL!ExternalPattern (
                        dname   <- 'ObjectPascal',
                        eptext  <- 'around_advice_call',
                        ptoken  <- 'ObjectPascal',
                        phead   <- ph
                ),
                ph : RSL!PatternHead (
                        name    <- 'around_advice_call',
                        params  <- Sequence {pp1,pp2,pp3,pp4,pp5,pp6}
                ),
                pp1 : RSL!PatternParameter (
                        name     <- 'program',
                        referTo <- 'ObjectPascal'
                ),
                pp2 : RSL!PatternParameter (
                        name     <- 'method_name',
                        referTo <- 'IDENTIFIER'
                ),
                pp3 : RSL!PatternParameter (
                        name     <- 'proceed_call',
                        referTo <- 'IDENTIFIER'
                ),
                ...
    }
```

Fig. 12. ATL specification (snippet) used to generate lower-order transformation rules (RSL) for weaving an Object Pascal source program

```
rule BeforeAdvice2Pattern {
    from
            s : AFortran!BeforeAdvice
    to
            t : RSL!Pattern (
                    phead  <- ph,
                    ptoken <- 'execution_part_construct_list',
                    ptext  <- spt
            ),
            ph : RSL!PatternHead (
                    name <- 'before_advice_stmt'
            ),
            ...
}

rule AfterAdvice2Pattern {
    from
            s : AFortran!AfterAdvice
    to
            t : RSL!Pattern (
                    phead  <- ph,
                    ptoken <- 'execution_part_construct_list',
                    ptext  <- spt
            ),
            ph : RSL!PatternHead (
                    name <- 'after_advice_stmt'
            ),
            ...
}

lazy rule PointCutToExternalPattern {
    from
            s : AFortran!Pointcut
    to
            t : RSL!ExternalPattern (
                    dname   <- 'FORTRAN',
                    eptext  <- 'around_advice_call',
                    ptoken  <- 'Fortran90_program',
                    phead   <- ph
            ),
            ph : RSL!PatternHead (
                    name    <-  'around_advice_call',
                    params <- Sequence {pp1,pp2,pp3,pp4,pp5,pp6}
            ),
            pp1 : RSL!PatternParameter (
                    name    <- 'program',
                    referTo <- 'Fortran90_program'
            ),
            pp2 : RSL!PatternParameter (
                    name    <- 'method_name',
                    referTo <- 'NAME'
            ),
            pp3 : RSL!PatternParameter (
                    name    <- 'proceed_call',
                    referTo <- 'NAME'
            ),
            ...
}
```

Fig. 13. ATL specification (snippet) used to generate lower-order transformation rules (RSL) for weaving a FORTRAN source program

For example, in the ATL rule `BeforeAdvice2Pattern`, the *before advice* in the source aspect metamodel is mapped to a *RSL pattern* in the target RSL metamodel that consists of a pattern head (`phead`), a pattern token (`ptoken`) and the pattern text (`ptext`). Similarly, a *RSL external pattern* is translated from a source *pointcut* specification and has the same LHS signature (`dname`, `eptext`, `ptoken`, `phead`) for both Object Pascal and FORTRAN generators. The main difference lies in the concrete syntax (*right-hand side*) of the base language grammar as referred in the transformation rules (e.g., an `execution_part_construct_list` in FOR-TRAN is similar to a `statement_list` in Object Pascal). Obviously, there are other non-terminal and terminal tokens in both the Object Pascal and FORTRAN grammar that have similar structural representation and meaning, but differ by name in their grammar form. The strategy is always to follow a common abstract structure (or substructure) to translate a particular join point from an aspect description to RSL. However, in certain cases, where the difference in signature or concrete syntax between two language grammars differ significantly, it may not be directly possible to map to a generic interface. Instead, the mapping can then conform to sub-structures or sub-interfaces.

Steps to Construct a New Weaver

Using the current methodology, in order to construct a new weaver for a language that is not supported by the framework, the following steps have to be performed:

- The aspect metamodel extension for the new language must be designed. Firstly, the new weaver should extend the language-specific aspect metamodel for the new language by inheriting from the generic aspect metamodel provided by the framework. Figures 9 and 10 show how this extension is done for Object Pascal and FORTRAN. This metamodel represents the abstract syntax of the newly constructed aspect language and is implemented using KM3, as shown in Figure 4. However, in some situations, representing common concepts between aspect languages may require the extension of the generic aspect metamodel.

- After the abstract syntax is defined, the corresponding concrete syntax that defines the syntactic structure of the aspect language should be designed. In our case, this was done using TCS, as shown in Figure 5. The choice of the metamodeling technology may slightly alter these first two steps.

- Apart from the generic metamodel, the framework provides a library of model transformation rules (i.e., ATL rules) that need to be customized based on the design of the new aspect language. Figures 12 and 13 show snippets of ATL transformation rules that are customized for Object Pascal and FORTRAN. In general, the model transformation rules differ in their concrete syntactical representation from one language to another and this difference is shown in Figure 17. In our future work, we plan to automate this customization by capturing the differences using a model mapper, thereby reducing the accidental complexity associated in this step.

- No changes are required for the back-end rules metamodel. After the model transformation rules are defined, the corresponding program transformation rules can be generated, as shown in Figure 7. The generated program transformation rules perform the actual weaving on the source code. The weaver constructor can automate this entire process by providing appropriate Ant scripts [30] such that the end-user is fully oblivious to the two-level transformations (i.e., first model transformation and then program transformation) taking place. This virtually completes the tasks for constructing a new weaver.
- The end-user only has to write their aspect program as shown in Listing 3 or Listing 5; they are shielded from the internal complexities. The opaque statements appearing in the aspect program thrust some accidental complexity on the end-user, which is a limitation of the current implementation, but is intended to reduce the burden of the front-end parser.

As an alternative approach to model-to-model (M2M) transformation followed by TCS extraction, an interesting technique that can be used is model-to-text (M2T) transformation [37]. In the M2T approach, models of particular software solutions are refined and transformed into source code (e.g., Java, C++). Such transformations generally make use of "templates." A template is a text sequence interspersed with commands that extract information from a model. The Jet or Acceleo template languages can be used for such a purpose [37]. We recognize that this is an interesting solution and could serve as an alternative approach towards constructing the RSL rule generator. However, using M2T, we may lose the precise concept mapping between the source and the target model, and rely on mapping concepts to strings. Nevertheless, many alternative approaches can still benefit from the technique described in this paper.

In the following section, we present two case studies that use our model-driven aspect weaving framework to construct aspect weavers for two different GPLs. In particular, we construct aspect weavers for Object Pascal and FORTRAN and make comparative studies of reuse of their front-end, the rule generator and the back-end. The observations made in the case studies help to illustrate the potential of the techniques presented so far. It also reveals some of the limitations of the current implementation of the framework and offers lessons learned during the process that can be applied for future improvements.

4   Case Studies – Object Pascal and FORTRAN

In order to experiment with the approach presented in the previous sections, we constructed two aspect weavers – one for Object Pascal and another for FORTRAN – using our generic model-driven framework. A subset (e.g., primitive pointcuts like call, execution, loop) of standard AOP features was built into both weavers in an AspectJ-like style. The FORTRAN weaver was constructed after the completion of the Aspect Pascal weaver and reused several functionalities, code and knowledge from the previous construction without much alteration to the core artifacts. For example, both weavers shared the generic front-end, which constituted around 50% of the overall front-end lines of code (LOC) written in KM3 and TCS. Moreover, the FORTRAN weaver reused 30% of the Object Pascal rule generator code without any alteration, and another 25% with minor customization. Most of the time and effort on building the FORTRAN weaver was spent on understanding the concrete syntax of the language and on the conceptual design of the weaver. The rest of the section is devoted to evaluating the basic functionalities of these weavers through sample case study applications.

4.1   Object Pascal Weaver Examples

The initial experimentation towards evaluating our Aspect Pascal weaver was realized within the scope of a commercial distributed application written in Object Pascal. The case study application and all the examples discussed here were first introduced in [12]. One specific application used for evaluation was a utility that assisted in upgrading a database after a schema change. The first example presented in this section is concerned with updating a processing dialog meter within the schema evolution tool. The second example relates to synchronization between various database error-handlers.

4.1.1   Processing Dialog Meter

Utilities such as a schema evolution tool provide feedback to the user in the form of a processing dialog, or meter, which indicates the progress of the overall task. The updating of the progress meter represents a crosscutting concern because the code to increment the meter is spread across the methods that perform much of the functionality (e.g., deleting database triggers, compiling new stored procedures, and other evolution tasks). Lines 2-8 in Listing 2 contain a redundant code fragment that appears in 62 different places of the schema evolution utility. This code is necessary to update the processing dialog after each database evolution task is completed. Technically, this happens after every call to the predefined Inc procedure.

```
1.  Inc(TotalInsertionsPerformed);
2.  if not ProcDlg1.Process(TotalInsertionsPerformed /
3.          TotalInsertionsCalculated) then
4.    begin
5.      ProcDlg1.Canceled := True;
6.      Result := True;
7.    exit;
8.  end; // if not Process
```

Listing 2: Progress meter updating

Listing 3 shows the UpdateProgressMeter aspect that encapsulates the crosscutting concern shown in Listing 2. The pointcut IncrCall_ captures all calls to procedure Inc. The advice code shown between Lines 5-13 is triggered after the "procedure call join point" is reached. It may be noted that the entire conditional 'if statement' (defined internally as an OpaqueStatement between <! and !>) is not parsed by the front-end but delegated to the back-end parser.

```
1.  aspect UpdateProgressMeter
2.    begin
3.      pointcut IncrCall_() :
              call(procedure *.Inc(Integer));
4.
5.    after() : IncrCall_()
6.    begin
7.      <!if not ProcDlg1.Process(TotalInsertionsPerformed /
8.            TotalInsertionsCalculated) then
9.        begin
10.         ProcDlg1.Canceled := True;
11.         Result := True;
12.       exit;
13.     end;!>
13.     end
14. end
```

Listing 3: Aspect to capture progress meter updating

Following TCS injection on the above source program (Listing 3), the corresponding Aspect Pascal model is generated (shown in Figure 14). The model (represented in XMI format) conforms to the APascal and GAspect metamodels introduced in Section 3 (this representation is never seen by the end-user). After applying an ATL transformation (*method call*) to this Aspect Pascal model, the resulting RSL model is generated that conforms to the target RSL metamodel. Finally, the lower-order RSL transformation rule is extracted from the RSL model using TCS extraction. The complete RSL model and the RSL transformation rule are available at [30]. Note that the complete transformation scenario was initially introduced in Section 2.3 of the paper (also refer to Figure 7) and is fully automated using Ant scripts.

```
<APascal xmlns="APascal" xmlns:_1="GAspect" name="UpdateProgressMeter">
  <domain name="ObjectPascal"/>
  <pointcut name=" IncrCall_">
    <pctexpr xsi:type="CallExpr">
      <funcOrProcSig xsi:type="ProcedureDef" name="Inc" classifier="*">
        <paramdefs name="*" type="Integer"/>
      </funcOrProcSig>
    </pctexpr>
  </pointcut>
  <advice xsi:type="_1:BeforeAdvice" pctname="//@pointcut.0">
    <advStmt xsi:type="_1:OpaqueStatement" stmt="..."/>
  </advice>
</APascal>
```

Fig. 14. Aspect Pascal model (snippet) generated from Aspect Pascal source program

The next example in our case study shows how a synchronization aspect is captured using the Aspect Pascal weaver constructed from our model-driven framework.

4.1.2 Database Error Handler Synchronization
Often, a commercial application must support databases from several different vendors (e.g., Oracle, Interbase, and SQL Server). In such a situation, exception handling

of database errors is a major difficulty because each database has its own way of raising exceptions. The same conceptual error (e.g., a null value in a required field) may
be raised in completely different ways with dissimilar error codes. Moreover, the exception handling code must be thread-safe because numerous clients may access the
database at the same time. The addition of this concurrency concern resulted in a manual invasive change to over 20 classes in the schema evolution utility [12]. An example error handler is shown in Listing 4. In this listing, lines 3-4 and 6-8 represent a
single synchronization concern. Furthermore, this exact code is replicated in all of the
entry and exit points of each type of error handler. Line 5 represents the actual database error handing code which is omitted for brevity.

```
1.  function TExNullField.Handle(ServerType: TServerType;
                                 E : EDBEngineError) : Integer;
2.  begin
3.     TExHandleColl(Collection).LockHandle;
4.     try
5.        <database error handling code omitted here>
6.        finally
7.           TExHandleColl(Collection).UnLockHandle;
8.        end;
9.  end;
```

Listing 4: Synchronization in a database error handler

Listing 5 shows the aspect to support a synchronization concern as stated above. The
pointcut funcHandler_ captures execution of all database handler functions.

```
1.  aspect SyncDBErrHandler
2.     begin
3.     pointcut funcHandler_() :
                  execution(function *.Handle(..));
4.     void around() : funcHandler_()
5.        begin
6.           <!TExHandleColl(Collection).LockHandle;!>
7.           try
8.              proceed ();
9.              finally
10.                <!TExHandleColl(Collection).UnLockHandle;!>
11.           end;
12.        end
13.     end
```

Listing 5: Aspect to capture synchronization in a database error handler

Synchronization is realized by an around advice that wraps calls to the LockHan-
dle and UnlockHandle methods inside a try/finally block. The proceed
statement allows the database error handling code to execute normally within the synchronization aspect. We applied the same steps as in the previous example to separate
this concern from the main code base. The example shows another special case of
using opaque statements that are not part of the aspect metamodel. Such statements

are not parsed by the front-end and instead delegated to the back-end transformation engine for further processing. This may add some accidental complexity for the end-user who needs to have prior knowledge about which concrete syntax are supported by the metamodel and which are actually delegated as opaque statements. This is a limitation in the implementation of the current approach but intended to keep the syntax of the aspect language separated from the syntax of the base language. The idea is to parse the base language syntax using the already available back-end parser (i.e., without having to extend them with new constructs) and implement the front-end parser incrementally to handle aspect-specific constructs. We recognize that the use of notation <!..!> raises the accidental complexity for the end-user and is not a desirable solution. In future implementation, we intend to improve the representation of opaque statements such that it is oblivious to the end-user.

The Aspect Pascal model shown in Figure 15 is obtained by applying TCS injection on the above source program. The complete ATL transformation (*method exec*) and generated RSL code is available at [30]. It should be noted that it is this lower-order RSL code that does the actual weaving on the base program, but the general user of this framework is oblivious to its presence. Instead, the front-end aspect language acts as a façade to the back-end PTE and hides all the accidental complexity associated with it (*Challenge C3*).

The XMI (Figure 14 and Figure 15) is only an internal representation of the Aspect Pascal model and is used for analyzing and transforming the aspect specification. A software developer does not see this internal representation. However, the information is useful for more advanced users (e.g., weaver constructor) for debugging and analysis purposes.

```
<APascal xmlns="APascal" xmlns:_1="GAspect" name="SyncDBErrHandler">
  <domain name="ObjectPascal"/>
  <pointcut name="funcHandler_">
    <pctexpr xsi:type="ExecExpr">
      <funcOrProcSig xsi:type="FunctionDef" name="Handle" classifier="*">
        <paramdefs name="*" type="*"/>
      </funcOrProcSig>
    </pctexpr>
  </pointcut>
  <advice xsi:type="_1:AroundAdvice" pctname="//@pointcut.0">
    <advStmt xsi:type="_1:OpaqueStatement" stmt="..."/>
    <advStmt xsi:type="_1:TryCatchFinallyStatement">
      <stmts xsi:type="_1:ProccedStatement"/>
      <finallyStmts xsi:type="_1:OpaqueStatement" stmt="..."/>
    </advStmt>
  </advice>
</APascal>
```

Fig. 15. Aspect Pascal model (snippet) generated from Aspect Pascal source program

4.2   FORTRAN Weaver Examples

Although most AOP research is centered around Java, we believe several numerical and scientific computing applications that are written in legacy languages like FORTRAN can benefit from AOP. There has been prior AOP / metaprogramming research conducted in the area of parallel programming [45, 47], especially with optimization of FORTRAN code [46]. To evaluate our framework in this regard, we constructed a

FORTRAN weaver and was able to reuse a majority of the code generator libraries that were previously written for Object Pascal. The front-end of the FORTRAN weaver is based on the same Generic Aspect Metamodel that was used by the Object Pascal weaver. We evaluated our weaver in a FORTRAN application using the Message Passing Interface (MPI) [29] written for high-performance scientific computing. The first example shows how a security concern can be weaved into such applications and the second example illustrates how to monitor and weave an aspect around loops.

4.2.1 Security Aspect

MPI is a library specification for message-passing and is largely used in high-performance scientific computing applications [29]. MPI provides more than 125 core functions that include all the basic functionalities to assist in writing parallel programs. There are several implementations of MPI written in various languages (e.g., C, FORTRAN, C++ and Java). In order to provide security to FORTRAN-based MPI applications, it is often required to encrypt/decrypt messages while they are sent or received across the network. Listing 6 shows a snippet of a FORTRAN MPI program, in which lines 9 and 12 illustrate how a security concern (i.e., a call to the encrypt function) is added before each call to MPI_SEND. The implementation of the security concern is scattered over the entire code base for all messages that require encryption during MPI_SEND.

Listing 7 shows the aspect program required to enable security for all messages during MPI message send and receive. The pointcut captures all calls to MPI_SEND and passes the message to be encrypted as an argument. In a similar way, security to messages may be enabled during calls to MPI_RECV. The internal representation of the generated artifacts (e.g., Aspect FORTRAN model, RSL model and RSL transformation rule) is not shown here but the transformation process is similar to previous descriptions.

```
1.    program send_recv_with_MPI
2.    ...! original code
3.    real :: a_msg
4.    real :: b_msg
5.    ...! original code
6.    allocate (a_msg(msg_len))
7.    allocate (b_msg(msg_len))
8.    ...
9.    call encrypt(a_msg)
10.   call MPI_SEND(a_msg,...)
11.   ...
12.   call encrypt(b_msg)
13.   call MPI_SEND(b_msg,...)
14.   ...
15.   deallocate (a_msg)
16.   deallocate (b_msg)
17.   ...! original code
18.   End
```

Listing 6. Encryption of messages during MPI_SEND

```
1.    aspect enable_encryption
2.      pointcut mpi_send_(real :: orig_msg) ::
3.        call(MPI_SEND(real,*)) && args(orig_msg)
4.      before(real :: orig_msg):: mpi_send_(orig_msg)
5.        call encrypt(orig_msg)
6.      endbefore
7.    endaspect
```

Listing 7. Aspect to enable encryption during MPI Calls

4.2.2 Join Point for Loops

It is often desired to monitor the performance of loops for some high-performance scientific applications. Harbulot et. al. first introduced this concept in an extension to AspectJ [25]. We borrowed from their definition and added this feature into our FORTRAN and Object Pascal weavers. According to our definition, the join point for a loop has the following signature:

```
<loop_name>(init::<val>, exit::<val>, stride::<val>)
```

Init specifies the loop initialization value, exit specifies the loop termination value and stride specifies the loop increment counter. Listing 8 shows an implementation of MPI_GATHER written in FORTRAN.

```
1.      program gather_vector
2.      ... ! original code
3.      parameter(niters=10)
4.      parameter(xmax=100,ymax=100)
5.      parameter (totelem=xmax*ymax)
6.      ...
7.      ! start timer
8.      time_begin = MPI_Wtime()
9.      do iter = 1,niters
10.        ...
11.          do i=1,totelem
12.            ...
13.          enddo
14.      enddo
15.      ! stop timer
16.      time_end = MPI_Wtime()
17.      ... ! original code
18.      end
```

Listing 8: Adding a timer around do loops

```
aspect AddTimerAroundLoops
  pointcut loop_timer_() ::
    execution(do(init::1,exit::10,stride:*))
  around():: loop_timer_()
    time_begin = MPI_Wtime()
    call proceed()
    time_end = MPI_Wtime()
  endaround
endaspect
```

Listing 9: Aspect to add a timer around do Loops

In MPI, messages can be forwarded by intermediate nodes where they are split (for scatter) or concatenated (for gather). Often, it is required to measure timing statistics around critical parts of program execution. One such case is shown in Listing 8. Lines 9-14 show the execution of the outer do loop, which has initial value as 1, exit value as 10 and a default stride as 1. In a manual approach, it is required to invasively add the timer information (Lines 8 and 16 shown in *italics*) and change the source program at every place whenever the program runs into the execution of a loop join point that matches the loop conditions.

Listing 9 shows the aspect program that can automatically add the timing functions during the execution of the loop join point. The join point for loops matches any loop expression in the base program that satisfies the loop initialization value, the loop finalization value (exit) and the loop stride value. The wildcard '*' may be interpreted as 'any.' Currently, both integer and string value types are supported, but future extensions can support other value types. However, as a side effect, the behavior of a base program may be altered if there are logical errors (init=1, exit=1, stride=2) in the loop expression and there is a corresponding match. Such a situation may be avoided in the future by adding semantic validations to the existing pattern matching functionality.

```
<AFortran xmlns="AFortran" xmlns:_1="GAspect" name="AddTimerAroundLoops">
 <domain name="FORTRAN"/>
 <pointcut name="loop_timer_">
  <pctexpr xsi:type="_1:LoopExpr">
   <loopStmt xsi:type="DoLoop">
       <loopInitCond xsi:type="1:IntLoopInitCond" condition="1"/>
       <loopExitCond xsi:type="1:IntLoopExitCond" condition="10"/>
       <loopStrideCond xsi:type="1:StringLoopStrideCond" condition="*"/>
   </loopStmt>
  </pctexpr>
 </pointcut>
 <advice xsi:type="_1:AroundAdvice" pctname="//@pointcut.0">
  <advStmt xsi:type="_1:OpaqueStatement" stmt="time_begin = MPI_Wtime()"/>
  <advStmt xsi:type="_1:ProceedStatement">
  <advStmt xsi:type="_1:OpaqueStatement" stmt="time_end = MPI_Wtime()"/>
 </advice>
</AFortran>
```

Fig. 16. Aspect FORTRAN model generated from source aspect program

The Aspect FORTRAN model (XML format) corresponding to the aspect specification (Listing 9) is shown in Figure 15. The model conforms to the Aspect FORTRAN metamodel from Figure 10. The corresponding ATL transformation for loops and the generated RSL code can be found at the project website [30].

4.3   Discussion of Experimental Results

In terms of reusability, all the examples listed in Section 4 reuse the same generic aspect metamodel (GAspect). Moreover, the ATL transformation for translating a particular join point reveals non-trivial reuse among weavers constructed for different GPLs. This was illustrated in Section 3.2 through Figures 12 and 13 (i.e., an ATL transformation for translating a method call join point in FORTRAN and

Object Pascal). In that particular example, 230 lines of model transformation code (out of 280 LOC) were reused without any modification. The remaining 50 LOC were reused with minor customization.

Similarly, for translating a `loop execution join point` in FORTRAN and Object Pascal, 265 LOC out of 305 were reused without any modification, while the remaining 40 LOC were reused with minor customization. Examples of an ATL rule for translating a `loop execution join point` for Object Pascal is shown in [30].

A visual comparison between the ATL rules (`loop execution join point`) for Object Pascal and FORTRAN weavers is shown in Figure 17[2], which suggests the level of reuse among the two ATL rules. This level of reuse is a direct benefit of using the framework, which enforces the model transformation rules to conform to a common abstract structure. The yellow lines show the difference between two rules, which is mostly due to the dissimilarity in the grammars (terminal and non-terminal symbols) of the two languages (Object Pascal and FORTRAN). Although these parts seem to be tangled in the current implementation (weak copy/paste reusability), a future improvement (strong reuse) would capture the mapping information (i.e., the concrete syntax or grammars of the base languages) in a model weaver [39] and apply the mapping information to automatically generate part of this model transformation library. From our own experience in constructing aspect weavers using the generalized framework, we realize that a large part of the generic front-end and program transformation rule generator is reusable across languages with little customization. A comparative analysis between other ATL rules for the Aspect Pascal and Aspect FORTRAN weaver is available at the GenAWeave website [30].

```
199       pp1 : RSL!PatternParameter (          199       pp1 : RSL!PatternParameter (
200           name <- 'program',                 200           name <- 'program',
201           referTo <- 'ObjectPascal'          201           referTo <- 'Fortran90_program'
202       ),                                     202       ),
203       pp2 : RSL!PatternParameter (          203       pp2 : RSL!PatternParameter (
204           name <- 'proceed_bef',            204           name <- 'proceed_bef',
205           referTo <- 'statement_list'       205           referTo <- 'execution_part_construct_list'
206       ),                                     206       ),
207       pp3 : RSL!PatternParameter (          207       pp3 : RSL!PatternParameter (
208           name <- 'proceed_after',          208           name <- 'proceed_after',
209           referTo <- 'statement_list'       209           referTo <- 'execution_part_construct_list'
210       ),                                     210       ),
211       pp4 : RSL!PatternParameter (          211       pp4 : RSL!PatternParameter (
212           name <- 'withincode',             212           name <- 'withincode',
213           referTo <- 'IDENTIFIER'           213           referTo <- 'NAME'
214       ),                                     214       ),
215       pp5 : RSL!PatternParameter (          215       pp5 : RSL!PatternParameter (
216           name <- 'init',                   216           name <- 'init',
217           referTo <- 'NATURAL_NUMBER'       217           referTo <- 'LABEL'
218       ),                                     218       ),
219       pp6 : RSL!PatternParameter (          219       pp6 : RSL!PatternParameter (
                                                 220
220           name <- 'exit',                   221           name <- 'exit',
221           referTo <- 'NATURAL_NUMBER'       222           referTo <- 'LABEL'
                                                 223
222       )                                     224       )
223 ;                                           225 ;
```

Fig. 17. A comparative analysis of model transformation rules

Likewise, the front-end of all weavers share a generic metamodel (i.e., GAspect). Out of 550 LOC used for defining the front-end metamodel (KM3 and TCS specifications), nearly 280 LOC were shared among the two weavers. However, it should be

---

[2] In the right-hand side of Figure 17, there is an extra carriage return on line 220 that caused the gray line to appear in the left-hand side of the figure.

noted that the current weavers have limited functionalities and the reuse may decrease with mutually exclusive functionalities (e.g., *with* join point is present only in Object Pascal and not in FORTRAN). Nevertheless, the purpose of the Aspect Pascal and Aspect FORTRAN weavers were to experimentally evaluate the generality of the model-driven framework for building aspect weavers. The main objective was to evaluate the reusability of features that can be shared among multiple weavers without writing them from scratch. In the current stage of our investigation, we have adopted a simple join point model (a subset of AspectJ) with primitive pointcuts like `call`, `execution`, `loop`, `withincode`, `with`, `within` and `args` and advice declarations like `before`, `after` and `around`. It was observed that the Aspect FORTRAN weaver that was constructed after the completion of the Aspect Pascal weaver reused a majority of the available front-end artifacts (e.g., generic metamodel and ATL specifications).

In addition to front-end reuse, the framework provides a reusable library of back-end external functions that can be used to provide low-level transformation support for new aspect weaver construction. These functions provide efficient tree traversal strategies in addition to AST manipulation [12]. Currently, there are 11 such functions that are shared by the Object Pascal and FORTRAN weavers. However, not all external functions are reusable or shared, especially, the ones that are dependent on the syntax of the base language. In such cases, the functions adopted by multiple weavers generally use identical algorithms and conform to a common abstract structure to increase their reusability.

Figure 18 shows the reusability summary for the FORTRAN and Object Pascal weavers. It can be observed that the front-end reusability is considerably larger than the back-end reusability. Overall, approximately 55-65% of the artifacts were reused between the two weavers.

FRONT-END REUSABILITY			
METAMODEL	KM3+TCS (LOC)	Shared LOC	Percentage
Aspect Pascal	565	280	**49.5**
Aspect FORTRAN	550		**50.1**
MODEL TRANSFORMATION	ATL (LOC)	Shared LOC	Percentage
Aspect Pascal	1890	1290	**68.2**
Aspect FORTRAN	1585		**81.3**
BACK-END REUSABILITY				
PARLANSE FUNCTIONS	Total LOC	Shared LOC	No. of Shared Functions	Percentage
Aspect Pascal	873	310	11	**35.5**
Aspect FORTRAN	775			**40**
OVERALL REUSABILITY			
OVERALL	LOC	Shared LOC	Percentage
Aspect Pascal	3328	1880	**56.4**
Aspect FORTRAN	2910		**64.6**

Fig. 18. Reusability summary for FORTRAN and Object Pascal weavers

4.4   Limitations to Current Framework

Although more advanced pointcuts like control flow (`cflow`) and reflection (`this-JoinPoint`) were omitted from the current investigation due to limited control flow analysis in DMS for Object Pascal and FORTRAN, future research aims to introduce them at a later stage. It should be noted that the join point model in our implementation is AST based, where join points are mapped to specific nodes or control points in the AST. Using the underlying AST based infrastructure, a control flow graph for a specific language in DMS can be implemented by using an attribute grammar evaluator that propagates control points around the AST and assembles those control points into a completed graph. Additional context information like `thisJoinPoint` can be added at specific nodes or control points in the AST. One can construct these evaluators by using a DMS Control Flow graph domain and a supporting library of control flow graph facilities that it provides. These evaluators are currently available off-the-shelf for the more popular C++, C and Java domains. Since building an attribute evaluator for Object Pascal and FORTRAN is purely engineering and less scientific in nature, we chose to introduce them at a later stage. However, we understand that with the addition of reflective capabilities and more advanced pointcut mechanisms, there might be a reduction in the overall reusability of model transformation rules in another language or platform context, but the goal of this research has been to show a technique to construct reusable aspect weavers by utilizing most of the software artifacts (e.g., existing parsers and analysis engines) that are already available for a variety of legacy and modern programming languages. The science and theory to construct such tools are already well-established and it would require considerable engineering effort to build them from scratch without gaining any additional scientific knowledge. On the other hand, new language-independent techniques like .Net CLI / CodeDOM are not always feasible to support various legacy languages like FORTRAN, COBOL and Object Pascal due to their non-conformance to the .Net specification. Unless those languages are forced to comply with a language-independent CLI specification, new experimentation to impart AOP features to such languages is very challenging. Currently, DMS provides more mature analysis engines for languages like C++ and Java. As part of possible future extensions, we plan to experiment with such advanced pointcut mechanisms (`cflow`, `reflection`) for these two languages. Another limitation in our current aspect metamodel is the absence of inter-type declaration (ITD). This was primarily due to the reason that we intended to experiment with a smaller subset of AOP language features and introduce others gradually at a later stage. This was more of a design choice than a limitation of the framework or the underlying program transformation engine, which has the necessary machinery to support ITDs.

Language-specific weavers will have a distinct advantage in their initial implementation of new features because they are direct extensions of their base language (low complexity). However, if one has to repeat those features in another language and platform context, there is no technique to support reuse of such features (low reusability). In our framework, the complexity is high on the part of the weaver constructor because of multiple levels of transformation. However, it is possible to pass on already implemented features from one language to another (high reusability). From the end-user's point of view, the complexity is similar for both language-specific and language-independent techniques, except the fact that a better mechanism is needed to handle opaque statements (i.e., statements that are not parsed by the front-end).

5   Related Work

In addition to Weave.Net [18], SourceWeave.Net [17], and Compose* [44] (presented in Section 3), another framework that aims toward language-independent AOP is Aspicere [16]. Currently, Aspicere's weaver transforms a C program by manipulating an XML-representation of its Abstract Syntax Tree (AST), but future extensions aim to combine Aspicere with the Gnu Compiler Collection (GCC). The technique plans to introduce two new intermediate representations: GENERIC and GIMPLE trees. Each different language front-end produces a forest of GENERIC trees, which are then turned into GIMPLE for optimizations and eventually fed to the back-ends. Aspicere aims at expressing the weaver's semantics in terms of generic trees that can eventually lead to language-independent AOP.

An initial prototype that brings aspects to COBOL was developed through a collaboration of academic and industrial partners [31]. The implementation reuses a pre-existing COBOL front-end to construct an AST that is persisted as XML. The Aspect COBOL weaver operates on the XML representation using a DOM-based approach. The weaver has similar semantics to AspectJ join points [8], but uses an imperative language that is closer to COBOL syntax. The weaver provides ad hoc type analysis (e.g., use-to-def site navigation) for more sophisticated data join points.

A related challenge emerging from representing the source model in the form of an XML representation (as seen in Weave.Net, SourceWeave.Net, and AspectCobol) concerns the issue of scalability. The verbosity of an XML code representation may hamper the size of an application that can be weaved. It has been reported that an XML representation is up to 50 times larger than other internal representations and much slower to transform [32]. The verbosity of XML may influence the ability of SourceWeave.Net, Aspicere and AspectCobol to handle very large applications.

More recently, Heidenreich et al. showed a generic approach for implementing aspect orientation for arbitrary languages using invasive software composition. However, their technique is more useful for declarative DSLs than for GPLs [26].

Morin et al. presented a generic aspect-oriented modeling framework to represent aspects that can be adapted to any modeling domain [27]. Although our work tends to capture the generality of aspect languages and not individual aspects, nevertheless, it can gain interesting insights from such an approach.

Within the AOSD-Europe project, a metamodel for aspect-oriented programming languages was developed [42]. The metamodel presented in that project consisted of four different metamodels; namely, the join point metamodel, join point selector metamodel, selector advice binding metamodel and advice metamodel. We believe this to be useful information and may be used to enhance the metamodel described in this paper.

A recent addition to the class of language extension tools is MetaBorg [33], which provides an ability to embed domain-specific languages into general-purpose languages. However, the embedding permitted by MetaBorg is focused on localized adaptations, and cannot accommodate the global effects of aspects. MetaBorg also requires specific transformation rules to be written for each GPL. Based on the Meta-Borg approach, an extensible kernel language for multi-language AOP called Reflex was developed [43].

In [34], advanced pattern detection techniques are suggested by applying a logic-based query language that uses concrete source code templates to match against a combination of structural and behavioral program representations, including call-graphs, points-to analysis results and abstract syntax trees. This is similar to the rule specification language available in DMS that is used for pattern matching. RSL also provides external patterns and conditions that make calls to external functions written in DMS PARLANSE (a parallel language for manipulating symbolic expressions) for more advanced program analysis.

Ramos et al. propose a framework for expressing patterns as *model-snippets* and show how pattern matching can be performed with model-snippets for any given metamodel [35]. In our current framework, all pattern matching and analysis is done through the back-end, where the metamodel is used to express the front-end aspect language and its generic extensions. All of the higher-order aspect specifications are translated to lower-order back-end program transformation code that does the actual weaving.

6 Conclusion

The research presented in this paper raised several key challenges (identified in Section 1.1) in designing a generic framework to construct aspect weavers. In particular, the paper describes a model-driven framework that combines program transformation with model-driven engineering to construct aspect weavers for modern and legacy programming languages. We showed how *Challenges C1 (parser construction problem)* and *C2 (weaver construction problem)* were resolved through adoption of a mature program transformation engine as the back-end of the framework. The paper also illustrated how accidental complexities (*Challenge C3*) that are generally associated with a program transformation system can be reduced using a model-driven front-end. The last challenge (*Challenge C4*) deals with generality, reusability, and transfer of knowledge from one weaver to another. In our opinion, this is the most difficult challenge of the four. We demonstrated that by making the front-end generic, along with a systematic program transformation rule generator, significant inroads have been made to address this challenge. To evaluate the usefulness of the generic framework, two aspect weavers were constructed for Object Pascal and FORTRAN. The FORTRAN weaver was built after the successful construction of the Object Pascal weaver. When constructing the second weaver, we observed that we could reuse more than 50% of the artifacts (generic front-end and rule generator) that were created during the construction of the Aspect Pascal weaver.

The current approach is focused on a simple join point model. More advanced pointcuts like control flow and reflective techniques like `thisJoinPoint` are currently not available. However, with the availability of a mature control flow analysis engine for Object Pascal and FORTRAN in DMS, we can extend the weavers to support advanced aspect language features. Note that most of the analysis and pattern matching is realized through the back-end program transformation engine and the front-end only acts as a wrapper to the back-end. If the back-end PTE can support advanced program analysis, it is possible to wrap those features through the front-end, avoiding all the accidental complexities (*Challenge C3*) that are generally associated with complex PTEs.

In summary, this research provides an initial solution to several challenges listed in Section 1 by reusing most of the existing software artifacts (e.g., lexers, parsers, analyzers, evaluators) that are already available for a variety of GPLs. Thus, our framework enables new experimentation with advanced software engineering principles like AOP for existing legacy languages. The research also addresses new challenges that arise from the usage of complex PTEs like DMS by providing a suitable front-end that hides most of the accidental complexity.

6.1 Lessons Learned

In this section, we summarize the seven main lessons that we have learned while working on the research presented in this paper. These lessons are enumerated below:

- *Lesson 1 - Generalizing the front-end:* We realized that parts of the aspect language front-end can be reused by making it generic. By generalizing the front-end metamodel, several aspect languages can extend a single core (e.g., GAspect) while the differences can be captured within their specific part. The solution can be achieved using MDE techniques like metamodel extension.
- *Lesson 2 - Improving the generic metamodel:* The current generic metamodel (i.e., GAspect) generalizes what is common between APascal and AFortran (i.e., the aspect languages for Object Pascal, and FORTRAN). Figure 19a shows this current design. If we consider the construction of ARuby (i.e., an aspect language for Ruby) using our framework, this new language could directly extend GAspect as shown in Figure 19a. However, it is expected that both ARuby and APascal will have some commonality (e.g., related to the object paradigm) not shared with AFortran. Figure 19b shows the structure of the new improved design. The commonalities between APascal and ARuby are extracted into OO-A (the common object-oriented constructs of ARuby and APascal), which extends GAspect. In [36], a proposal for typing models as a collection of interconnected objects is discussed. The formalism described there is an extension to object-oriented typing, but suitable to a model-oriented context. Our approach of defining an abstract metamodel and its conformance between other metamodels via metamodel extensions is similar to the concept described in [36].

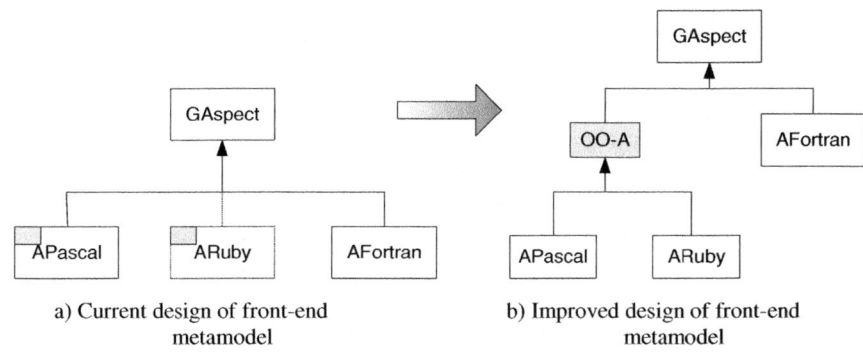

a) Current design of front-end
metamodel

b) Improved design of front-end
metamodel

Fig. 19. Improving the front-end metamodel design

- *Lesson 3 – Use of generic interfaces in the rule generator:* The concept of generic interface was introduced in Section 3.2 to generalize the design of the rule generator. As a result, the rule generator library can be reused across languages with minimum customization.
- *Lesson 4 - Modeling can be suitably applied to PTEs:* From our research, we realized that it is possible to model and transform program transformation re-write-rules using MDE. The combination of both technical spaces offers more possibilities than each considered separately.
- *Lesson 5 - Changing the target PTE:* The source aspect metamodel need not be altered even if one chooses to opt for a different target PTE (e.g., ASF+SDF). In such a case, a new PTE metamodel needs to be developed, as well as a new rule generator for this new target. We expect that it may be possible to generalize part of the transformation code by introducing a PTE pivot metamodel that abstracts common properties of many PTEs.
- *Lesson 6 - Changing the source language:* Conversely, for every new aspect language, one needs to add the appropriate metamodel extensions to the GAspect metamodel, but no change to the target metamodel is needed.
- *Lesson 7 - Automation of rule generator:* We realized that most of the time and effort on building a new weaver is spent on understanding the concrete syntax of the base language. We believe that it should be possible to extract the join point model from transformation rules, and model it in terms of the concrete syntax. Then, a significant part of the transformations could be automatically generated.

6.2 Future Work and Possible Extensions

The following represent areas of future investigation that can extend the capabilities of the model-driven weaver construction techniques introduced in this paper:

- *Improving reusability:* We would like to improve the reusability of features among aspect weavers by further enhancements to the existing design of our framework. For example, we would like to create a generic metamodel for object-oriented constructs, from which the weavers constructed for object-oriented languages can inherit. Similarly, we would like to create a generic metamodel for Join Point Models (JPMs). All weavers can inherit from the generic JPM, and (if required) add new join point extensions to their specific JPM.

- ***Constructing weavers for other GPLs:*** Another possible extension of our work is to construct aspect weavers for other GPLs including object-oriented scripting languages like Ruby, JavaScript and Python. We can also experiment with adding new types of join points (e.g., loops and conditional statements) to existing general-purpose programming languages like Java and C++.
- ***Applying the approach to DSALs:*** Although the majority of research in the AOSD community focuses on general-purpose aspect languages (e.g. AspectJ), there have been a number of influential investigations on domain-specific aspect languages (DSALs) (e.g., COOL for concurrency management and RIDL for serialization [38]). So far, we have only considered the construction of general-purpose aspect languages using our framework, but it would be interesting to investigate how the framework can also accommodate the development of weavers targeting DSALs.

Acknowledgement

This work is supported in part by an NSF CAREER award (CCF-1052616) and by the OpenEmbeDD project.

References

1. Kiczales, G., Lamping, J., Mendhekar, A., Maeda, C., Lopes, C., Loingtier, J., Irwin, J.: Aspect-Oriented Programming. In: Liu, Y., Auletta, V. (eds.) ECOOP 1997. LNCS, vol. 1241, pp. 220–242. Springer, Heidelberg (1997)
2. Clarke, S., Harrison, W., Ossher, H., Tarr, P.: Subject-Oriented Design: Towards Improved Alignment of Requirements, Design, and Code. In: Object-Oriented Programming, Systems, Languages, and Applications (OOPSLA), Denver, CO, October 1999, pp. 325–339 (1999)
3. Jacobson, I., Ng, P.: Aspect-Oriented Software Development with Use Cases. Addison-Wesley, Reading (2005)
4. France, R., Ray, I., Georg, G., Ghosh, S.: Aspect-Oriented Approach to Design Modeling. IEE Proceedings - Software (Special Issue on Early Aspects: Aspect-Oriented Requirements Engineering and Architecture Design) 151(4), 173–185 (2004)
5. Schmidt, D.: Guest Editor's Introduction: Model-Driven Engineering. IEEE Computer 39(2), 25–31 (2006)
6. Lämmel, R., Verhoef, C.: Cracking the 500 Language Problem. IEEE Software, 78–88 (November/December 2001)
7. Ulrich, W.: Legacy Systems: Transformation Strategies. Prentice-Hall, Englewood Cliffs (2002)
8. Kiczales, G., Hilsdale, E., Hugunin, J., Kersten, M., Palm, J., Griswold, W.: Getting Started with AspectJ. Communications of the ACM, 59–65 (October 2001)

9. Baxter, I., Pidgeon, C., Mehlich, M.: DMS: Program Transformation for Practical Scalable Software Evolution. In: International Conference on Software Engineering (ICSE), Edinburgh, Scotland, May 2004, pp. 625–634 (2004)

10. Fradet, P., Südholt, M.: Towards a Generic Framework for Aspect-Oriented Programming. In: Demeyer, S., Dannenberg, R.B. (eds.) ECOOP 1998 Workshops. LNCS, vol. 1543, pp. 394–397. Springer, Heidelberg (1998)

11. Aßmann, U., Ludwig, A.: Aspect Weaving with Graph Rewriting. In: International Symposium on Generative and Component-Based Software Engineering, Erfurt, Germany, September 1999, pp. 24–36 (1999)

12. Gray, J., Roychoudhury, S.: A Technique for Constructing Aspect Weavers using a Program Transformation Engine. In: International Conference on Aspect-Oriented Software Development (AOSD), Lancaster, UK, March 2004, pp. 36–45 (2004)

13. van den Brand, M., Heering, J., Klint, P., Olivier, P.: Compiling Rewrite Systems: The ASF+SDF Compiler. ACM Transactions on Programming Languages and Systems, 334–368 (July 2002)

14. Cordy, J.: The TXL Source Transformation Language. Science of Computer Programming 61(3), 190–210 (2006)

15. Akers, R., Baxter, I., Mehlich, M., Ellis, B., Luecke, K.: Case Study: Re-engineering C++ Component Models via Automatic Program Transformation. Information & Software Technology 49(3), 275–291 (2007)

16. Adams, B.: Language-independent Aspect Weaving. Summer School on Generative and Transformational Techniques in Software Engineering, Braga, Portugal (July 2005)

17. Jackson, A., Clarke, S.: SourceWeave. In: Karsai, G., Visser, E. (eds.) GPCE 2004. LNCS, vol. 3286, pp. 115–135. Springer, Heidelberg (2004)

18. Lafferty, D., Cahill, V.: Language-Independent Aspect-Oriented Programming. In: Object-Oriented Programming, Systems, Languages, and Applications (OOPSLA), Anaheim, CA, October 2003, pp. 1–12 (2003)

19. Lämmel, R.: Declarative Aspect-Oriented Programming. In: ACM SIGPLAN Workshop on Partial Evaluation and Semantics-Based Program Manipulation, San Antonio, TX, January 1999, pp. 131–146 (1999)

20. Jouault, F., Bézivin, J.: KM3: a DSL for Metamodel Specification. In: Gorrieri, R., Wehrheim, H. (eds.) FMOODS 2006. LNCS, vol. 4037, pp. 171–185. Springer, Heidelberg (2006)

21. Kurtev, I., Bézivin, J., Jouault, F., Valduriez, P.: Model-based DSL Frameworks. In: Object-Oriented Programming, Systems, Languages and Applications, Portland, OR, October 2006, pp. 602–616 (2006)

22. Barbero, M., Jouault, F., Gray, J., Bézivin, J.: A Practical Approach to Model Extension. In: European Conference on Model Driven Architecture Foundations and Applications (ECMDA), Haifa, Israel, June 2007, pp. 32–42 (2007)

23. Jouault, F., Bézivin, J., Kurtev, I.: TCS: A DSL for the Specification of Textual Concrete Syntaxes in Model Engineering. In: Generative Programming and Component Engineering (GPCE), Portland, OR, October 2006, pp. 249–254 (2006)

24. Jouault, F., Allilaire, F., Bézivin, J., Kurtev, I.: ATL: A Model Transformation Tool. Science of Computer Programming 72(1-2), 31–39 (2008)

25. Harbulot, B., Gurd, J.: Using AspectJ to Separate Concerns in Parallel Scientific Java Code. In: International Conference on Aspect-Oriented Software Development (AOSD), Lancaster, UK, March 2004, pp. 122–131 (2004)

26. Heidenreich, F., Johannes, J., Zschaler, S.: Aspect Orientation for Your Language of Choice. In: 11th International Workshop on Aspect-Oriented Modeling, Nashville, TN (September 2007)
27. Morin, B., Barais, O., Jézéquel, J., Ramos, R.: Towards a Generic Aspect-Oriented Modeling Framework. In: Workshop on Models and Aspects (ECOOP), Berlin, Germany (July 2007)
28. Klint, P., Lämmel, R., Verhoef, C.: Toward an Engineering Discipline for Grammarware. ACM Transactions on Software Engineering and Methodology 14(3), 331–380 (2005)
29. Gropp, W., Lusk, E., Doss, N., Skjellum, A.: A High-Performance, Portable Implementation of the MPI Message Passing Interface Standard. Parallel Computing 22(6), 789–828 (1996)
30. GenAWeave project website, http://www.cis.uab.edu/softcom/genaweave
31. Lämmel, R., De Schutter, K.: What Does Aspect-Oriented Programming Mean to Cobol? In: International Conference on Aspect-Oriented Software Development (AOSD), Chicago, IL, March 2005, pp. 99–110 (2005)
32. Germon, R.: Using XML as an Intermediate Form for Compiler Development. In: XML Conference and Exposition, Orlando, FL (December 2001)
33. Bravenboer, M., Visser, E.: Concrete Syntax for Objects: Domain-specific Language Embedding and Assimilation without Restrictions. In: Object-Oriented Programming, Systems, Languages, and Applications (OOPSLA), Vancouver, Canada, October 2004, pp. 365–383 (2004)
34. De Roover, C., Brichau, J., Noguera, C., D'Hondt, T., Duchiena, L.: Behavioural Similarity Matching using Concrete Source Code Templates in Logic Queries. In: ACM SIGPLAN Workshop on Partial Evaluation and Program Manipulation (PEPM 2007), Nice, France, January 2007, pp. 92–101 (2007)
35. Ramos, R., Barais, O., Jézéquel., J.: Matching Model-Snippets. In: Engels, G., Opdyke, B., Schmidt, D.C., Weil, F. (eds.) MODELS 2007. LNCS, vol. 4735, pp. 121–135. Springer, Heidelberg (2007)
36. Steel, J., Jézéquel, J.: On Model Typing. Journal of Software and Systems Modeling (SoSyM) 6(4), 452–468 (2007)
37. Eclipse Model to Text (M2T) project, http://www.eclipse.org/modeling/m2t/
38. Lopes, C.: D: A Language Framework for Distributed Programming. Ph.D. Dissertation, College of Computer Science, Northeastern University, December 1997 (1998)
39. Jossic, A., Del Fabro, M., Lerat, J., Bézivin, J., Jouault, F.: Model Integration with Model Weaving: A Case Study in System Architecture. In: International Conference on Systems Engineering and Modeling, Haifa, Israel, March 2007, pp. 79–84 (2007)
40. Hilsdale, E., Hugunin, J.: Advice Weaving in AspectJ. In: International Conference on Aspect-Oriented Software Development (AOSD), Lancaster, UK, March 2004, pp. 26–35 (2004)
41. Schult, W., Tröger, P.: Loom.NET - An Aspect Weaving Tool. In: Cardelli, L. (ed.) ECOOP 2003. Schult, W., Tröger, P, vol. 2743. Springer, Heidelberg (2003)
42. Brichau, J., Mezini, M., Noyé, J., Havinga, W., Bergmans, L., Gasiunas, V., Bockisch, C., Fabry, J., D'Hondt, T.: An Initial Metamodel for Aspect-Oriented Programming Languages, Deliverable D39. In: AOSD-Europe (2006)
43. Tanter, E.: An Extensible Kernel Language for AOP. In: AOSD Workshop on Open and Dynamic Aspect Languages, Bonn, Germany (2006)

44. de Roo, A., Hendriks, M., Havinga, W., Durr, P., Bergmans, L.: Compose*: A Language-
    and Platform-Independent Aspect Compiler for Composition Filters. In: Workshop on
    Advanced Software Development Tools and Techniques, Pahpos, Cyprus (July 2008)
45. Chalabine, M., Kessler, C.W.: Parallelisation of Sequential Programs by Invasive
    Composition and Aspect Weaving. In: Cao, J., Nejdl, W., Xu, M. (eds.) APPT 2005.
    LNCS, vol. 3756, pp. 131–140. Springer, Heidelberg (2005)
46. Irwin, J., Loingtier, J., Gilbert, J., Kiczales, G., Lamping, J., Mendhekar, A., Shpeisman,
    T.: Aspect-Oriented Programming of Sparse Matrix Code. In: Sun, Z., Reynders, J.V.W.,
    Tholburn, M. (eds.) ISCOPE 1997. LNCS, vol. 1343, pp. 249–256. Springer, Heidelberg
    (1997)
47. Herrmann, C., Lengauer, C.: Using Metaprogramming to Parallelize Functional
    Specifications. Parallel Processing Letter 12(2), 193–210 (2002)

A System of Patterns for Reusable Aspect Libraries

Maarten Bynens, Eddy Truyen, and Wouter Joosen

DistriNet, K.U. Leuven
Maarten.Bynens@cs.kuleuven.be
http://distrinet.cs.kuleuven.be

Abstract. A key direction for achieving mainstream adoption of aspect-oriented (AO) programming is the availability of reusable aspect libraries that can be easily applied across a wide range of applications. This paper presents a pattern system for AO design that provides solutions for recurring problems in the design of such reusable aspect libraries. We have focused on libraries using AspectJ. The requirements for setting up reusable aspect libraries are first sketched. Subsequently, an architectural pattern and four design patterns addressing key design problems are identified: managing aspect-awareness, enabling join point abstraction and adaptation, decomposition, and mediation. Each design pattern leads to a set of programming idioms to address the related design problem. The pattern system aggregates the four sets of idioms that include a specific section to guide selection of a specific idiom. The implementation of an aspect library for access control is discussed to illustrate how the system of patterns can be used and how the different patterns and idioms can be combined. The format of the pattern catalogs is based on pattern writing advice provided by the Hillside group. We have analyzed and integrated related work in design patterns for aspects. Furthermore, we present an initial validation of the patterns with respect to their stability, versatility, and ease-of-use. To the best of our knowledge, this is the first comprehensive system of AOP patterns that supports the construction of aspect libraries.

1 Introduction

Separation of concerns is a central principle in the design of software [22]. The presence of crosscutting concerns is a barrier in complying with that principle. A crosscutting concern is a concern that conceptually is logically coherent but that in practical implementations is scattered over different software modules and therefore tangled with other concerns that are implemented within those modules. Well-known examples of such concerns are persistence, transactions, logging, etc.

Aspect-oriented software development (AOSD) puts forward the concept of an aspect to modularize crosscutting concerns, to achieve a better conformity between concerns and modules. At the programming level, aspects are somehow

S. Katz et al. (Eds.): Transactions on AOSD VIII, LNCS 6580, pp. 46–107, 2011.

similar to classes - they can consist of fields, methods - but have the additional
capability of intervening in the normal program control flow and structure - by
means of pointcuts, advice, and inter-type declarations (ITDs).

As always with the introduction of new programming mechanisms, an important question is how to put these facilities to good use. For aspect-oriented programming (AOP) this is particularly important now that AOP has become more
mature and increasingly more developers have started to use this technology [66].
Guidelines and concrete examples help developers to understand the benefits of
using the paradigm and its facilities. As design patterns for object-oriented software [19] helped programmers to deal with late binding and encapsulation, we
believe there is also a need for design patterns for aspect-oriented software that
support programmers with expressive aspect-oriented composition, which has
the power to change the behavior of a program drastically. With pointcuts and
advice, programmers are often uncertain about which code is going to execute
when, similar to the days when late binding was a relatively new concept: programmers were often unsure about which method was going to execute. It is
important to note that, without a careful design, using aspects can be prob-
lematic and a threat to stable, adaptable designs [72, 14, 46]. As a result, AOP
needs its own system of design patterns: effective design solutions for recurring
design problems [9].

Another important factor in the adoption of AOP by non-experts is the availability of reusable aspects. Similar to COTS components, such reusable aspects
can be used as basic building blocks for application development. This evolution
has been identified as one of the key conditions for adoption of AOP [83]. Some
reusable aspects, targeted at a specific concern, have recently been presented.
Examples include transactions [43], concurrency [15], and persistence [65]. Traditionally, non-functional concerns such as the ones mentioned are the main candidates to become reusable components. However, nothing prevents functional
concerns to become reusable components as well. Especially in product-line environments and more mature domains.

The goal of this paper is to provide the developer with a system of design
patterns to guide the use of AOP, especially with reusability and stability of
aspects in mind. We use AspectJ as the representative of a family of AOP languages that have a Java-like language background and support pointcuts, advice
and ITD's. Preferably, also type parameters and annotations are available.

Existing works by various authors have already presented design solutions for
AOP [29, 50, 40, 62, 25, 51, 24, 68]. This paper builds of course upon such work
in several ways. Apart from the inspiration for the patterns themselves, these
works also prove the relevance of the need for design patterns. The design patterns described in existing literature are however fragmentary contributions that
are not targeted towards a common goal or problem context. A coherent system
that unites and integrates these fragmentary contributions is therefore needed:
often interesting links between different design solutions are not discussed. Also,

documentation of known uses and guidance in selecting patterns are typically not well addressed in these works. Our proposed system of patterns therefore aims to address this fragmentary nature by making the following contributions.

– We describe a pattern system for design problems related to one coherent problem context, namely, how to design reusable aspect libraries that can be easily deployed in various applications, and that are stable in the presence of evolution.
– Our pattern system consists of 3 layers: an architectural pattern, 4 design patterns focusing on a specific sub-problem, and for each design pattern a set of programming idioms that can be used to implement the design pattern in AspectJ.

  • Our pattern system also adds forces and variation points that guide the interested application developer in choosing which solution is best suited for a particular problem context.
  • We identify uses of these patterns in academic and industry contexts.
  • Some patterns now have a more general description than their counterpart in related work. It makes the patterns more generally applicable by elevating the description from a specific problem context.

– We illustrate how the pattern system can be used together by presenting a case study that employs a multiple of the presented patterns. Furthermore, we present an initial validation of using the patterns and idioms with respect to the requirements.

To the best of our knowledge, this is the first comprehensive system of AOP patterns that supports the construction of libraries. We obviously build upon earlier publications that contain initial description of design patterns, and possible small collections of these [29, 40, 50, 24, 25, 62, 69, 68], as well as lessons learned from developing reusable aspects [42, 15, 82, 65], some empirical studies [37, 61] and proposed language extensions for AOP [4, 34, 64]. Clearly this work is not about supporting classical OO design patterns by using AOP [31, 21].

Structure of the Paper

The second section presents the requirements that are essential for the success of reusable aspects, namely versatility and stability of the aspect design and the ease of using the library. Section 3 gives a quick overview of aspect-oriented programming. More concretely, we introduce the main constructs in AspectJ, necessary to understand the examples in the rest of the paper. Section 4 gives a high level overview of the pattern system. It introduces the architectural pattern, four design patterns and the associated programming idioms. Section 4 also includes the template we use to describe the patterns and idioms, and elaborates on the case of access control, which we use as a running example throughout the paper. Section 5 describes the individual patterns and idioms following the structure discussed in the preceding section. Section 6 shows how the different patterns and idioms can be used in combination by presenting a complete, reusable implementation of the access control aspect. Section 7 presents an initial validation. It reports on the setup and presents a comparison between the aspect libraries with and without the patterns with respect to the requirements outlined in Section 2. Section 8 summarizes the content of the paper and discusses future work.

2   Requirements

The success of reusable aspect libraries will mainly depend on three kinds of requirements, namely the stability of the aspect library design, the versatility of the library and the ease of using the library. Each of these requirements is necessary to achieve true reusability. The key challenge of reusability is composition of the aspect library with applications. *Versatility* is about the feasibility of that composition, *Ease-of-use* is about the difficulty of making that composition and *Stability* about the consequences of the composition on evolution.

Stable Design

Loose coupling is important for reusable aspects. Both the aspect and the base program should be able to evolve independently, with a minimal impact on each other. Loose coupling between modules in the context of AOP means more than just not referring to internal specifics of other modules. Because of the quantifying abilities of AOP (one module can have an effect on multiple other modules) there is a need for a stable, but flexible, definition of the relation between aspect and base, in order to make it resistant against modification of a related module. It is the pointcut that embodies this coupling. It's hard to find a good balance between making this coupling either too explicit (like enumerating all method signatures) or too implicit (like using a lot of wildcards). This problem leads to *fragile pointcuts*, which has received significant attention [76, 45, 73, 38].

Consider for example that we have a reusable aspect that implements access control functionality[1]. An important relation in this aspect describes the sensitive entities in the application. It is crucial that when the software evolves, the resulting relation (which is modified or extended accordingly), is still the one intended originally.

Versatility

Versatility means that the aspect design can be reused across a range of different applications. The opposite of versatility is inflexibility, i.e., the inability to refine the abstractions of aspect to a broad range of application requirements. Typically, the cause of such inflexibility is that certain design choices, that are fixed by the aspect, conflict with the requirements of the application. As a result, the

---

[1] We will use the case of access control as a running example throughout the rest of this paper.

application developer has to workaround this problem by reimplementing the aspect functionality, leading to duplicated code.

A key to reusable aspect libraries is thus support for defining stable abstractions that can encapsulate later refinements to the needs of various applications. Different AOP languages differ in their support for incremental refinement of abstractions (e.g. in AspectJ only abstract aspects can be extended and pointcuts cannot be refined while in CaesarJ [5] it is possible to specialize and compose with non-abstract pointcuts through a super keyword). Even with good language support however, it is still hard to come up with partial definitions of aspects that leave open the right set of variation points to accommodate the needs of an open set of applications. Depending on the used AOP language and the different forces at play, the appropriate programming idioms must thus be used to realize reusable and stable aspect designs.

Ease-of-Use

Reusable aspects are meant to be used also by developers without much expertise in AOP. Easing the use of reusable aspects thus requires that composition of aspects can be done based on guidelines and examples of good practice.

What we need is that complex aspect compositions are easy to deploy. Such compositions are mainly accomplished by means of pointcuts, advice and ITD's, mechanisms that can get the non-expert developer into trouble. Design patterns will help the developer to manage the complexity of these new mechanisms and prevent the occurrence of unintended and harmful situations.

For instance, in the situation where a user wants to deploy a reusable aspect implementing access control, the user needs to configure which objects in the application are sensitive and the access rules that determine whether an action is allowed or not. One way to do this, is by providing the relevant annotations in the base code. Any complex aspect composition might be based on those annotations.

In realistic situations, a reusable aspect will not just be one aspect. It will be a collection of aspects, classes, interfaces, ... For the user, the reusable aspect should be a unit of configuration. Therefore, ease-of-use is also applicable to the configuration of the aggregate of aspects as a whole. As a result, the user is offered a powerful composition mechanism.

In summary, experience has taught us that it is hard to define aspects so that they are

- expressive: able to describe the intended join points to interact at in a concise way
- robust: not overly dependent on changes in the base program
- composable: in order to define aspects in terms of other aspects

As a result, reusable aspects should abstract from their dependencies and specify both their structure and behavior in terms of these abstractions.

3   Aspect-Oriented Programming

This section gives a short introduction to the principles of AOP. More concretely, we introduce the main constructs in AspectJ, which we use as the language of choice for the rest of this paper to present the idioms and the examples. AOP provides new constructs to dynamically intervene in the control flow of a program and to statically alter the structure of a program. We will first address the dynamic facilities of AOP and the static facilities afterwards.

3.1   Behavioral Crosscutting

An aspect intervenes in the control flow by attaching extra functionality at certain join points. A join point is a well-defined point in the execution of a program. Examples are the call or execution of a method, reading or writing an instance variable, . . .

A pointcut is a description of a set of join points that share one or more characteristics using a pointcut language (PCL). For example, the following pointcut matches all the join points of the execution of a method `foo()` as declared in a type `Sensitive`.

```
pointcut sensitive(): execution(public void Sensitive.foo());
```

AspectJ offers a number of primitive pointcuts (such as `execution` in the example above) that can be used and combined to define more complex pointcuts. Besides the primitives concerning methods and fields, other primitive pointcuts match join points related to object creation, exception handling, advice execution, and control flow. Also more dynamic primitives that relate to the actual identity or run-time type of a certain object or parameter are available. Typically, pointcut declarations then consist of a combination of these primitive constructs by means of logical operators.

To make the description of pointcuts more expressive, the use of wildcards and type patterns is allowed. For example, the following pointcut matches all calls to getter methods on types `Sensitive` or `Confidential` regardless of access modifier[2], return type or number or types of parameters.

```
pointcut getters(): call(* (Sensitive || Confidential).get*(..));
```

AspectJ also supports the use of annotations to describe method signatures (e.g. within a call or execution primitive) and types. E.g. the following pointcut matches all execution join points of methods with a `Sensitive` annotation.

```
pointcut sensitive(): execution(@Sensitive * *(..));
```

Additionally, AspectJ supports a number of annotation-based pointcut primitives which can be used to match, based on the presence of an annotation at runtime or to expose the annotation value as context.

---

[2] By default a pointcut matches any access modifier (it is the same as using a wildcard). To capture package-protected methods, the following pattern has to be used: `execution(!private !public !protected * *(..))`.

The crosscutting functionality that needs to be executed at the join points depicted by a pointcut is defined in a construct called advice. For instance, the following piece of advice specifies that before each join point described by the pointcut `sensitive()`, the method `checkAccess()` will be called.

```
before ():  sensitive (){
  checkAccess ();
}
```

As control flow passes each join point twice (on the way in and on the way out), we need to not only specify at which join points, but also if the advice has to execute before, after, or around the join point. Before and after advice are self-explanatory, around advice replaces the original behavior at the join point but has the ability to call that original behavior by using `proceed` - comparable with a `super` call in a method override.

If the advice needs context information from the intercepted join point, there are two main options. Within the advice block the keyword `thisJoinPoint` can be used to access reflective information available at the join point. A more explicit alternative is to expose the needed context information by using pointcut parameters. These parameters behave like output parameters (as e.g. in C#) that get bound in the pointcut, rather than parameterizing the pointcut, and can subsequently be used in the advice. In the following example, the pointcut exposes the sensitive entity as a parameter, which can be used to check access rights in the advice.

```
pointcut sensitive (Sensitive  entity):
  execution(public void  Sensitive.foo ()) && this (entity);

before(Sensitive  entity):  sensitive (entity){
  checkAccess (entity);
}
```

3.2   Structural Crosscutting

AOP offers inter-type declarations to alter the static structure of a program, e.g. by adding new fields or methods to a class or extending certain inheritance hierarchies. Member introductions can be defined on classes as well as interfaces. They look similar to normal member definitions, except that, additionally, the type where the member needs to be introduced is specified. For example, the following statement introduces the boolean field `isSensitive` to the `Entity` class.

```
public boolean Entity.isSensitive ;
```

Changes to an inheritance hierarchy can be made with `declare` statements. The following statement makes `Calendar` a subclass of `Resource`.

```
declare parents:  Calendar extends  Resource;
```

The `declare` statement can also be used to define the precedence between aspects in case they run advice at the same join point and to signal warnings or errors based on potentially harmful constructs in the base code.

3.3 Aspects

As stated above, aspects are similar to classes. They can contain methods, fields and can be part of an inheritance hierarchy. Additionally, aspects contain point-cut declarations, advice, and inter-type declarations (ITD). With these mechanisms aspects can intervene in both the structure and control flow of the base program. An important difference is that aspects are instantiated implicitly (e.g. in AspectJ one singleton aspect will be created but other instantiation schemes are supported).

Aspects may extend classes and implement interfaces. Classes, however, cannot extend aspects. Aspects may extend other aspects on the condition that the super-aspect is abstract. Abstract aspects cannot be instantiated and will thus not be active. They can contain abstract pointcuts, based on which, advice can be defined.

4 Pattern System Overview

This section presents the overall structure of the system of patterns. The patterns are loosely organized in three layers – architectural pattern, design patterns, and programming idioms – following patterns of software architecture [9]. A single architectural pattern is presented that represents the key architectural design decisions that are applicable to the recurring design problem of building a reusable aspect library. This architectural pattern subsequently makes use of 4 different design patterns that each deal with a particular sub-problem. For each of these design patterns we in turn distinguish between several programming idioms for implementing that design pattern in AspectJ[3].

This section is structured as follows. The architectural pattern is first presented. Thereafter a concise overview of the design patterns and associated idioms is presented. Subsequently the templates used for describing in more detail, the patterns and idioms as part of Sect. 5 is presented. Finally, we give more detail about the running example on an access control library.

4.1 Architectural Pattern

Figure 1 illustrates the architectural pattern for the design of reusable aspect libraries. The pattern distinguishes between multiple elements in the binding between aspect and base components, namely join point abstractions (provided and required) and join point bindings (connector or adapter).

---

[3] We also shortly discuss how to implement similar idioms in CaesarJ, Spring AOP and JBoss AOP.

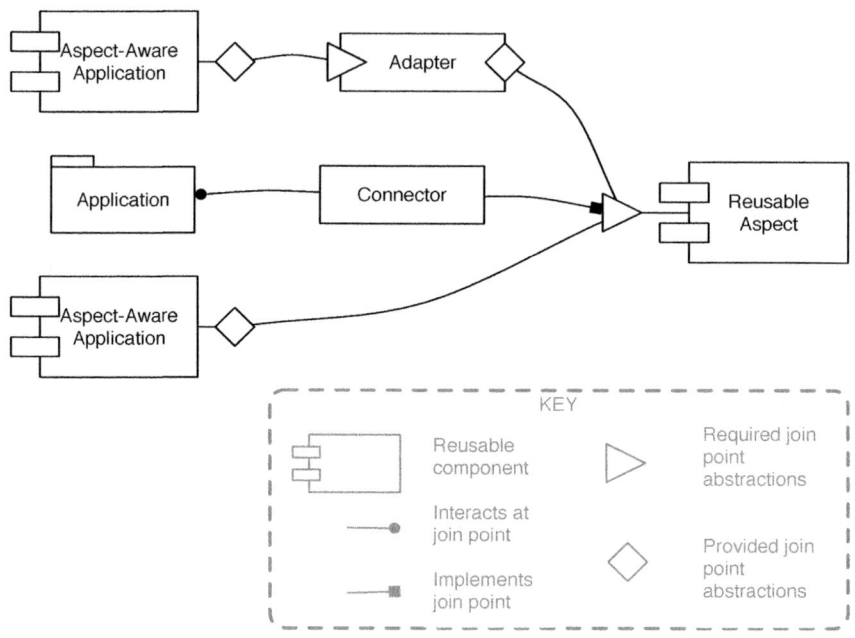

Fig. 1. Architectural pattern for reusable aspect libraries

A first key design decision underlying the architectural pattern is that the aspect-base binding should be defined in terms of the right join point abstractions. A *join point abstraction* (JPA) is part of an aspectual interface that exposes a set of crosscutting abstract structures or behaviors (represented by ▷). Join point abstractions are defined by reusable aspect components as some kind of expected interface. Optionally, the base application can also expose a set of provided join point abstractions (represented by ◇). A consequence of exposing join point abstractions, is that they make the base application aspect-aware instead of keeping it oblivious.

Making a good trade-off between aspect-awareness and obliviousness is difficult [16, 39, 81] and often depends on the particular software development context in which the aspect library will be used. As shown in Figure 1, the architectural pattern therefore manifests itself in three variants with respect to fully completing the binding of an aspect library to a base application. These three variants account for three different software development contexts. A first possibility is that the reusable aspect can be bound to an oblivious base application using a *connector*. An oblivious base program is defined as a program that is not aware that any aspects will be applied to it and therefore has not been prepared for providing any explicit join point abstractions to these aspects. An example scenario for this variant is binding an aspect to legacy code that does not provide explicit join point abstractions. The connector realizes the expected join point abstractions of the aspect library (represented with ——■) in terms of the available structure and syntax of base code (represented with ——•). The two other variants deal with an aspect-aware base application, i.e., a program that exposes a set of provided joint point abstractions. Either these provided join point abstractions match with the expected join point abstractions of the reusable aspect or they don't. If they match, the aspect and the base application can be composed as is. This is realistic e.g. in the context of a mature domain with a standard component model like Enterprise Java Beans, where provided join point abstractions are expressed as annotations that provide metadata related to persistence and transactions. In case the abstractions don't match, an adapter is needed to map the provided joint point abstractions to the expected join point abstractions required by the aspect. This will be a common situation in less mature domains. The adapter can be interpreted as a module that exposes both provided and required join point abstractions in such a way that they respectively match the required JPA of the reusable aspect and the provided JPA of the base code.

Indifferent of which variant is selected, to meet the requirements of stability and versatility, it is important that join point abstractions are abstract enough so that they can hide any changes in the implementation of the base application from the aspect components and, conversely, the aspect is applicable to a broad range of applications.

A reusable aspect library not only requires stability and versatility of the binding between aspect and base, but also the stability and versatility of the internal structure of the aspect library. The internal structure of the aspect libraries should therefore be decomposed into a set of common and open parts which can be refined into a set of sub-aspects. The aspect library also has to encapsulate support for orchestrating the run-time interaction between those sub-aspects.

As a result, the architectural pattern identifies four design problems: two related to the binding between aspect and base (how to abstract from concrete join points in aspect and base code respectively) and two related to the internal structure of the aspect (how to decompose the aspect and how to orchestrate the run-time interaction between the resulting sub-aspects). The next subsection will present the design patterns and associated programming idioms that deal with these four identified design problems.

4.2   Design Patterns and Programming Idioms

The architectural pattern itself depends upon 4 design patterns that each tackle a specific design problem related to the design and integration of reusable aspect libraries. Figure 2 gives an overview of the design patterns by linking them together. In this graph, circles represent design patterns or categories of related idioms and rectangles represent design problems. Edges connect problems and patterns. Initial nodes, indicated by the diamonds, specify the particular development context and the role of the developer involved, i.e., library designer, base developer, and system composer who is responsible for binding the aspect library to the base application. In some development contexts the base developer also plays the role of the system composer. Note that the solution to the design problem of how to connect the aspect library to the target application depends on the solution chosen by the base developer. This is depicted by the dotted line and corresponds with the different manifestations of the binding in Fig. 1.

Each design pattern in turn depends on a set of programming idioms. Different forces play a role in the particular software development context corresponding to the design pattern. These forces are contributory factors in the choice for the most suitable idiom or combination of idioms. This means that a force is neither a sufficient or necessary condition for applying an idiom. Multiple forces can be relevant in a particular problem context. Depending on the relative importance of the these forces, the developer needs to consider whether one force dominates the others and apply the associated idiom or that a combination of idioms is more appropriate. As a result, some idioms are positioned as different variants from which to choose one and other idioms are complementary strategies that each focus at a different dimension of the overall problem of the design pattern. The remainder of this section will now give a short overview of the different design patterns based on Figure 2 and the related idioms which the pattern depends on.

The *Join point abstraction* pattern is used by the library designer to tackle the first problem at hand, i.e. what is the appropriate set of expected join point abstractions on which the aspect library should depend. The table below lists the different alternative programming idioms for implementing this design pattern in AspectJ. We refer to Section 5.2 for a detailed overview of the design pattern and the idioms.

Join point abstraction idioms

Marker interface	A (usually) empty interface that can be used as a type abstraction
Type parameter	Abstract from type information using type parameters in a generic aspect
Abstract pointcut	Use an abstract pointcut to abstract from any crosscutting behavior
Annotation introduction	Use an annotation to abstract from structural join points

The Join point abstraction pattern depends further on a set of programming idioms for binding the expected join point abstractions of the aspect with the base application. As already stated above, there are 2 variants of the architectural pattern for which an additional element is needed for completing a full binding between a reusable aspect and a base application. In case a base application does not provide any join point abstraction, the system composer has to

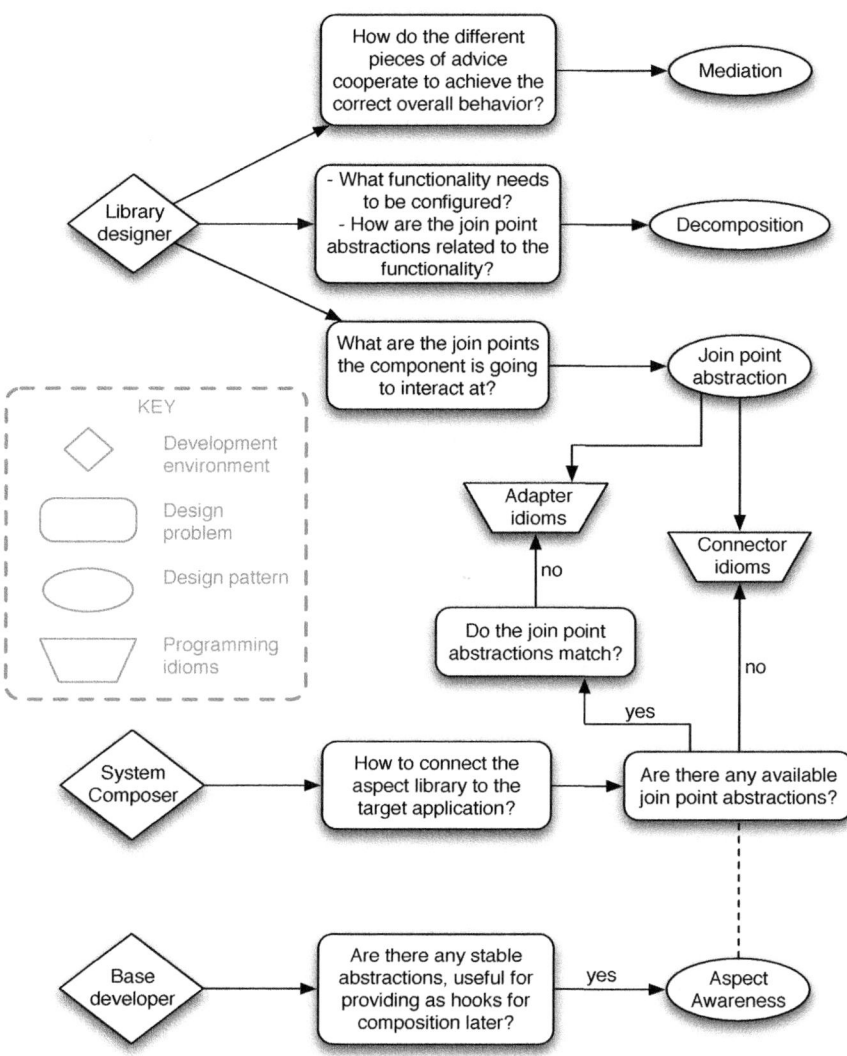

Fig. 2. High level overview of the design patterns

use a *Connector* idiom. In case both sides have an explicit interface with join point abstractions, but these join point abstractions do not match or are implemented using incompatible programming idioms, the system composer must use an *Adapter* idiom. For each Join point abstraction idiom there is one compatible Connector idiom and we refer to Section 5.2 for a detailed overview. We refer to Table 1 in Section 5.2.6 for an overview of the possible Adapter idioms. There exists a separate Adapter idiom for each element in the cartesian product of Join point abstraction and Aspect awareness idioms.

The *Decomposition* pattern targets the development of complex aspect components that are too large to be manageable as a single unit. The pattern proposes to decompose the aspect component in several smaller (more basic) elements. In the context of AspectJ such elements subject to decomposition can be aspects, but also, at a more fine-grained level, pointcuts, advice, and inter-type declarations. A detailed overview of the pattern and related idioms are presented in Section 5.3.

Decomposition idioms

Template pointcut	Decompose a pointcut into hook pointcuts, separating stable, and variable parts
Pointcut method	Encapsulate a dynamic condition in a method to be called from advice
Template advice	Decompose advice into hook methods, separating stable and variable parts
Participant connection	Instead of specifying the connection between aspect and base globally in one place, divide the connection in multiple participant connections, each integrated with a particular part of the base application

The *Mediation* pattern targets the behavior of a number of sub-aspects, which are meant to behave as a single unit. This pattern is typically applied after the decomposition pattern as it brings the decomposed sub-aspects back together to let them cooperate and achieve a common goal. The overview of this pattern and related idioms are presented in Section 5.4.

Mediation idioms

Chained advice	Let the cooperating aspects interact at the same join point and specify an order between their pieces of advice
Mediation data introduction	Introduce mediation-specific data members into base objects and mediate the cooperating aspects using these data members.
Dynamic annotation introduction	Attach an annotation to a certain control flow by annotating advice and mediate the cooperating aspects using this attached annotation.

The single design pattern which is relevant for the base developer is the *Aspect awareness* pattern. This pattern targets the development of the base application that exposes a set of provided join point abstractions at which aspects might interact. Aspect awareness does not mean that the base application is specific to some particular aspect, but that it is prepared for composition with aspects. It is aware of the concept of aspectual composition. A detailed overview of this pattern and its related idioms is presented in Section 5.1.

Aspect-awareness idioms

Pointcut interface	Expose a set of stable crosscutting behaviors as named pointcut signatures
Naming convention	Consistently use a stable naming scheme in the base code
Annotation convention	Consistently use a stable annotation scheme in the base code
Structural convention	Expose a crosscutting concern by consistently applying the same structure to implement a particular concern

4.3   Pattern Template and Catalog Structure

This section will present the structure of the description of the design patterns and idioms in Sect. 5. We describe each design pattern and its associated idioms in a separate subsection. For reasons of clarity, Connector and Adapter idioms are presented in the same section as the Join point abstraction idioms.

The template we use to describe the patterns and idioms is loosely based on the style described by Meszaros and Doblein [56]. The template for describing design patterns is as follows:

- *Problem.* What problem is addressed by the pattern?
- *Context.* The circumstances that impose constraints on the solution are called the context of the pattern and determines the relative importance of its forces.
- *Abstract solution.* How is the problem solved by using this pattern? The pattern gives an abstract solution which is refined or extended by the idioms.
- *Abstract forces.* Considerations that must be taken into account when choosing the solution are called forces. The pattern description presents the abstract forces which describe in general, when this pattern is applicable. These considerations should not be interpreted as a set of necessary conditions for applying the pattern.
- *Rationale.* Discusses why the pattern is an appropriate solution. The rationale refines the problem, motivates the solution and introduces an example.
- *Related work and known uses.* This paragraph enumerates known uses and related descriptions of this design pattern.
- Next, each idiom is described by refining and/or extending the general description of the design pattern. It consists of the following elements:

  - *Name.* Every idiom has a name by which it can be referenced.
  - *Problem.* Only present if the idiom solves a more specific problem than its design pattern.
  - *Solution.* How is the problem solved by using this idiom?
  - *Forces.* The forces of an idiom discuss when the idiom is applicable in comparison to the other idioms for the same pattern.

- *Rationale.* Why is this idiom an appropriate solution? It completes the example and discusses related issues.
- *Implementation in other AOP technologies.* Discusses how this idiom could be implemented in other AOP languages and framework besides AspectJ. CaesarJ, JBoss AOP and Spring AOP are included.
- *Related work and known uses.* The last paragraph enumerates known uses and descriptions of this idiom.

- *Usage of associated programming idioms.* Clarifies how the related idioms are typically applied to solve the problem. Further guidance is given on using the appropriate idioms for implementing the design pattern depending on the specific development context and forces that need to be resolved.
- *Ease-of-use.* Discusses the impact of each idiom on the ease-of-use requirement. Some idioms result into more easy-to-use aspect libraries then other idioms.

4.4   Running Example

In the rationale section of each pattern description we continue with the access control aspect and use the calendar system from Verhanneman et al. [80] as a running example. This calendar system allows users to book appointments and resources (like laptops, projectors, ...). Three main types of users can be distinguished: calendar owners, secretaries and employees. Their access rights can be determined as follows:

- the owner of a calendar can book, edit and delete entries, but cannot book a resource;
- a secretary can edit entries and book resources;
- all employees can view the entries in a calendar but cannot change them.

For instance, if we look at the Calendar interface, methods showEntries, newEntry and deleteEntry require access control, while getOwner doesn't. showEntries is accessible to all Employee objects, but newEntry and deleteEntry are only accessible to the registered owner of the Calendar object.

```
public interface Calendar {
  Entry [] showEntries ();
  void newEntry ( TimeInterval t , Resource [] r );
  void deleteEntry ( Entry e );
  Employee getOwner ();
}
```

Listing 1. Calendar interface from the access control example

5   Pattern Descriptions

This section gives a template-based description of each pattern and related programming idioms in a separate subsection.

5.1 Aspect Awareness Pattern

Problem. How to design base code that is not tightly coupled to aspects while still facilitating the expressive power of AOP? How to get a grip on fragile pointcuts from the base code perspective?

Context. Development of base code that can be easily composed with multiple aspects at once and reused in combination with different aspects over time.

Abstract Solution. Explicitly expose relevant join points in the base code, which aspects can use to interact with. These exposed join points include context information and encapsulate the positions where this information is relevant.

Abstract Forces. Use an aspect awareness pattern when

- the application depends on aspects to implement certain crosscutting concerns not handled by the base code;
- the base program should not be specific to one particular aspect;
- the program abstractions currently representing the crosscutting concern are not stable. Using them could result in fragile pointcuts;
- it doesn't take much effort to explicitly expose relevant join points.

Rationale. A good place to start looking for join points to expose are intrinsic properties of the program. In our access control example the notion of sensitive operations is an important intrinsic property. An access control component needs to know which objects or operations are sensitive and thus must check access to. Whether it is an aspect or any other technology that implements the authorization behavior, it would benefit significantly if such a notion is exposed.

The fragile pointcut problem will not be solved by using abstract awareness patterns, but it will become more controllable. As the join point abstraction (whether it is a pointcut or something else) is closer to the join points themselves, the impact of a discrepancy between them will be localized.

Related Work and Known Uses. Opening up base code is not new. For instance, C# provides event handling with delegates to enable future extensions. Ptolemy [64] is a language with quantied, typed events that aims to combine the advantages of event-based programming and AOP. Also related are *explicit join points* [34, 35] that make base code aspect-aware and allows explicit interaction in order to increase aspect modularity.

Noble et al. describe patterns for AOSD on an architectural level [62]. Their *extension* pattern corresponds to our aspect-awareness design pattern. In requirements engineering, the principle of preparing the base requirements is called *scaffolding* [13].

In practice, the principle of opening up some modules for future extension is well known, e.g. in white-box frameworks, Eclipse extension points, etc. Spring Insight [70] supports visibility into web application performance through instrumenting Spring and demonstrates the value of having code that is consistently structured by frameworks. It basically is an aspect library with a user interface on top that leverages the consistent structure of Spring applications.

5.1.1 Pointcut Interface

Solution. A *pointcut interface* exposes a set of stable crosscutting behaviors as named pointcut signatures.

Forces. Use a *pointcut interface* to expose join points when

- the abstraction to be exposed captures certain points in the control flow of the program, as opposed to certain points in the static structure of the program. We call them behavioral join points;
- the join points to be exposed can be adequately expressed in a PCL;
- the abstractions are exposed with aspect-based composition explicitly in mind.

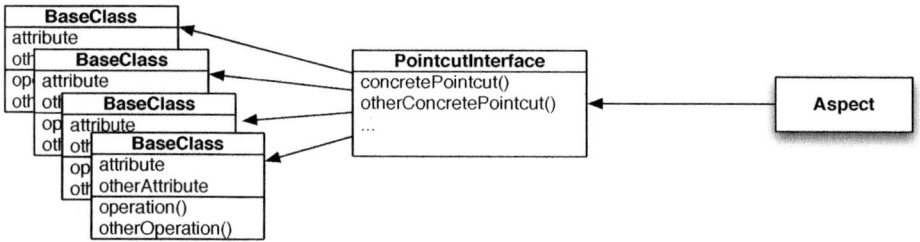

Fig. 3. Structure of *pointcut interface*

Rationale. Using a *pointcut interface*, we could expose the notion of sensitive operations as follows:

```
public interface SensitiveOperations {
    pointcut sensitive(Object caller): call(* Calendar.*(..)) &&
        this(caller) && (call(* showEntries())  ||
                         call(* newEntry(..))    ||
                         call(* deleteEntry(..)));
}
```

Listing 2. *Pointcut interface* that captures sensitive operations

Since a pointcut interface exposes certain behaviors instead of the operations themselves, we must make a choice whether to capture the execution of the operation or the calls to it. Because in the context of access control, caller info might be important, we choose to expose the calls to sensitive operations as a crosscutting behavior.

In other contexts this might result in *pointcut interface* not being useful. E.g. if we expect that an aspect will need to add members using an ITD, a pointcut interface is of no use.

A benefit of *pointcut interface* is that it can be used hierarchically. E.g. when a program consists of a number of subsystems (packages, classes), each exposing its own pointcut interface, an umbrella interface can combine the exposed behaviors into a single pointcut interface.

Implementation in other AOP technologies. Classes in CaesarJ can contain pointcuts. If the pointcut is public, it can be reused just as in AspectJ, otherwise mixin composition will do the trick. JBoss AOP and Spring can provide a pointcut interface either in an XML file or as annotations in an aspect class.

Related Work and Known Uses. The notion of a pointcut interface was first presented by Gudmundson and Kiczales [25]. Grisworld et al. [24] refine this notion as crosscutting interfaces (or XPI). A crosscutting interface decouples aspect code from the unstable details of advised code in a similar way as a pointcut interface. Furthermore, an XPI imposes a contract and design rules.

The notion of providing pointcuts in the base code is also presented as a programming language construct. The underlying theory is called *Open Modules* [4].

Example usage of *pointcut interface* can be found in the DigiNews application [77, 63]. A domain-driven methodology was used to find stable abstractions for the design with pointcut interfaces [78]. The same methodology was applied to a common case study for AO modeling [79]. In the context of extending OO frameworks, extension join points [47] are used to denote the hot-spots of the framework. The reference documentation of the Spring application framework [3] shows how to share common pointcut definitions. They recommend defining a `SystemArchitecture` aspect that captures common pointcut expressions, which is similar to *pointcut interface*.

5.1.2 Naming Convention

Solution. Consistently use a stable naming scheme for types and methods in the base program.

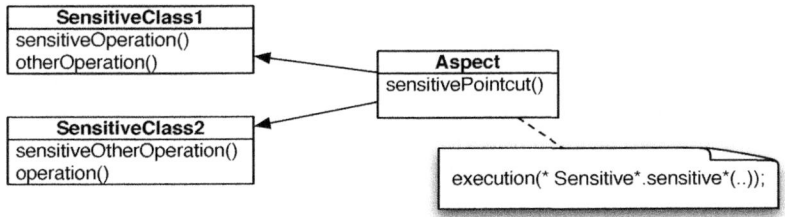

Fig. 4. Structure of naming convention

Forces. Use *naming convention* to expose join points when

- the program structure aligns well with the join points to be exposed. The join points map easily to certain methods, types, ... ;
- it is the dominant join point abstraction for the program elements (it is cumbersome to expose multiple join point abstractions for the same program element using a naming convention);
- other tools or technology can benefit from the exposed abstraction.

Rationale. If there are no other concerns that interfere, we can expose all sensitive operations by starting their name with `sensitive` and making sure that other methods do not. As a result a PCL can easily express the notion of sensitive operations using a syntax pattern. The `Calendar` interface could then be specified as follows:

```
public interface SensitiveCalendar {
  Entry [] sensitiveShowEntries ();
  void sensitiveNewEntry (TimeInterval t, Resource [] r);
  void sensitiveDeleteEntry (Entry e);
  Employee getOwner ();
}
```

Listing 3. *Naming convention* that captures sensitive operations

These naming conventions can then easily be exploited in an aspect as follows:

```
pointcut sensitiveCalls: call (* sensitive *(..));
```

Implementation in other AOP technologies. With few exceptions CaesarJ uses the same pointcut language. Naming conventions can be used without any difference. Also in JBoss AOP and Spring, naming conventions can be taken advantage of. They provide wildcards and JBoss AOP even provides some powerful patterns to describe types.

Related Work and Known Uses. Kiczales and Mezini briefly discuss naming conventions [40] and compare them with a number of other implementation strategies for achieving separation of concerns. Laddad [50] mentions the benefits of using naming conventions to simplify pointcut expressions. Subject-oriented programming techniques [32, 74, 6] uses names as the basis to compose programming elements from the different subjects.

Naming conventions were one of the implementation strategies that Wampler used when developing Contract4J [82].

5.1.3   Annotation Convention

Solution. Consistently use a stable annotation scheme in the base code.

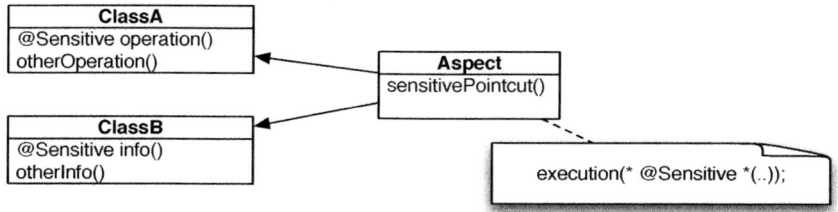

Fig. 5. Structure of *annotation convention*

Forces. Use *annotation convention* to expose join points when

- the program structure aligns well with the join points to be exposed. The join points map easily to certain methods, types, . . . ;
- some program elements need to expose multiple join point abstractions;
- there are other uses for the exposed join points besides aspect-based composition.

Rationale. No matter which other concerns interfere, we can annotate sensitive operations with a designated annotation (e.g. @*Sensitive*()). The Calendar interface could then be specified as follows:

```
@Sensitive public interface Calendar{
    @Sensitive Entry [] showEntries ();
    @Sensitive void newEntry(TimeInterval t, Resource[] r);
    @Sensitive void deleteEntry(Entry e);
    Employee getOwner ();
}
```

Listing 4. *Annotation convention* that captures sensitive operations

Additionally, annotation parameters can be used to specify sensitivity levels, accepted roles, . . .

These annotations can then easily be exploited in an aspect as follows:

```
pointcut sensitiveCalls: call(@Sensitive * *(..));
```

Implementation in other AOP technologies. As CaesarJ is based on Java2, there is no support for annotations (yet). Annotations are available in JBoss AOP and Spring and can be captured in pointcuts.

Related Work and Known Uses. Kiczales and Mezini briefly discuss annotation conventions [40] and compare them with a number of other implementation strategies for achieving separation of concerns. Laddad [48, 49] describes the use of annotations in combination with aspects in more detail.

In practice, annotations are commonly used, e.g. in Junit [36] or in EJB [57] to configure container services like persistence and authentication. Also Spring

Roo makes extensive use of annotations to add extra behavior to Java applications [71] (by generating aspects in the background).

5.1.4   Structural Convention

Solution. Expose a crosscutting concern by consistently applying the same structure to implement a particular concern.

Forces. Use *structural convention* to expose join points when

- the join points to be exposed are difficult to express using a PCL;
- the join points to be exposed do not correspond well with available method and type names and annotations;
- there are other uses for the exposed join points besides aspect-based composition.

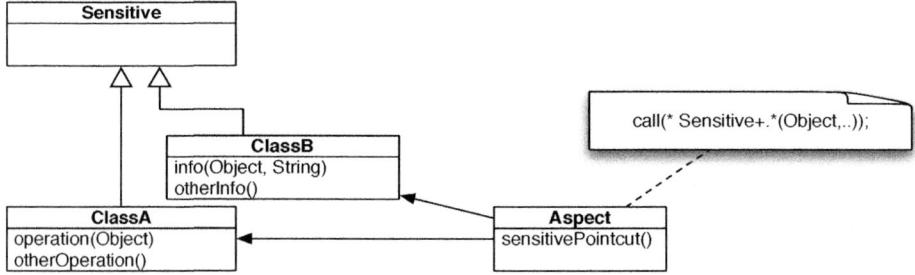

Fig. 6. Example structure of *structural convention*

Rationale. To expose sensitive operations by means of a structural convention, we need some pattern of behavior that can be recognized and apply it to every sensitive operation.

```
public interface Calendar implements Sensitive{
    Entry[] showEntries(Object caller);
    void newEntry(Object caller, TimeInterval t, Resource[] r);
    void deleteEntry(Object caller, Entry e);
    Employee getOwner();
}
```

Listing 5. *Structural convention* that captures sensitive operations

The pattern we use here, is that every method that is called on a subtype of Sensitive with the caller object as first parameter, is a sensitive operation. This pattern of behavior can be captured by an aspect and the caller object can be used to determine access rights. The aspect can also be used to check that the first parameter is in fact the caller object.

```
pointcut  sensitiveCalls(Object  caller):
   call(* Sensitive+(Object ,..) && callerArgument(caller ,*);
pointcut callerArgument(Object  caller ,Object  arg):
   this(caller) && args(arg ,..) && if(caller==arg);
```

Implementation in other AOP technologies. Any structural convention that is limited to constructions from Java2 can be used in CaesarJ (e.g. no annotations or type parameters). Structural conventions are very suitable in JBoss AOP and Spring, also because JBoss AOP provides powerful constructs to define types.

Related Work and Known Uses. The most common structural convention is providing method hooks for interesting join points [37, 61]. This can even lead to the extraction of an empty method, just for the sake of providing a join point. In requirements engineering, this is called scaffolding [13]. Another example of a structural convention is the use of OO design patterns. They have known names and structures and are thus ideal candidates, as e.g. shown by Chakravarty, Regehr and Eide [12].

The standard practice in Java of implementing certain interfaces (e.g. Remote, Serializable) can be considered a structural convention.

5.1.5   Summary Aspect Awareness

To finish the description of the Aspect Awareness design pattern, we give an overview of the main forces that drive the selection for the most appropriate idiom or combination thereof and briefly discuss their impact on ease-of-use.

Usage of associated programming idioms. The main variation point is the use of explicit base-level pointcuts (written using a PCL) versus the consistent use of a convention. Important factors regarding this decision are the ability of the PCL to capture the needed crosscutting behavior and whether the exposed abstractions should have other purposes besides aspect-based composition. For example, other program transformation tools or middleware already rely on certain annotations in the base program. Annotations could also be used for creating domain-specific languages or for verification or analysis purposes. The use of a convention can be based on:

- providing annotations;
- naming of program elements (classes, methods, . . .);
- program structure (calling certain methods, implementing interface, . . .).

The use of *naming conventions* is discouraged especially if the AOP language supports annotations. Both techniques attach additional semantics to a method or type, but annotations are less error-prone.

It is perfectly possible that multiple forces are relevant. It is then up to the application developer to decide whether one force is dominant or applying a combination of idioms is a better solution. For instance, a pointcut interface can have pointcuts based on an annotation convention.

Ease-of-use. Aspect awareness has a positive impact on the ease of integrating an aspect with the base code, because the exposed abstractions can be leveraged when defining the binding of the aspect. With respect to definition of the exposed abstractions *pointcut interface* requires some knowledge and experience of the PCL. Otherwise, structural conventions potentially require synthetic code structures. The use of annotations offers a very flexible and lightweight composition technique.

5.2   Join Point Abstraction Pattern

Problem. How to design an aspect that is not tightly coupled to the join points at which it interacts.

Context. Development of an aspect that can be easily composed with multiple base components at once and reused in combination with different base applications over time.

Abstract Solution. Define pointcuts in terms of join point abstractions and expose these abstractions to form some sort of expected interface for the composition of this aspect.

Abstract Forces. Use a join point abstraction pattern when

- a versatile aspect is needed, which should be applicable to a wide range of applications. As a result we cannot depend on knowledge about the available join points;
- the stability of the available join points is not guaranteed;
- the available join points are known, but do not align well with the program structure;
- base code might already have exposed the necessary abstractions (e.g. EJB annotations);

Rationale. A join point abstraction can come in many shapes and forms as both behaviors and structures can be abstracted. The join point does not have to be entirely abstract. By giving a partial definition of a join point, we can put more constraints on the structure of the binding between aspects and base.

A reusable aspect for access control will interact at join points related to sensitive objects, objects in the application that need protection against unauthorized access. Instead of making assumptions about the name, structure and other characteristics of these join points, we can make abstraction of some or all of these characteristics.

Related work and Known Uses. Making abstraction of the base code or i.e. the join points at which an aspect interacts is not new. E.g. model-based pointcuts [38] have been proposed as an approach to manage the fragile pointcut problem. Also aspect integration contracts [52], an interface-based approach towards more robust AO composition, include base code properties.

5.2.1 Abstract Pointcut

Solution. Use an abstract pointcut to abstract from any crosscutting behavior.

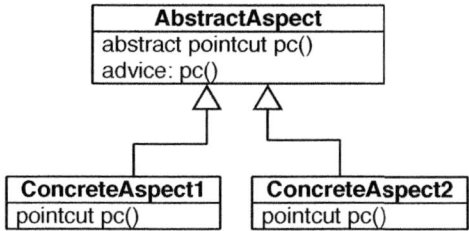

Fig. 7. Structure of abstract pointcut

Forces. Use an abstract pointcut to abstract from join points when

- there is no knowledge on the kind of join point the aspect is going to interact at;
- different kinds of behavioral join points are abstracted (method join points, join points on certain objects, control flows, . . .);
- the abstraction is only used to bind advice (not for ITD's);
- the join point abstraction is shared between related aspects (they could share a super-aspect);
- the join point abstraction describes a heterogeneous concern (i.e. advice may vary depending on the concrete definition for the pointcut).

Rationale. An abstract pointcut is the most straightforward mechanism to abstract from join points. This pattern leaves it up to the base developer or aspect composer to specify the correct pointcut declaration. As a result, an abstract pointcut is a very flexible technique, but offers no means to restrict the range of join points. In such a case, documentation is vital.

```
public abstract aspect AccessControl {
    // . . .
    abstract pointcut checkAccess ( AccessSubj s , AccessObj o ) ;
}
```

Listing 6. Abstract pointcut example

Connect the abstract pointcut by giving it a concrete definition in a sub-aspect. E.g.,

```
public aspect MyAccessControl extends AccessControl {
    pointcut checkAccess ( AccessSubj s , AccessObj o ) :
        call( * AccessObj + .*( .. ) ) && this (s) && target (o) ;
}
```

Implementation in other AOP technologies. Abstract pointcuts are available in CaesarJ. They are even more flexible as CaesarJ supports mixin composition and not only abstract aspects can be refined further. In JBoss AOP it is not possible to define abstract pointcuts. However, because binding of advice to pointcut is specified separately, this is not always a limitation. Spring supports abstract aspects using AspectJ or the @AspectJ development style.

Related Work and Known Uses. The concept of an abstract pointcut stems directly from the language [75] and is therefore a straightforward idea. It is described in more detail by Hanenberg [29], who also elaborates on what its role could be in a bigger picture [28].

Example uses of an abstract pointcut can be found a.o. in Cunhas framework for concurrency [15], Hannemans implementation of the GoF design patterns [31] and the ajlib incubator project [8], which implements some AspectJ aspects which are meant to be reusable.

5.2.2   Marker Interface

Solution. Separate type information from a pointcut or ITD and refer to a marker interface instead. The marker interface is a (usually empty) interface that serves as an abstraction for these types in the base program.

Forces. Use *marker interface* to abstract from join points when

- the join points are described using type information;
- the abstraction is used in both advice and ITD's;
- the join point abstraction is shared between multiple non-related aspects (i.e. the marker interface can be used also to describe other concerns);
- the aspect makes callbacks on the object underlying the JPA;
- the join point abstraction describes a homogeneous concern (i.e. the same advice applies to all connections of the marker interface).

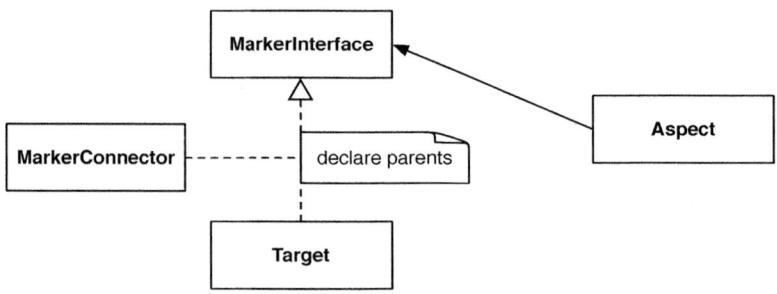

Fig. 8. Structure of *marker interface*

Rationale. We can observe that the structure of join points related to the sensitive operations is always the same: the call of a method on a type `AccessObject` from an object of type `AccessSubject`. Only the exact interpretations of these types need further specification.

```
public aspect AccessControl {
  //...
  pointcut checkAccess(AccessSubject s, AccessObject o):
    this(s) && call(* AccessObject+.*(..)) && target(o);
}
public interface AccessObject {}
public interface AccessSubject {}
```

Listing 7. Using *marker interface* to abstract from types that define join points

If the marker interfaces are not defined locally (as in List. 7), they can also be used in other aspects. Adding methods to a marker interface puts more constraints on the join points at which the aspect might interact.

The marker interfaces from List. 7 could be connected as follows:

```
declare parents: Calendar || Resource extends AccessObject
declare parents: Employee extends AccessSubject
```

Listing 8. Connecting marker interfaces to concrete application types

The fact that a marker interface is an upper bound, means that it can be used to connect an aspect to multiple types at once, but also that advice cannot be made specific depending on a certain connection as the marker interface describes the same join points wherever it is used.

If a marker interface is used within a member introduction, this is sometimes referred to as a separate idiom named *Container Introduction*. For example, we could add to each protected resource a log in which all access attempts to that resource can be stored.

```
List<String> AccessObject.accessAttempts;
```

Implementation in other AOP technologies. CaesarJ supports bindings (wrapper construction). These can be used to introduce behavior (comparable to introductions). Unfortunately, these bindings cannot be used to abstract from join points. Advice in CaesarJ is part of the binding and will always be application-specific (in terms of the join points it interacts at, not in terms of the functionality it provides). JBoss AOP and Spring support inheritance declarations just as AspectJ (only by means of XML or annotations).

Related Work and Known Uses. Hanenberg, Unland, and Schmidmeier have described *marker interface* and its connection [29], also under the name *indirect pointcut connection*[4][26]. The AspectJ Cookbook [58] describes the *director* pattern and is very related. It consists of an abstract aspect with multiple roles as nested interfaces. These roles have the same purpose as a marker interface. *Marker interface* is an important concept in many of the refactorings in the catalogue of Monteiro [59, 60].

As *marker interface* is one of the most well known practices in AO design, it can be found in many open-source applications. To name a few: the AspectOP-TIMA framework for transactions and concurrency [41]; the GoF design pattern implementations by Hanneman [31]; AJHotDraw [55], an AO implementation of JHotDraw [2]; HealthWatcher [23]; NVersion [7].

5.2.3 Type Parameter

Solution. Abstract from type information using type parameters in a generic aspect. These type parameters can be used in pointcuts and ITD's.

Forces. Use a type parameter to abstract from join points when

- the join points are described using type information;
- the abstraction captures the relation between multiple types;
- the abstraction is used in both advice and ITD's;
- the join point abstraction describes a heterogeneous concern (i.e. advice may vary depending on the concrete type for the type parameter);
- the join point abstraction is shared between related aspects (they could share a super-aspect);
- the abstraction captures certain methods and using wildcards is not helpful.

Rationale. Suppose we want to extend the aspect from List. 7 with a pointcut `accessAllowed` that describes which accesses should be allowed. Looking at the access rules from our example (Sect. 4.4), we see that the decision is based on who accesses what. Listing 9 shows how this can be represented in a pointcut using type parameters.

Connecting a generic aspect to a concrete base application is accomplished through an (empty) aspect that extends the generic aspect with concrete types for its type parameters. E.g. binding the generic aspect from List. 9 could look as follows:

---

[4] And *indirect introduction* for *container introduction*.

```
public abstract aspect AccessControl<AllowedSubj , AllowedObj>{
  // . . .
  pointcut accessAllowed ( AllowedSubj  s ,  AllowedObj  o ) :
    this ( s )  &&  call ( ∗  AllowedObj . ∗ ( . . ) )  &&  target ( o ) ;
}
```

Listing 9. Using type parameters in a generic aspect to abstract from types that define join points

```
public aspect ResourceAccess extends
  AccessControl<Secretary , Resource>{}
public aspect CalendarAccess extends
  AccessControl<Employee , Calendar>{}
```

Listing 10. Independent connections of a type interaction using type parameters

Each concrete sub-aspect represents an access rule, e.g. `ResourceAccess` defines that a secretary can access a resource. Using marker interfaces (Sect. 5.2.2) it would not be possible to implement multiple independent rules. Because marker interfaces have a global meaning, the result would be that all types representing an `AllowedSubj` are allowed access to all types representing an `AllowedObj`.

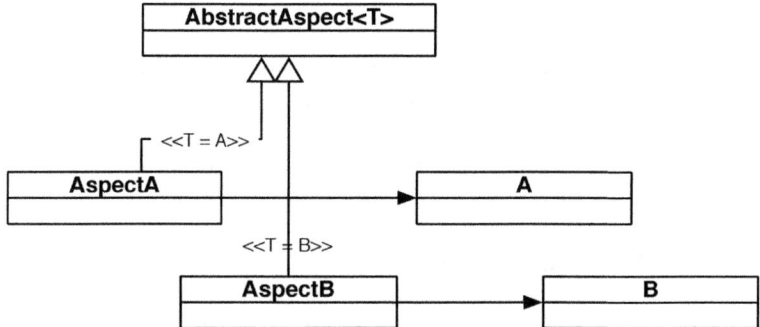

Fig. 9. Structure of type parameter abstraction and connection

A type parameter can also be used to parameterize a pointcut in terms of which methods to match. E.g. in List. 10 `CalendarAccess` defines the rule that each employee can access all calendar operations. How can we use type parameters if only a subset of calendar operations should be allowed to each employee? Listing 11 specifies this subset of methods in a separate interface and declares it to be a super-type of the target type. As a result it is able to use this interface as target type in the pointcut[5].

```
public abstract aspect
  AccessControl<AllowedSubj , AllowedObj , AllowedOps> {
  //...
  declare parents AllowedObj implements AllowedOps ;
  pointcut accessAllowed (AllowedSubj s, AllowedObj o):
    this(s) && call(* AllowedOps.*(..)) && target(o);
}

public aspect AccessConnector{
  interface AccessOperations{
    Entry [] showEntries ();
  }

  aspect ConcreteAccessControl extends
    AccessControl<Employee , Calendar , AccessOperations >{}
}
```

Listing 11. Using a type parameter to abstract from method information

Implementation in other AOP technologies. CaesarJ doesn't include type parameters, it provides virtual classed instead. They are too limited to be used as abstraction for join points. Also in JBoss and Spring, type parameters are not available.

Related Work and Known Uses. The need for genericity when designing aspects had been discussed already before AspectJ introduced generic aspects [30, 54, 11, 44].

Hoffman and Eugster apply type parameters in their empirical study [35] and show their benefits with respect to the reusability of aspects.

5.2.4   Annotation Introduction

Solution. Use an annotation to abstract from structural join points. Connect it to the base code by introducing the annotation using an ITD (or using a workaround if the relevant join points are only available as a pointcut).

Forces. Use *annotation introduction* to abstract from join points when

- the join points are described by annotatable program elements[6];
- the join point abstraction is shared between multiple non-related aspects;

---

[5] This idiom works because of the semantics a type has in the different primitive pointcuts. Within a `call()` or `execution()` pointcut, the semantics of the type is that of a set of methods, while for instance in a `this()` or `target()` pointcut, a type represents a set of objects.

[6] Currently these are methods, types and other class members.

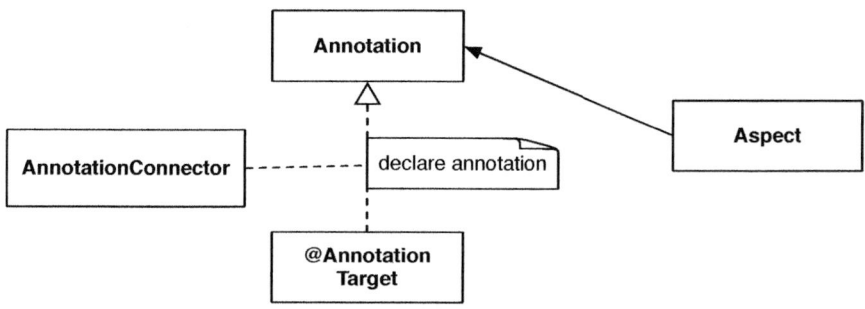

Fig. 10. Structure of *annotation introduction*

- the abstraction is used in both advice and ITD's;
- the join point abstraction describes a homogeneous concern (i.e. the same advice applies to all connections of the marker interface).

Rationale. Annotations provide a flexible mechanism to add metadata to program elements. Multiple annotations can be attached and parameters can encapsulate metadata items.

We could for example define our `checkAccess()` pointcut in terms of annotations that are available in the base program.

```
public aspect AccessControl {
    //...
    pointcut checkAccess(): call(@CheckAccess * *(..));

    @Retention(RetentionPolicy.RUNTIME) @interface CheckAccess{}
}
```

Listing 12. An annotation that abstracts from sensitive method join points

Additionally, the aspect developer needs to define the annotation (usually with run-time retention[7]). The aspect is then defined in terms of this annotation as though it is part of the base program.

The following ITD's illustrate the introduction of the annotation `checkAccess` on both types and methods.

```
declare @type: Resource || Calendar: @CheckAccess;
declare @method: * Calendar.showEntries(): @CheckAccess;
declare @method: * Resource.book(Entry): @CheckAccess;
```

Implementation in other AOP technologies. CaesarJ has no support for annotations (yet). In JBoss AOP and Spring annotations can be introduced just like in AspectJ.

---

[7] So aspects have access to annotations attached to objects at run-time (necessary for `@this`, `@target` and `@args`).

Related Work and Known Uses. The AspectJ notebook [75] describes how annotations are used, while Laddad elaborates on their potential [48, 49]. The combination of aspects and annotations is not exclusive to AspectJ, e.g. Havinga,
Nagy and Bergmans discuss the use of annotations in Compose* [33].

Wampler uses annotations as one of the implementation strategies in Con-
tract4J [82]. Annotations are also used by Cunha in his framework for parallel
computing [15] and in the ajlib incubator project [8].

5.2.5   Summary Join Point Abstraction

To wrap up the description of the Join Point Abstraction design pattern, we give
an overview of the main forces that drive the selection for the most appropriate
idiom or combination thereof and briefly discuss their impact on ease-of-use.

Usage of associated programming idioms. The main factors that drive the selection are the way the join point abstraction (JPA) is used and whether the JPA
is used by various aspects (which are not in an inheritance hierarchy). If the
JPA is used in both advice and ITD's, *abstract pointcut* cannot be used. If the
JPA is used by various aspects, *marker interface* and *annotation introduction*
are most appropriate. *Abstract pointcut* is most appropriate when there is no
(known) common structure among the join points. *Type parameters* are most
suitable when the relation between multiple type needs to be captured (e.g. in
the access control example the relation between the caller and the object that is
called could be captured with type parameters). Also for this pattern, the most
suitable solution can be a combination of idioms, e.g. an abstract pointcut that
is refined by a pointcut using annotations in a sub-aspect.

Ease-of-use. In terms of ease-of-use, the idioms either require an AO construction or some changes to the base code. These changes are the addition of annotations and marker interfaces. The required AO constructions can be as easy
as an inter-type declaration (for binding a marker interface or annotation) or
an empty aspect definition that binds a type parameter. Only abstract pointcut
may require more knowledge about AO technology.

5.2.6   Connecting the Abstractions

Table 1 summarizes how each abstraction can be connected to the base application in terms of the kind of join points that are exposed. Essentially, it points out
how the adapter in Fig. 1 is implemented in terms of the interfaces it connects.

Most of these cases are similar to what has been explained before (in the descriptions of the aspect awareness and join point abstraction patterns), except
for *dynamic type wrapper* and *dynamic annotation introduction*. These are used
in the case of a connection between a structural abstraction as provided join
points (type parameter, marker interface, and annotation) and a pointcut interface as exposed join point abstraction (e.g. base application provides a pointcut
interface). The structure of both these workarounds is essentially the same. We
need to wrap some run-time behavior into a program element. These techniques
make the code rather complicated and should be avoided if possible. Let's have
a look at *dynamic annotation introduction* first.

Table 1. Overview of the adapter idioms

	Exposed join point			
Join point abstraction	Structural convention	Naming Convention	Annotation Convention	Pointcut interface
Type parameter	Concrete type parameter	(ITD)*		Dynamic Type Wrapper
Marker Interface	Subtype/ITD			
Annotation	*Annotation Introduction*			*Dynamic Annotation Introduction*
Abstract Pointcut	Concrete pointcut			

*if the convention applies to the names or annotations of types

So, we have a pointcut with an annotation abstraction, e.g. from List. 12:

```
pointcut checkAccess(): call(@CheckAccess * *(..));
```

and we need to connect it to a pointcut exposed by a pointcut interface, e.g. from List. 2

```
public interface SensitiveOperations {
  pointcut sensitive(Object caller);
}
```

We therefore need to do two things: make sure that join points captured by `sensitive` appear to be method calls and that the method carries the annotation.

```
public aspect AnnotationConnector {
  interface SensitiveCall {
    @CheckAccess doProceed();
  }

  Object around(Object caller):
    SensitiveOperations.sensitive(caller) {
      new SensitiveCall(){
        @CheckAccess void doProceed() {
          return proceed(caller);
        }
      }.doProceed();
  }
}
```

Listing 13. Connection of an annotation to the join points of a pointcut

To make it look like a method call we need to use an anonymous inner class with the annotated method that incorporates the proceed context. The same structure can be used for *dynamic type wrapper* by making `SensitiveCall` a subtype of the type abstraction.

If the original aspect developer (of the aspect in List. 12) is able to anticipate such a situation, he can use a more general pointcut declaration that captures both annotated methods and annotated advice. For example,

pointcut checkAccess () : **@annotation** (CheckAccess) ;

uses the `@annotation` construct that matches any join point of which the subject has a certain annotation.

5.3   Decomposition Pattern

Problem. How to deal with aspects, pointcuts or advice of high complexity, that are implemented monolithically, compromising reusability and variability.

Context. Developing an aspect that might evolve and be composed with other aspects.

Abstract Solution. Decompose aspects into manageable parts according to one or more properties (variability, location, run-time dependency).

Abstract Forces. Use a decomposition pattern when

- the aspect defines basic functionality, used by multiple other aspects via extension;
- the aspect needs to separate between stable and variable parts;
- the aspect embodies too many dependencies:

  - aspect is connected to many base modules;
  - its pointcuts represent many concepts;
  - its advice specifies many actions.

Rationale. As an example of an aspect with high complexity, let's again take the `AccessControl` aspect. It should throw a security exception when an unauthorized access to a protected resource occurs. The aspect contains a pointcut that describes the unauthorized accesses and advice that throws the exception.

```
public aspect AccessControl {
  pointcut calendarAccessDenied(Object e, Calendar c):
    target(c) && this(e) &&
    !(this(Employee) && call(* Calendar.showEntries ())) &&
    !(this(Employee) && call(* Calendar.*Entry(..))
      && if(c.owner==e));

  pointcut resourceAccessDenied():
    target(Resource) &&
    !(this(Secretary) && call(* Resource.book()));
```

```
Object around ( ) :  calendarAccessDenied ( ∗ ,∗ )  | |
    resourceAccessDenied ( )  {
       throw new  SecurityException ( ) ;
  }
}
```

Listing 14. Plane sailing implementation of the access control aspect

We can see that the implementation of this aspect makes it difficult to adapt to future changes or to reuse it in a different context. There are multiple reasons for this. The behavior of the aspect is fixed. This hampers reuse of the aspect since its functionality cannot be refined when used in another context. The locations where this behavior is injected are specified by the pointcuts. They contain too much information, making them hard to understand and not easy to reuse or adapt.

Related Work and Known Uses. Noble et al describe some sort of decomposition on the architectural level and call it heterarchical design [62].

The AspectOPTIMA framework [41, 43, 42] uses coarse-grained decomposition by providing a large number of small aspects to enable configurability.

5.3.1   Template Advice

Problem. How to manage advice definitions that should specify behavior that, traditionally, would be defined in multiple methods or classes?

Solution. Decompose the behavior of a piece of advice into one or more *hook* methods. The advice itself specifies the stable structure of the behavior while the hook methods contain the variable parts of the behavior.

Forces. Use *template advice* when

- advice is subject to refinement;
- advice needs to be reused in different situations with some variability;
- advice functionality should be available as a method (so it can be called explicitly).

Rationale. In general, the advice only retains the basic structure of the cross-cutting functionality, which is not expected to change. Hook methods contain the variable parts (and can be left abstract).

Instead of giving our response to unauthorized accesses, a fixed implementation in the advice body, it is better to delegate the actual response to a method that implements the appropriate behavior (as in List. 15). Even better would be to define this behavior in its own class and, thus, releasing it from the restrictions that aspects have with respect to reuse and evolution. Although *template*

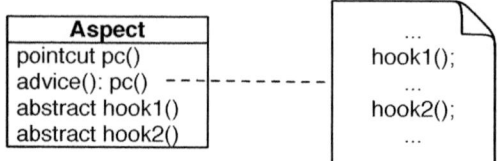

Fig. 11. Structure of *template advice*

```
public abstract aspect AccessControl {
  // ...
  Object around() : accessDenied() {
    handleUnauthorizedAccess();
  }

  void handleUnauthorizedAccess() {
    throw new SecurityException();
  }
}
```

Listing 15. *Template advice* example

advice is vital in the context of anonymous advice (as in AspectJ), it also has its value on its own. By defining crosscutting functionality in a separate module and calling it from within advice, it is also accessible for other aspects and even ordinary classes.

If the behavior that needs to be activated by a certain `around` advice is defined in a separate class and needs to call the original behavior at the current join point (i.e. call `proceed`), how can we accomplish this? Because the keyword `proceed` is only available inside the body of the advice, we have to use a variant of the *Worker Object* idiom [50].

```
public abstract class UnauthorizedAccessHandler {
  public abstract Object doProceed();
  public void handleUnauthorizedAccess() {
    // ...
    doProceed();
    // ...
  }
}

public abstract aspect AccessControl {
  // ...
  Object around() : accessDenied() {
    new UnauthorizedAccessHandler() {
      public Object doProceed() {
        proceed();
      }
```

```
  } . handleUnauthorizedAccess () ;
 }
}
```

Listing 16. *Template advice* based on Worker Object idiom

The class that defines the crosscutting behavior (`UnauthorizedAccessHandler` in List. 16) represents the behavior from the base program that it needs to call, with an abstract method (`doProceed()`). The problem is that calling this behavior is only possible from within the advice by using `proceed`. Our only option is to use an anonymous inner class in the advice that extends the abstract class and implements the abstract method as a call to `proceed`.

Implementation in other AOP technologies. Template advice can be used in CaesarJ exactly the same way as in AspectJ. The same is true for JBoss AOP and Spring as there is no difference between advice and methods.

Related Work and Known Uses. Hanenberg et al. present *template advice* [29, 26, 27], but do not describe the opportunity of defining crosscutting behavior in separate classes and the issues and benefits of doing so.

Example uses of *template advice* can be found in Cunhas concurrency framework [15], the Eclipse JDT weaving service [1] and Hannemans implementation of the GoF design patterns [31]. Examples where the implementation of proceed is outsourced to another class can be found in the worker object creation idiom [50] and the ajlib incubator project [8].

5.3.2 Template Pointcut

Solution. Define the general structure of a pointcut by decomposing it into more basic hook pointcuts. These hook pointcuts describe the variable parts of the pointcut while the template itself remains stable.

Forces. Use *template pointcut* when

- the pointcut is too complex (it represents more than 1 concept, which compromises reusability);
- the pointcut contains both stable and variable parts.

Rationale. The template pointcut is decomposed into a number of (abstract) hook pointcuts, which can be overridden in sub-aspects. For instance, each sub-aspect could be appropriate for a different base application.

Let us look back at the pointcuts from List. 14. A standard approach to determine unauthorized accessed is to define the total scope of access control and explicitly list all accesses that should be allowed. Therefore, the pointcut intercepts all calls to sensitive objects, except those actions that are explicitly allowed. The pointcuts, as they are now, use the notion of sensitive objects, but

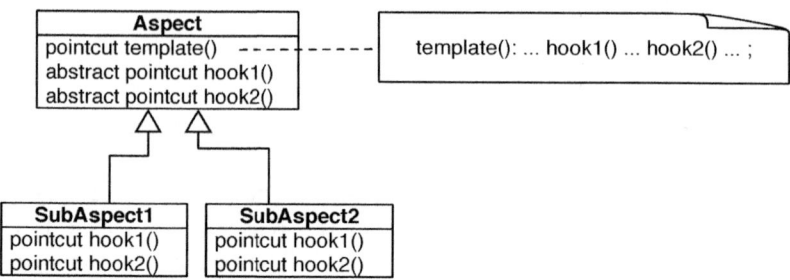

Fig. 12. Structure of *template pointcut*

this notion is not available as an abstraction because it is tangled with the access rules within the pointcut. How can we improve this situation?

We can define the general structure of the `accessDenied` pointcut in terms of two hook pointcuts: `checkAccess` and `accessAllowed`.

```
public abstract aspect AccessControl {
    pointcut accessDenied(): checkAccess() && !accessAllowed();
    abstract pointcut checkAccess();
    abstract pointcut accessAllowed();

    Object around(): accessDenied() {
      throw new SecurityException();
    }
}
```

Listing 17. *Template pointcut* example

As a result, the notion of sensitive objects and the access rules are specified separately and are thus reusable and evolvable. Of course, this pattern can be applied recursively in case a hook pointcut is still too complex.

The reusability of the super-aspect is largely determined by the general structure that is defined by the template pointcut. If the decomposition into hook pointcuts is orthogonal, these hooks become reusable and modifiable separately, without affecting each other.

Implementation in other AOP technologies. CaesarJ has better support for *template pointcut* than AspectJ. Not only abstract aspects can be reused; pointcuts can be refined, also in terms of the 'super' pointcut. Composite pointcut[8] can be used in JBoss AOP, but not *template pointcut* as there are no abstract pointcuts and pointcuts cannot be overridden. In Spring *template pointcut* can be used the same as in AspectJ.

---

[8] Composite pointcut decomposes a concrete pointcut definition into a number of smaller concrete pointcut definitions. No abstract pointcuts are used.

Related Work and Known Uses. This pattern is inspired by the classic *Template Method* design pattern from the GoF [19], which decomposes a method into hook methods for the same reasons. Lagaisse et al. describe the *template pointcut* pattern in more detail under the name of *elementary pointcut* [51, 10]. It elaborates on the consequences of applying the pattern in the context of pointcut inheritance and on the principles of how to decompose a pointcut into hook pointcuts (or elementary pointcuts). Hanenberg et al. describe the *composite pointcut* pattern [29, 26], which is very similar, but does not take aspect or pointcut refinement into account.

Santos describes the use of *template pointcut* to implement modular hotspots in frameworks [68]. In the ajlib incubator project, the tracing aspect also applies the *template pointcut* pattern.

5.3.3 Pointcut Method

Solution. Pointcut method postpones part of the decision whether a certain join point should be advised until that advice is actually run, by first calling a method, the pointcut method.

Forces. Use *pointcut method* when

- a pointcut contains both static and run-time decisions;
- a partially different advice execution is needed depending on the outcome of a run-time decision.

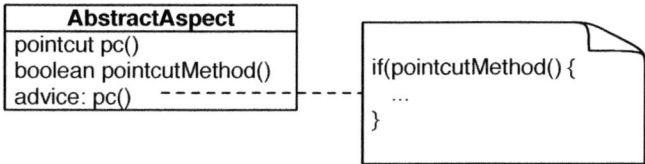

Fig. 13. Structure of *pointcut method*

Rationale. Pointcut method is a variant of *template advice* (5.3.1), but since it is commonly used and has a specific purpose totally different from *template advice*, it is described separately.

The problem that *pointcut method* addresses is the presence of a dynamic condition. AspectJ offers a number of primitive pointcut constructs to capture run-time information. Examples are `this()` and `args()` which capture the type or identity of the current executing object and the current arguments respectively. For more general conditions concerning run-time information, the AspectJ pointcut language provides the `if()` construct. However, the if-expression that represents the dynamic condition cannot call non-static methods, which severely limits its potential for reuse.

With respect to our access control example, dynamic conditions are needed e.g. to check the access to a calendar for adding a new entry (as in the pointcut `calendarAccesDenied` in List. 14). This decision cannot be based on the types of the objects alone, because only the registered owner of the calendar can add new entries. If we expect this dynamic condition to change in the future, how can we prepare for it? By separating the dynamic condition in a method. As part of the pointcut is now represented as a method, it is more susceptible to future changes.

In the access control example, we can separate the ownership check into a pointcut method (`condition` in List. 18).

```
public aspect AccessAllowed extends AccessControl {
    pointcut calendarAccessAllowed(Employee e, Calendar c):
        this(e) && call(* Calendar.*Entry(..)) && target(c);

    boolean condition(Calendar c, Employee e){
        return e==c.owner;
    }

    Object around(Employee e, Calendar c): accessAllowed(e,c) {
        if (!condition(c,e))
            throw new SecurityException();
        proceed(e,c);
    }
}
```

Listing 18. Using *pointcut method* to capture a dynamic condition.

A common pitfall is the combination of *pointcut method* and around advice. As around advice totally replaces the original functionality at the current join point, `proceed()` (or any other default behavior) needs to be called explicitly in case the pointcut method decides the advice doesn't apply after all.

Implementation in other AOP technologies. As, mechanically, *pointcut method* is only a specific case of *template advice*, CaesarJ also supports it. The same is true for JBoss AOP and Spring.

Related Work and Known Uses. Hanenberg, Unland and Schmidmeier give an extensive description of *pointcut method* [29, 27]. Example usage of *pointcut method* can be found in AJHotDraw [55], an AspectJ implementation of JHot-Draw [2], in the CommandObserver aspect. Also, the mobility aspect pattern [20] uses *pointcut method* in its implementation.

5.3.4   Participant Connection

Solution. Instead of specifying one global connection for the whole base program, divide the connection in multiple participant connections, each integrated with a particular part of the program.

Forces. Use a *participant connection* when

- a pointcut becomes coupled to too many base modules;
- evolution of certain parts of the base program is important.

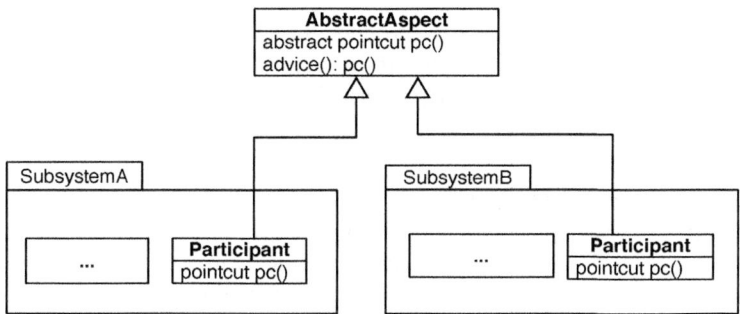

Fig. 14. Structure of *participant connection*

Rationale. Participant connection is based on the Participant pattern described by Laddad [50], which proposes an abstract pointcut (Sect. 5.2.1) being implemented independently for each subsystem. The same reasoning can also be applied to the other join point abstractions.

Referring to the access control example, describing all accesses that need authorization in a single pointcut would lead to a fragile design. Because, in that case, nearly every change in the base program would have an effect on that pointcut.

The core structure of the pattern is as follows: specify one main abstract aspect that defines the main behavior, but is based on an abstract pointcut. Subsequently, for each subsystem, specify a sub-aspect that gives a concrete definition of the pointcut for that specific subsystem. Because the pointcut is now local to the join points it describes, it will be both simpler and more robust.

If we consider each class a subsystem, the participant aspect can be defined as a nested aspect in that class. E.g. binding an abstract pointcut `checkAccess` that represents all the sensitive operations, could look as follows:

```
public class Calendar {
    //...
    static aspect CalendarAccess extends AccessControl{
        pointcut checkAccess(): execution(* Calendar.*(..)) &&
```

```
        (execution(* showEntries())||execution(* newEntry(..))||
          execution(* deleteEntry(..)));
    }
}
```

Listing 19. Participant connection of an abstract pointcut.

Implementation in other AOP technologies. Participant connections are also possible in CaesarJ. Since, Caesar classes can contain pointcuts, there is no need for the inner class construction. Using XML, separate bindings can be specified for advice in JBoss AOP and Spring.

Related Work and Known Uses. One specific case of a participant connection (which connects an abstract pointcut in a participant) is described by Laddad [50]. It is the original design pattern *Participant* and is later discussed in the context of annotations [48, 49].

5.3.5   Summary decomposition
To wrap up the description of the Decomposition design pattern, we give an overview of the main forces that drive the selection for the most appropriate idiom or combination thereof and briefly discuss their impact on ease-of-use.

Usage of associated programming idioms. When choosing a decomposition idiom one needs to know what to decompose (pointcuts, advice) and based on which principle. If advice is a key element in the aspect *template advice* can be used to decompose it. For decomposing a pointcut there are three options. If the pointcut represents more than one concept, with both stable and variable parts, *template pointcut* is the solution. If the variable part is a run-time decision *pointcut method* is a better alternative. In the case that the pointcut is coupled to too many different base modules, *participant connection* can be used to provide a separate connection for each subsystem. Similar to the other design patterns, multiple decomposition idioms can be combined. E.g. a pointcut can be decomposed into a template, multiple hook pointcuts and a run-time decision using *template pointcut* and *pointcut method* respectively.

Ease-of-use. Decomposition patterns allow the developer to hide the aspectual elements from the user of the aspect library; or, at least, to make them more basic and thus easier to implement. *Template advice* and *pointcut method* enable to see respectively advice and pointcuts as normal method calls. *Template pointcut* and *participant connection* respectively make the pointcut to connect and the connection itself smaller in scope. Decomposition idioms will thus increase the ease-of-use of complex aspects.

5.4   Mediation Pattern

Problem. How to coordinate the behavior of a group of aspects that need to cooperate to achieve a shared goal?

Context. Aspect behavior is spread over multiple aspects, e.g. as the result of using a decomposition pattern.

Abstract Solution. Provide a mechanism to regulate if and when an aspect needs to be activated (with respect to other aspects).

Abstract Forces. Use a mediation pattern when

- decomposed aspects need to be coordinated to work as a team;
- aspect behavior is difficult to control if not coordinated;
- it is not feasible to bring the aspects back together into a single aspect.

Rationale. The need for mediation is often the result of the use of a decomposition pattern. E.g. if *template pointcut* (Sect. 5.3.2) is used, there can be multiple sub-aspects having their own implementation of a shared hook pointcut. For instance, based on the abstract aspect from List. 17, we can implement multiple sub-aspects, that, if we are not careful, will counteract each other. Let us take a look at List. 10. It defines two aspects based on the same generic aspect (List. 9). It is not apparent straight away, but these two aspects are in conflict (the overall behavior is that each access will be denied). The problem is that both aspects take a decision autonomously, which is allowing access in some specific cases and denying access in all other cases. Since allowing access is implemented as proceeding to the next aspect and denying access as throwing an exception, all accesses result in an exception.

The root of the problem is that each aspect has its own effect on the base program. We must achieve that each aspect can indicate its intentions and that a resulting action based on all the intentions takes effect in the application.

Related Work and Known Uses. The principle of making cooperation explicit also applies to objects, as shown by the *Mediator* design pattern [19]. More closely related is the work of Schmidmeier [69] in which he describes two core patterns of aspects interacting and cooperating with other aspects.

5.4.1 Chained Advice

Solution. Let the cooperating aspects interact at the same join point and define a chain of advice. The order of the chain can be defined explicitly (with a precedence declaration) or implicitly (when each chain element provides a join point for the next one).

Forces. Use *chained advice* when

- advice runs or can be attached at the same join point;
- there is a clear and fixed order between the different pieces of advice.

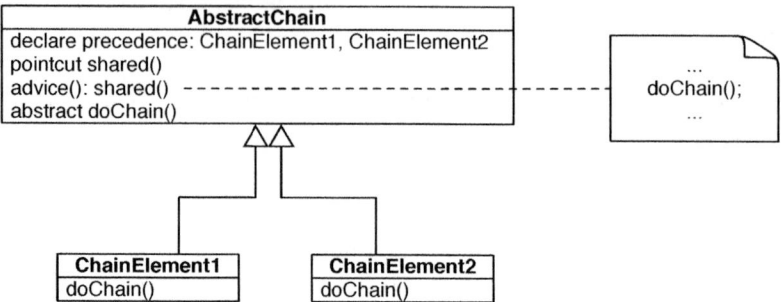

Fig. 15. Possible structure of *chained advice*

Rationale. When two or more aspects define advice that might be activated at the same join point, the order in which the different pieces of advice will run is undefined. Therefore, the developer should anticipate all possible interactions between such aspects and control their execution order.

Specifying the order of execution between the chain elements can be done explicitly or implicitly. An explicit order is specified using a precedence declaration. This keeps the chain elements independent of each other, but the declaration itself is static and unique per concrete composition of aspects.

If the chain elements don't necessarily have to be independent, the order of execution can also be specified more implicitly. In this case each chain element provides a join point for the next. Since advice is not a single identifiable join point, a workaround is necessary; e.g. by annotating the advice or using *template advice* (Sect. 5.3.1). Instead of the shared pointcut, the join point from the previous chain element needs to be specified in each aspect.

We can apply *Chained advice* to the access control example. We use it to enforce that all aspects first check the access rule they implement before a resulting action is taken. We therefore make a distinction between aspects that check the access rules and the aspect that will eventually grant or deny access. In List. 20 the abstract aspect from List. 17 is now split into three aspects. The aspect `AccessControl` is now only used to specify the precedence between the two other aspects, making sure that all access checks have occurred before access is definitely granted or denied.

`AccessChecker` uses the `accessAllowed` pointcut to indicate the intention of allowing this access. After all `AccessChecker` aspects have performed their task, `AccessGranter` finally takes action based on all the intentions. `AccessControl` and `AccessGranter` run at the same join points because the join points captured by `accessAllowed` are a subset of those captured by `checkAccess`.

What is missing from the *chained advice* pattern is the information flow between the chain elements. E.g. in our access control example, how do the `AccessChecker` aspects provide the necessary information to `AccessGranter`

```
public aspect AccessControl {
  declare precedence: AccessChecker , AccessGranter ;
}

public aspect AccessChecker {
  pointcut accessAllowed () :  ...
}

public aspect AccessGranter {
  pointcut accessDenied () :  ...

  Object around () :  accessDenied () {
    throw new SecurityException () ;
  }
}
```

Listing 20. Using *chained advice* to impose a certain order between different aspects

so that it can take the appropriate action? The other two mediation patterns (*dynamic annotation introduction* in Sect. 5.4.2 and *mediation data introduction* in Sect. 5.4.3) can be used in combination with *chained advice* to accomplish this.

Implementation in other AOP technologies. Pointcuts can be shared in CaesarJ, Spring and JBoss AOP and also the precedence between different aspects can be declared, so there is no difference in implementation.

Related Work and Known Uses. Hanenberg, Unland, and Schmidmeier describe the *chained advice* pattern [29, 27].

5.4.2   Dynamic Annotation Introduction

Solution. Attach metadata to a certain control flow by using an annotated `around` advice that only calls `proceed`. The `cflow` primitive can then be used to check whether some property holds for a certain control flow.

Forces. Use *dynamic annotation introduction* when

- aspects interact at different join points;
- aspects cooperate within one message flow;
- different objects are used throughout the message flow.

Rationale. If we return to the example, we want to achieve that when one aspect decides access is allowed, the other aspect should no longer intervene. One way to

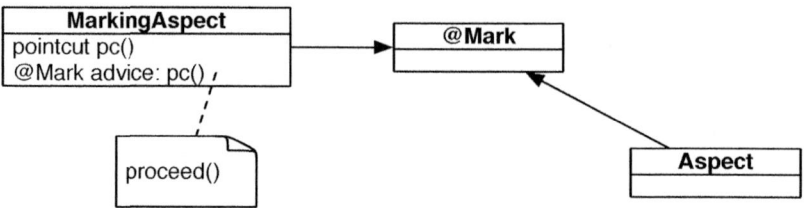

Fig. 16. Structure of *dynamic annotation introduction*

do this is to annotate the control flow as being safe. We can now fully implement the aspect `AccessChecker` from List. 20 by adding an advice that annotates the control flow of join points in `accessAllowed` as being safe.

```
public aspect AccessChecker {
  abstract pointcut accessAllowed ();

  @Safe Object around(): accessAllowed (){
    proceed ();
  }
}
public @interface Safe {}
```

Listing 21. *Dynamic annotation introduction*

The pointcut `accessDenied` from the aspect `AccessGranter` could then be implemented as follows (in combination with *template pointcut*, 5.3.2):

```
pointcut accessDenied (): checkAccess () && !marked ();
abstract pointcut checkAccess ();
pointcut marked (): cflowbelow(@annotation (Safe ));
```

Implementation in other AOP technologies. There are no annotations in CaesarJ. A more general construction can be used: the combination of a hook method and `cflow`. Instead of annotating the advice, the advice will call the hook pointcut (i.e. a *structural convention*). JBoss AOP supports all the necessary mechanisms to implement *dynamic annotation introduction*. Due to the way weaving is implemented in Spring, *dynamic annotation introduction* cannot be implemented directly. Because aspects cannot be advised themselves, another indirection is needed to make things work.

Related Work and Known Uses. De Fraine, Quiroga, and Jonckers present control flow policies to statically verify aspect interactions [17]. *Dynamic annotation introduction* can be seen as one implementation technique to realize such policies at run-time.

5.4.3   Mediation Data Introduction

Solution. Introduce some mediation-specific data members into base objects and let each cooperating aspect manipulate this data. In the end, a final action can be taken based on the final value of these data members.

Forces. Use *mediation data introduction* when

- aspects interact at different join points;
- the aspect cooperation spans multiple message flows;
- same object(s) is/are used by the cooperating aspects.

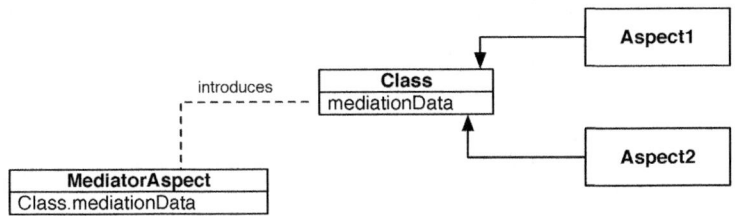

Fig. 17. Structure of *mediation data introduction*

Rationale. Let's see how this pattern can be applied to resolve the conflict in the example. What we want to achieve is that if one aspect decides access is allowed, the other aspect should no longer intervene. *Mediation data introduction* solves this by attaching extra information to the base object that is being handled (in this case an Employee object). What happens is that when an aspect decides to allow access, it marks the employee as being allowed (e.g. setting a boolean flag to true). Now, before throwing an exception, the other aspect can inspect this information and act accordingly. Aspect `AccessChecker` would then be completed as follows:

```
public aspect AccessChecker {
    abstract pointcut accessAllowed (Employee e);

    boolean Employee.allowed = false;

    Object around(Employee e): accessAllowed (e){
        e.allowed = true;
        proceed(e);
        e.allowed = false;
    }
}
```

Listing 22. *Mediation data introduction*

The pointcut `accessDenied` from the aspect `AccessGranter` could then be implemented as follows (in combination with *template pointcut*, 5.3.2):

```
pointcut accessDenied () : checkAccess () && !marked(*);
abstract pointcut checkAccess ();
pointcut marked(Employee e) : this(e) && if(e.allowed);
```

Of course, if we want this aspect to be more reusable, we better replace the explicit reference to `Employee` with a marker interface (i.e. applying *container introduction*, 5.2.2) to reduce coupling.

Implementation in other AOP technologies. Because bindings in CaesarJ are unique for each aspect, the data that is introduced is not shared and can thus not be used for mediation. In JBoss AOP and Spring, this pattern can be implemented the same way as in AspectJ.

Related Work and Known Uses. Example usage of *mediation data introduction* is the AspectOPTIMA framework [41] where some aspects introduce data to cooperate with other aspects (e.g. name, locks and checkpoints).

5.4.4   Summary Mediation

To finish the description of the Join Point Abstraction design pattern, we give an overview of the main forces that drive the selection for the most appropriate idiom or combination thereof and briefly discuss their impact on ease-of-use.

Usage of associated programming idioms. For the relatively simple coordination of aspects running at the same join point and having a fixed order, *chained advice* provides an easy solution. Otherwise, *mediation data introduction* or *dynamic annotation introduction* is needed, depending on whether the same objects are present throughout the interaction and whether the interaction spans multiple message flows. Since *mediation data introduction* works by injecting data into base objects, it only works when the same object(s) is/are used throughout the interaction. *Dynamic annotation introduction* works by annotating the message flow, which makes it inappropriate for interactions spanning multiple message flows.

For more complex interactions, the current pattern definitions are probably not sufficient. E.g. it can become quite difficult to express the intention of an aspect without the aspect actually carrying it out. This probably requires a set of idioms on its own. Another issue that makes mediation a difficult design problem is the combination of determining execution order and resolution of conflicts between aspects. Conflict resolution is about determining which intentions of the aspects will take effect. Execution order is about which intention will take effect first. Currently, the mediation idioms don't handle this distinction well. Further discussion is however beyond the scope of this paper.

Ease-of-use. To have an easy-to-use aspect library, the designer specifies the cooperation of the aspect elements upfront as much as possible. Otherwise, precedence declarations can be used to define simple user policies. *Mediation data introduction* and *dynamic annotation introduction* are less adequate for letting users configure the aspect library.

6   Example Case: A Reusable Aspect for Access Control

This section presents a reusable implementation of an aspect for access control. This case has been used throughout the paper as a running example. Here, we will put together the pieces. The main goal is to give an example of how the different patterns and idioms can be combined. First we present the general framework of access control aspects (Sect. 6.1), which we will then use to apply access control to an oblivious base program (Sect. 6.2) and a base program that exposes sensitive operations by means of annotations (Sect. 6.3).

6.1   A Reusable Access Control Aspect

Based on the philosophy of stepwise refinement, the design of the aspect library consists of a common layer and two incremental layers that add new functionality, respectively, for managing more complex access control policies and for improving the ease-of-use of the overall aspect library.

Listing 23 shows the design of the common layer. As discussed in Sect. 5.4.1 on *chained advice*, we distinguish two distinct phases to allow multiple aspects to perform their checks before a decision is taken on granting the action. Therefore aspect `AccessControl` declares the precedence between these two phases. The precedence declaration uses the super-types `AbstractAccessChecker` and `AbstractAccessGranter` to make sure that every checking aspect executes before the aspect that grants the access. `AbstractAccessChecker` is an empty abstract aspect, used only to declare the precedence. `AbstractAccessGranter` contains the core functionality. It defines a template pointcut (Sect. 5.3.2) that specifies unauthorized accesses based on two abstract hook pointcuts. Furthermore it contains an abstract method that will be executed around each unauthorized access (by applying template advice, Sect. 5.3.1).

```
public abstract aspect AccessControl {
   declare precedence: AbstractAccessChecker+,
       AbstractAccessGranter+;
}

public abstract aspect AbstractAccessGranter {
   pointcut accessDenied(): checkAccess() && !accessAllowed();
   abstract pointcut checkAccess();
   abstract pointcut accessAllowed();                    Template pointcut

   Object around(): accessDenied() {
      handleUnauthorizedAccess();
   }
```

```
  public abstract void handleUnauthorizedAccess ();   Template advice
}
public abstract aspect AbstractAccessChecker {}
```

Listing 23. Core functionality of a reusable aspect for access control

The next layer adds support for dynamic conditions. In List. 24 we therefore extend `AbstractAccessGranter` with `DynamicAccessGranter` to take into account the marks that will be set by `DynamicAccessChecker` (we included type parameters because we expect that dynamic conditions will be type specific, Sect. 5.2.3). Also a marker interface `AccessSubject` is introduced to abstract from all types that require access control. A boolean flag is added to this marker interface to enable marking the access decisions. This is achieved by combining mediation data introduction (Sect. 5.4.3) and marker interface with container introduction (Sect. 5.2.2).

```
public abstract aspect DynamicAccessGranter
    extends AbstractAccessGranter {
      pointcut accessAllowed (): marked(*);
      pointcut marked( AccessSubject subj ):
        this(subj) && if(subj.allowed);      Mediation data introduction

      private boolean AccessSubject.allowed = false;

                                              Container introduction
}

public interface AccessSubject {}                   Marker interface
```

Listing 24. Adding support for dynamic conditions

In List. 25 `DynamicAccessChecker` uses pointcut method (Sect. 5.3.3) to enable the users of the aspect to implement a dynamic condition (the default implementation always returns true, i.e. by default there is no dynamic condition). Based on this condition it marks the subject by applying mediation data introduction.

```
public abstract aspect
  DynamicAccessChecker<AllowedSubj , AllowedObj> extends
  AbstractAccessChecker {

    declare parents : AllowedSubj implements AccessSubject ;

    abstract pointcut checkAllowed ( AllowedSubj subj ,
      AllowedObj obj );

    Object around(AllowedSubj subj , AllowedObj obj ):
```

```
      checkAllowed(subj, obj) {
        if(condition(subj,obj)){
          ((AccessSubject)subj).allowed = true;
          proceed(subj, obj);                    Mediation data introduction
          ((AccessSubject)subj).allowed = false;
        }
        else proceed(subj, obj);                 Pointcut method
      }

      public boolean condition(AllowedSubj s, AllowedObj o){
        return true;
      }                                          Pointcut method
    }
```

Listing 25. Implementing dynamic conditions using *mediation data introduction* and *pointcut method*

The final layer adds support for easy composition with oblivious base code. In List. 26) pointcut checkAccess is given a generic structure, easily made concrete by connecting both marker interfaces (another marker interface AccessObject is added). To support easy configuration of the access rules, the pointcut checkAllowed is given a generic structure based on three type parameters, describing the caller, the callee and the allowed actions respectively. AccessChecker uses a type parameter (Sect. 5.2.3) as an abstraction for method signatures.

```
public interface AccessObject {}                  Marker interface

public abstract aspect AccessGranter extends
  DynamicAccessGranter {
    protected pointcut checkAccess(): this(AccessSubject) &&
      call(* AccessObject+.*(..)) && target(AccessObject);
}

public abstract aspect
  AccessChecker<AllowedSubj, AllowedObj, AllowedAction> extends
  DynamicAccessChecker<AllowedSubj, AllowedObj> {

    declare parents: AllowedObj implements AllowedAction;
                                                  Type parameter

    pointcut checkAllowed(AllowedSubj s, AllowedObj o):
      this(s) && target(o) && call(* AllowedAction.*(..));
}
```

Listing 26. Adding support for easy composition of access control with an oblivious application

Note that the last two layers are optional. They can be skipped if not necessary for the application developer. For example the common layer can be directly used by refining the hook pointcuts of the *template pointcut* idiom. If dynamic conditions are needed, the second layer can be used which adds a pointcut method. If ease-of-use is important, the bottom layer is appropriate. By deciding on a structure for the join points, the library can be easily configured by specifying the type parameters.

To summarize the design of the reusable aspect for access control, we now give an overview of the idioms that were used to implement each design pattern.

Join point abstraction. To implement the join point abstraction design pattern, we used a combination of *abstract pointcut* (in the common layer) and *marker interface* and *type parameter* (in the bottom layer). Marker interface and type parameter require a certain structure of the join points to interact with. To ensure versatility of the aspect library, abstract pointcut was used to enable connection to applications that do not satisfy this structure. We have chosen for type parameters to be able to capture the combination of caller and callee types, which is important for access control decisions. Marker interfaces were chosen to define the total scope of access control. Annotations would have been a suitable choice as well, since no callbacks are needed on the target join points. Additionally, a type parameter is also used to enable method-level access control instead of type-level access control.

Decomposition. Both pointcuts and advice were decomposed in this example. We used *template advice* to make abstraction of the action to be taken on unauthorized accesses. *Template pointcut* was used to split the concept of unauthorized accesses in two easier to define concepts (total scope and authorized accesses respectively). Furthermore, we separated the concept of a dynamic condition for authorized accesses using *pointcut method*.

Mediation. In this example we used a combination of *chained advice* and *mediation data introduction*. Two clear, distinct phases can be distinguished for access control. First, each rule determines its intention and second, a collective decision is taken and made effective in the system. *Chained advice* takes care of keeping the two phases separated, while *mediation data introduction* makes it possible to specify intentions without having an effect in the system. In this example, *dynamic annotation introduction* could be used as well for this purpose.

6.2   Composition with Oblivious Base Program

Listing 27 shows how the reusable aspect described above can be connected to a base program that is not specifically prepared. First, we configure the total scope of access control by connecting the marker interfaces `AccessSubject` and `AccessObject` and activate the access granter by adding a non-abstract sub-aspect. Next, we specify the concrete access rules by providing empty aspects that only give concrete types for the type parameters of `AccessChecker` and adding a dynamic condition if needed, by overriding the `condition()` method.

```
public aspect AccessAllowed {

  declare parents: Employee implements AccessSubject;
  declare parents: Resource || Calendar
   implements AccessObject;                          Marker interface

  static aspect ActivateGranter extends AccessGranter{}

  interface ResourceOperations {
    void book(Entry e);
    void cancel(Entry e);
  }

  interface ShowEntries {
    Entry[] showEntries();
  }

  interface SecretaryCalendar {
    void newEntry(TimeInterval t, Resource[] r);
    void editEntry(Entry e);
  }

  interface OwnerCalendar extends SecretaryCalendar {
    void newContinualEntry(TimeInterval first, Date last,
        Resource[] resources);
    void deleteEntry(Entry e);
  }

  static aspect Rule1 extends AccessChecker
  <Secretary, Resource, ResourceOperations>{}
  static aspect Rule2 extends AccessChecker
  <Employee, Calendar, ShowEntries>{}
  static aspect Rule3 extends AccessChecker
  <Secretary, Calendar, SecretaryCalendar>{}
  static aspect Rule4 extends AccessChecker
  <CalendarOwner, Calendar, OwnerCalendar>{
    public boolean condition(CalendarOwner co, Calendar c){
      return c.owner==co;
    }
  }
}
```

Listing 27. Example connector for an oblivious application to add access control

6.3   Composition with Aspect-Aware Base Program

How to compose access control with an aspect-aware base program depends strongly on the techniques used. Listing 28 shows how to connect the access

control aspect with a base program that provides annotations to determine validity of accesses. Therefore we need to implement the hook pointcuts `checkAccess`
(which specifies all accesses that need to be checked) and `accessAllowed` (which
specifies all accesses that need to be granted). We also need a helper pointcut
(`correctAnnotation`) to be able to use variables that were not introduced by
`accessAllowed`.

```
public aspect AnnotationGranter extends AbstractAccessGranter{
    pointcut checkAccess(): call(@Sensitive * *(..)) && @target(
        Sensitive);
    pointcut accessAllowed(): correctAnnotation(*,*);
    pointcut correctAnnotation(Sensitive s, Allowed role):
        @target(s) && @this(role) &&
        if(role.code().equals(s.allowed()));
}
```

Listing 28. Connecting an aspect-aware application using a sub-aspect leveraging
annotations

6.4 Revisiting the Requirements

We conclude the presentation of the integrated example with a brief discussion
on how this implementation meets the requirements.

Versatility of the aspect library is achieved by defining the aspects in terms of
join point abstractions. Abstract pointcuts in the common layer make it easy to
connect the library to any base application by giving concrete definitions of the
hook pointcuts. E.g. when the base application exposes stable abstractions using
Aspect awareness these hook pointcuts can be easily defined. For easy configuration of an oblivious base application, the library also defines more structured
join point abstractions. By deciding on a structure for the join points, the library
can be easily configured by specifying the type parameters. Stability of the design is a result of having the choice between different styles of connecting, most
suitable to a concrete context. Internal stability is achieved by decomposing the
library in small aspects with small pointcuts and advice.

With respect to implementation, we see that a combination of idioms is used
to realize each design pattern. We expect that this will be common for complex
aspect libraries that should meet the requirement of versatility, stability, and
ease-of-use.

7   Validation

In this section we present an initial validation of the benefits of the patterns in
our pattern system with respect to the requirements listed in Section 2. This is
not meant as a conclusive empirical study, but aims to give a first impression
of what the impact is of employing the patterns. This initial validation is based
on the results of a master thesis, in which two students applied the patterns

to define some reusable aspects and evaluated their applicability in the context of multiple applications. We used these results to perform some measurements based on a selection of external metrics for stability, versatility, and ease-of-use. External metrics measure an external attribute directly, by putting the system in a concrete context. Sant'Anna et al. performed a similar study [67] supplemented with a prediction using internal metrics.

7.1   Setup

The setup for our initial validation consists of three applications: USell, a prototype sales application; Cities Of Faith (COF), an online multiplayer game and Manage My Sales (MMS), an operational commercial web application. The aspects studied in these applications are pricing, authorization, and argument validation[9]. Most attention is given to the pricing aspect library. It provides support for adding extra price factors like, V.A.T., transportation costs, promotions, etc. For each aspect, there is an implementation without patterns and an implementation based on the patterns. For the pricing library, there are two alternative implementations based on the patterns. Both use *pointcut method, template advice,* and *mediation data introduction*, but version 1 adds *marker interface*, while version 2 adds *template pointcut* and *type parameter*.

Each implementation of each aspect is applied to each application, without changing the aspect library. We also have simulated a number of change requests (CR) that impose new requirements on the applications with respect to the different aspectual functionalities. For instance the following examples of change requests have been performed with respect to the pricing functionality:

- MMS application: summer-time discounts, promotion for premium business customers
- COF application[10]: paying players can perform more moves, moving a group of units together is less expensive
- USell application: providing a change log to visualize all price factors, extra costs for delivery, products involved in a couple promotion are not subject to other promotions.

7.2   Stability

To give an idea of the impact of the patterns on stability, we compared the number of changed and added pointcuts for each change request of the USell application[11].

---

[9] The source code of the aspects and the USell applications are available at http://distrinet.cs.kuleuven.be/software/aodesignpatterns. Source code for MMS and COF is available on request due to copyrights owned by third parties.

[10] In the context of COF, pricing is used to determine the cost of moving units (soldiers, ships) across the board. E.g. moving units through enemy territory is more expensive.

[11] The numbers for the other applications where not meaningful as they made extensive use of the *pointcut method* idiom.

Table 2. Added and changed pointcuts for each change request in the USell application

Added and changed pointcuts	Base	CR1	CR2	CR3	CR4	CR5	CR6	CR7	Total
Pricing (without patterns)	0	3	5	1	0	8	2	0	19
Pricing (patterns v1)	0	3	0	1	0	2	2	0	8
Pricing (patterns v2)	3	5	0	0	0	3	5	0	16

On average, the implementations using patterns require less pointcuts to be added or changed. Remark that for the third implementation some pointcuts were needed right from the beginning. The reason is that this implementation used a generic aspect with abstract pointcuts that need an implementation before it can become active.

7.3   Versatility

To give an idea of the impact of the patterns on versatility we have compared the degree of library use for the 3 alternative implementations of the pricing library. We show the trend in library use by giving the value after the first change request and the value after all change requests. The degree of library use is defined as the lines of code (LOC) that are actually used by an application divided by total LOC of the library.

We would expect that as more change requests have been performed, more functionality of the aspect library will be used. The results are as follows:

Table 3. Degree of library use for the pricing aspect after 1 change request and after all change requests

Degree of library use (%)	USell	MMS	COF
Pricing (without patterns)	57→23	50→23	40→17
Pricing (patterns v1)	89→99	99→99	89→99
Pricing (patterns v2)	77→85	84→85	76→84

Not only do we see that the degree of library use for the patterned versions is higher, also their trend is upward, while that of the version without patterns is downward. As the requirements for pricing become more complex with more change requests, more functionality of the pricing library is needed. As the implementation without patterns does not provide the necessary abstractions, that functionality cannot be reused.

This decreasing trend of library use can also be considered from the perspective of the amount of code duplication on top of the library. If an application cannot reuse the functionality from the library, we expect that the application will need to define this functionality itself, leading to a duplication of code. To confirm this expectation, we have measured the amount of duplicated code in the USell application before and after integrating the pricing library. We used the DuDe tool to count the amount of duplicated text blocks across the application source code[12]. The following table gives the amount of blocks of duplicated code after integrating the 3 alternative implementations of the pricing library. The USell application without the pricing library contains 11 blocks of duplicated code.

Table 4. Amount of duplicated code in USell application before and after integration of the pricing aspect

Amount of duplicated code blocks (%)	USell
Pricing (without patterns)	15→37
Pricing (patterns v1)	13→27
Pricing (patterns v2)	14→21

We see indeed that the pricing implementation without patterns triggers more duplication in the USell application code than the other versions.

7.4   Ease-of-Use

As shown in section 7.3, the additional coding effort for integrating an aspect library is smaller when the aspect library has been designed using patterns. This indicates that the overall ease-of-use of aspect libraries increases with the use of the patterns. In this subsection, we compare the different used programming idioms to each other with respect to their impact on ease-of-use. We perform this comparison by measuring the total LOC of the application before and after integrating the aspect.

For authorization, we compare the use of annotations with the use of participant connection. For argument validation, we compare annotation-based point-cuts with a traditional object-oriented implementation. As can be expected we see that the use of annotations requires a significantly lower LOC (and thus on ease-of-use). Annotations allow the developer to ignore boilerplate code for authorization and argument validation by providing metadata with the method signature or on the arguments themselves.

For the two implementations of the pricing aspect there are no significant differences in LOC. From these numbers no conclusion can be made with respect to the impact on ease-of-use for these different combinations of idioms.

---

[12] Dude (Duplication Detector) is a tool that uses textual comparison at the level of line of code in order to detect fragments of duplicated code. Its powerful detection engine can also cover various adaptations of the duplicated code (such as variables renaming or statement insertion/removal) – http://loose.upt.ro/iplasma/dude.html.

Table 5. Total LOC for different implementations of the aspects

Total LOC	USell	MMS	COF
Without pricing	1518	4828	38700
Pricing (patterns v1)	2213	5103	38888
Pricing (patterns v2)	2197	5109	38882
Authorization (participant)	n/a	5012	39203
Authorization (annotations)	n/a	4930	38799
Argument validation (OO)	1463	4922	39156
Argument validation (annotations)	1396	4813	38700

7.5   Threats to Validity

Although this initial validation is not meant as a conclusive empirical study, we believe that these results give a good impression on the applicability of the patterns and the benefits of applying them. To assess the real value of these results, we analyze the threats to the validity.

Construct Validity. Stability, reusability and ease-of-use are attributes that are difficult to measure. The metrics used for reuse [18] and stability [23] have been used before. The metric used for ease-of-use is less established, but size is always an important indicator for effort [53].

Internal Validity. The most important threats to internal validity are the bias of the students towards promoting the patterns and the learning effect as the implementations without patterns were implemented first.

External Validity. The size and number of the applications and aspects used is not sufficient to make general conclusions about the benefits of the patterns in a real-world context. Also, all code in the study was written in AspectJ, which limits the portability of the results to other AOP technologies.

8   Conclusion

8.1   Future Work

Even though some of the design patterns we describe are well known and used on a large scale, it is important to do a more proper evaluation. More case studies are needed, especially larger and more complex ones, to study the impact of these patterns on usability and reusability. For instance the mediation patterns need more study to evaluate their support for more complex policies that cause intricate interplay between different aspects.

   The patterns we present are based on the constructs available in AspectJ. Other AO languages, and also more advanced OO composition mechanisms, need to be studied in order to evaluate their potential to provide reusable solutions for the separation of crosscutting concerns. Candidate programming constructs are virtual classes, closures, mixins, implicit composition, ...

The pattern system we present, adds structure and selection guidance to the collection of patterns and idioms. More knowledge can be added to the system, e.g. relations between patterns and idioms. The ultimate goal is a genuine pattern language that defines an integrated process for designing reusable aspects. Additionally, other requirements can be taken into account to extend the pattern system. New patterns and idioms will become relevant and other forces will drive pattern selection.

8.2 Summary

In this paper we have presented a system of design patterns aimed at the development of reusable aspects. Our focus was on aspects applicable to various applications and application domains and the ease of configuring the aspect for a concrete context. Our pattern system consists of three layers: an architectural pattern, 4 design patterns, each focusing on a specific sub-problem, and for each design pattern a set of programming idioms that can be used to implement the design pattern. Each pattern additionally presents in general terms the forces and variation points that guide the application developer in choosing the appropriate idiom for implementing the pattern, depending on the specific development context.

We have described the patterns using a standard format and illustrated them by means of a running example regarding access control. We gave a holistic view on the running example which shows the use of the different patterns and the interplay between them. We also included the use of these patterns in academic and industry contexts and presented an initial validation with respect to the requirements. The major lessons learned from the validation are that versatility and stability improve with the use of patterns and that annotations are more easy-to-use than other idioms (a result that can be expected). The results give a good impression on the applicability of the patterns and the benefits of applying them. In combination with the fact that the patterns and idioms are used in real-world applications should give them sufficient credibility as worthwhile solutions to the design problem of reusable aspect libraries.

References

[1] Eclipse jdt weaving service, `http://wiki.eclipse.org/JDT_weaving_features`
[2] Jhotdraw as open-source project, `http://jhotdraw.org/`
[3] Spring reference documentation, `http://www.springsource.org/documentation`
[4] Aldrich, J.: Open Modules: Modular Reasoning about Advice. In: Black, A. (ed.) ECOOP 2005. LNCS, vol. 3586, pp. 144–168. Springer, Heidelberg (2005)
[5] Aracic, I., Gasiunas, V., Mezini, M., Ostermann, K.: An overview of CaesarJ. In: Rashid, A., Aksit, M. (eds.) Transactions on Aspect-Oriented Software Development I. LNCS, vol. 3880, pp. 135–173. Springer, Heidelberg (2006)
[6] Baniassad, E., Clarke, S.: Theme: An approach for aspect-oriented analysis and design (2004)
[7] Bodden, E.: An aspectj library for fault tolerance, `http://www.bodden.de/tools/#aspectj-ft`

[8] Bodkin, R., Schidmeier, A., Bodden, E.: The ajlib incubator project, http://fisheye.codehaus.org/browse/ajlib-incubator

[9] Buschmann, F., Meunier, R., Rohnert, H., Sommerlad, P., Stal, M.: Pattern-Oriented Software Architecture. A System of Patterns, vol. 1. Wiley, Chichester (1996)

[10] Bynens, M., Lagaisse, B., Joosen, W., Truyen, E.: The elementary pointcut pattern. In: BPAOSD 2007: Proceedings of the 2nd Workshop on Best Practices in Applying Aspect-Oriented Software Development, p. 2. ACM, New York (2007)

[11] Canal, J.A.: Parametric aspects: A proposal. In: RAM-SE, pp. 91–99 (2004)

[12] Chakravarthy, V., Regehr, J., Eide, E.: Edicts: implementing features with flexible binding times. In: AOSD, pp. 108–119 (2008)

[13] Chitchyan, R., Greenwood, P., Sampaio, A., Rashid, A., Garcia, A.F., da Silva, L.F.: Semantic vs. syntactic compositions in aspect-oriented requirements engineering: an empirical study. In: Sullivan, K.J. (ed.) AOSD, pp. 149–160. ACM, New York (2009)

[14] Clifton, C., Leavens, G.T., Noble, J.: MAO: Ownership and effects for more effective reasoning about aspects. In: Ernst, E. (ed.) ECOOP 2007. LNCS, vol. 4609, pp. 451–475. Springer, Heidelberg (2007)

[15] Cunha, C.A., Sobral, J.L., Monteiro, M.P.: Reusable aspect-oriented implementations of concurrency patterns and mechanisms. In: AOSD 2006: Proceedings of the 5th International Conference on Aspect-Oriented Software Development, pp. 134–145. ACM, New York (2006)

[16] Filman, R.E., Friedman, D.P.: Aspect-Oriented Programming is Quantification and Obliviousness. In: Position paper for the Advanced Separation of Concerns Workshop at the Conference on Object-Oriented Programming Systems, Languages, and Applications (OOPSLA). ACM, Minnesota (2000)

[17] De Fraine, B., Quiroga, P.D., Jonckers, V.: Management of aspect interactions using statically-verified control-flow relations. In: International Workshop on Aspects, Dependencies and Interactions, pp. 5–14 (2008)

[18] Frakes, W.B., Terry, C.: Software reuse: Metrics and models. ACM Comput. Surv. 28(2), 415–435 (1996)

[19] Gamma, E., Helm, R., Johnson, R., Vlissides, J.: Design Patterns, Elements of Reusable Object-Oriented Software. Addison-Wesley, Reading (1995)

[20] Garcia, A., Kulesza, U., Sardinha, J., Lucena, C., Milidi, R.: The mobility aspect pattern. In: Proceedings of the 4th Latin American Conference on Pattern Languages of Programming, SugarLoafPLoP 2004 (2004)

[21] Garcia, A.F., Sant'Anna, C., Figueiredo, E., Kulesza, U., de Lucena, C.J.P., von Staa, A.: Modularizing design patterns with aspects: a quantitative study. In: AOSD, pp. 3–14 (2005)

[22] Ghezzi, C., Jazayeri, M., Mandrioli, D.: Fundamentals of Software Engineering. Prentice Hall PTR, Upper Saddle River (2002)

[23] Greenwood, P., Bartolomei, T., Figueiredo, E., Dosea, M., Garcia, A., Cacho, N., Sant'Anna, C., Soares, S., Borba, P., Kulesza, U., Rashid, A.: On the impact of aspectual decompositions on design stability: An empirical study. In: Bateni, M. (ed.) ECOOP 2007. LNCS, vol. 4609, pp. 176–200. Springer, Heidelberg (2007)

[24] Griswold, W.G., Sullivan, K., Song, Y., Shonle, M., Tewari, N., Cai, Y., Rajan, H.: Modular software design with crosscutting interfaces. IEEE Softw. 23(1), 51–60 (2006)

[25] Gudmundson, S., Kiczales, G.: Addressing practical software development issues in aspectj with a pointcut interface. In: Advanced Separation of Concerns (2001)

[26] Hanenberg, S., Costanza, P.: Connecting Aspects in AspectJ: Strategies vs. Patterns. In: First Workshop on Aspects, Components, and Patterns for Infrastructure Software at AOSD (2002)

[27] Hanenberg, S., Schmidmeier, A.: Idioms for building software frameworks in aspectj. In: AOSD Workshop on Aspects, Components, and Patterns for Infrastructure Software (2003)

[28] Hanenberg, S., Unland, R.: Using and Reusing Aspects in AspectJ. In: Workshop on Advanced Separation of Concerns, OOPSLA (2001)

[29] Hanenberg, S., Unland, R., Schmidmeier, A.: AspectJ Idioms for Aspect-Oriented Software Construction. In: Proceedings of EuroPLoP, pp. 617–644 (2003)

[30] Hanenberg, S., Unland, R.: Parametric introductions. In: AOSD 2003: Proceedings of the 2nd International Conference on Aspect-Oriented Software Development, pp. 80–89. ACM, New York (2003)

[31] Hannemann, J., Kiczales, G.: Design pattern implementation in java and aspectj. In: OOPSLA, pp. 161–173 (2002)

[32] Harrison, W., Ossher, H.: Subject-oriented programming: a critique of pure objects. SIGPLAN Not. 28(10), 411–428 (1993)

[33] Havinga, W., Nagy, I., Bergmans, L.: Introduction and derivation of annotations in aop: Applying expressive pointcut languages to introductions. In: First European Interactive Workshop on Aspects in Software (2005)

[34] Hoffman, K., Eugster, P.: Bridging java and aspectj through explicit join points. In: PPPJ 2007: Proceedings of the 5th International Symposium on Principles and Practice of Programming in Java, pp. 63–72. ACM, New York (2007)

[35] Hoffman, K., Eugster, P.: Towards reusable components with aspects: an empirical study on modularity and obliviousness. In: ICSE 2008: Proceedings of the 30th International Conference on Software Engineering, pp. 91–100. ACM, New York (2008)

[36] JUnit.org. Resources for test driven development, http://www.junit.org/

[37] Kästner, C., Apel, S., Batory, D.S.: A case study implementing features using aspectj. In: SPLC, pp. 223–232 (2007)

[38] Kellens, A., Mens, K., Brichau, J., Gybels, K.: Managing the evolution of aspect-oriented software with model-based pointcuts. In: Hu, Q. (ed.) ECOOP 2006. LNCS, vol. 4067, pp. 501–525. Springer, Heidelberg (2006)

[39] Kiczales, G., Mezini, M.: Aspect-oriented programming and modular reasoning. In: ICSE 2005: Proceedings of the 27th International Conference on Software Engineering, pp. 49–58. ACM, New York (2005)

[40] Kiczales, G., Mezini, M.: Separation of concerns with procedures, annotations, advice and pointcuts. In: Black, A.P. (ed.) ECOOP 2005. LNCS, vol. 3586, pp. 195–213. Springer, Heidelberg (2005)

[41] Kienzle, J.: AspectOPTIMA,
http://www.cs.mcgill.ca/~joerg/AspectOPTIMA/AspectOPTIMA.html

[42] Kienzle, J., Duala-ekoko, E., Gélineau, S.: AspectOPTIMA: A case study on aspect dependencies and interactions. Transactions on Aspect-Oriented Software Development 5, 187–234 (2009)

[43] Kienzle, J., Gélineau, S.: Ao challenge - implementing the acid properties for transactional objects. In: AOSD 2006: Proceedings of the 5th International Conference on Aspect-Oriented Software Development, pp. 202–213. ACM, New York (2006)

[44] Kniesel, G., Rho, T., Hanenberg, S.: Evolvable pattern implementations need generic aspects. In: RAM-SE, pp. 111–126 (2004)

[45] Koppen, C., Stoerzer, M.: Pcdiff: Attacking the fragile pointcut problem. In: First European Interactive Workshop on Aspects in Software, EIWAS (2004)

[46] Kuhlemann, M., Kästner, C.: Reducing the complexity of AspectJ mechanisms for recurring extensions. In: Proc. GPCE Workshop on Aspect-Oriented Product Line Engineering, AOPLE (2007)

[47] Kulesza, U., Alves, V., Garcia, A., de Lucena, C.J.P., Borba, P.: Improving Extensibility of Object-Oriented Frameworks with Aspect-Oriented Programming. In: Morisio, M. (ed.) ICSR 2006. LNCS, vol. 4039, pp. 231–245. Springer, Heidelberg (2006)

[48] Laddad, R.: AOP and Metadata: A perfect match, part 1. IBM developerworks: AOP@Work,
http://www.128.ibm.com/developerworks/java/library/j-aopwork3/

[49] Laddad, R.: AOP and Metadata: A perfect match, part 2. IBM developerworks: AOP@Work,
http://www.128.ibm.com/developerworks/java/library/j-aopwork4/

[50] Laddad, R.: AspectJ in Action: Practical Aspect-Oriented Programming. Manning Publications Co., Greenwich (2003)

[51] Lagaisse, B., Joosen, W.: Decomposition into elementary pointcuts: A design principle for improved aspect reusability. In: SPLAT (2006)

[52] Lagaisse, B., Joosen, W., De Win, B.: Managing semantic interference with aspect integration contracts. In: International Workshop on Software-Engineering Properties of Languages for Aspect Technologies, SPLAT (2004)

[53] Li, W., Henry, S.M.: Object-oriented metrics that predict maintainability. Journal of Systems and Software 23(2), 111–122 (1993)

[54] Loughran, N., Rashid, A.: Framed aspects: Supporting variability and configurability for AOP. In: Dannenberg, R.B., Krueger, C. (eds.) ICOIN 2004 and ICSR 2004. LNCS, vol. 3107, pp. 127–140. Springer, Heidelberg (2004)

[55] Marin, M.: Ajhotdraw, http://swerl.tudelft.nl/bin/view/AMR/AJHotDraw

[56] Meszaros, G., Doble, J.: Metapatterns: A pattern language for pattern writing. In: 3rd Pattern Languages of Programming Conference (1996)

[57] Sun Microsystems. Enterprise javabeans technology,
http://java.sun.com/products/ejb/index.jsp

[58] Miles, R.: AspectJ Cookbook. O'Reilly Media, Inc., Sebastopol (2004)

[59] Monteiro, M.P., Fernandes, J.M.: Towards a catalog of aspect-oriented refactorings. In: AOSD 2005: Proceedings of the 4th International Conference on Aspect-Oriented Software Development, pp. 111–122. ACM, New York (2005)

[60] Monteiro, M.P., Fernandes, J.M.: Towards a catalogue of refactorings and code smells for aspectj. T. Aspect-Oriented Software Development 1, 214–258 (2006)

[61] Murphy, G.C., Lai, A., Walker, R.J., Robillard, M.P.: Separating features in source code: An exploratory study. In: ICSE, pp. 275–284 (2001)

[62] Noble, J., Schmidmeier, A., Pearce, D.J., Black, A.P.: Patterns of aspect-oriented design. In: Proceedings of European Conference on Pattern Languages of Programs (2007)

[63] Op de beeck, S., Van Landuyt, D., Truyen, E., Joosen, W.: A domain-specific middleware layer using AOSD: next-generation digital news publishing. In: Proceedings of the ACM/IFIP/USENIX Middleware 2008 Conference Companion, pp. 78–81. ACM, New York (2008)

[64] Rajan, H., Leavens, G.T.: Ptolemy: A Language with Quantified, Typed Events. In: Ryan, M. (ed.) ECOOP 2008. LNCS, vol. 5142, pp. 155–179. Springer, Heidelberg (2008)

[65] Rashid, A., Chitchyan, R.: Persistence as an aspect. In: AOSD 2003: Proceedings of the 2nd International Conference on Aspect-Oriented Software Development, pp. 120–129. ACM, New York (2003)

[66] Rashid, A., Cottenier, T., Greenwood, P., Chitchyan, R., Meunier, R., Coelho, R., Südholt, M., Joosen, W.: Aspect-oriented software development in practice: Tales from aosd-europe. Computer 43(2), 19–26 (2010)

[67] Sant'anna, C., Garcia, A., Chavez, C., Lucena, C., von Staa, A.v: On the reuse and maintenance of aspect-oriented software: An assessment framework. In: Proceedings XVII Brazilian Symposium on Software Engineering (2003)

[68] Santos, A.L., Koskimies, K.: Modular hot spots: A pattern language for developing high-level framework reuse interfaces. In: Proceedings of European Conference on Pattern Languages of Programs (2008)

[69] Schmidmeier, A.: Cooperating aspects. In: Proceedings of EuroPLoP (2005)

[70] SpringSource. Spring insight, http://www.springsource.com/products/tcserver/devedition

[71] SpringSource. Spring roo, http://www.springsource.org/roo

[72] Steimann, F.: The paradoxical success of aspect-oriented programming. SIGPLAN Not. 41(10), 481–497 (2006)

[73] Stoerzer, M., Graf, J.: Using pointcut delta analysis to support evolution of aspect-oriented software. In: ICSM 2005: Proceedings of the 21st IEEE International Conference on Software Maintenance (ICSM 2005), pp. 653–656. IEEE Computer Society, Washington, DC, USA (2005)

[74] Tarr, P., Ossher, H., Harrison, W., Sutton Jr., S.M.: N degrees of separation: multi-dimensional separation of concerns. In: International Conference on Software Engineering, p. 107 (1999)

[75] The AspectJ Team. The aspectj 5 development kit developer's notebook, http://www.eclipse.org/aspectj/doc/released/adk15notebook/index.html

[76] Tourwe, T., Brichau, J., Gybels, K.: On the Existence of the AOSD-Evolution Paradox. In: SPLAT Workshop, Boston, AOSD (2003)

[77] Van Landuyt, D., Op de beeck, S., Kemper, B., Truyen, E., Joosen, W.: Building a next-generation digital publishing platform using aosd, http://distrinet.cs.kuleuven.be/projects/digitalpublishing/

[78] Van Landuyt, D., Op de beeck, S., Truyen, E., Joosen, W.: Domain-driven discovery of stable abstractions for pointcut interfaces. In: Proceedings of the 8th ACM International Conference on Aspect-Oriented Software Development, AOSD 2009, pp. 75–86. ACM, New York (2009)

[79] Van Landuyt, D., Truyen, E., Joosen, W.: Discovery of stable domain abstractions for reusable pointcut interfaces: common case study for ao modeling. CW Reports CW560, Department of Computer Science, K.U.Leuven, Leuven, Belgium (August 2009)

[80] Verhanneman, T., Piessens, F., De Win, B., Truyen, E., Joosen, W.: Implementing a modular access control service to support application-specific policies in caesarj. In: AOMD 2005: Proceedings of the 1st Workshop on Aspect Oriented Middleware Development, ACM, New York (2005)

[81] Wampler, D.: Noninvasiveness and Aspect-Oriented Design: Lessons from Object-Oriented Design Principles (2004)

[82] Wampler, D.: The Challenges of Writing Reusable and Portable Aspects in AspectJ: Lessons from Contract4J. In: International Conference on Aspect Oriented Software Development (AOSD 2006)–Industry Track Proceedings (2006)

[83] Wiese, D., Meunier, R., Hohenstein, U.: How to convince industry of aop. In: AOSD 2007, Industry Track (2007)

A Real-World Perspective of AOP*

Ramnivas Laddad

Abstract. What is the real deal with AOP? Is it something that you should embrace or ignore? What do you gain with AOP, and what do you risk by adopting it? Let's address these important questions from a practitioner's point of view. We'll start with AOP in the context of the typical hype cycle. This will give us a historical perspective on AOP evolution and indicate what lies ahead. We also look at the landscape, focusing on the current situation and changes in last few years. While AOP is a more general concept, because our focus is the real world use of it, we'll focus on AspectJ—its most prominent implementation.

Keywords: Aspect-oriented programming, AOP, AspectJ, Spring, Java.

1 Mapping AOP onto the Hype Cycle

Every technology goes through a cycle that's well illustrated by the Gartner Hype Cycle (http://en.wikipedia.org/wiki/Hype_cycle). AOP is no exception. Understanding the hype cycle and the position of the technology you're considering to adopt is important. It allows you to offer a more accurate gauge of the benefits the technology is likely to offer and the risk you expose yourself to. In this section, I'll give my assessment of the hype cycle of AOP in five major phases: technology trigger, peak of inflated expectations, trough of disillusionment, slope of enlightenment, and plateau of productivity. The following figure depicts the hype cycle and how AOP maps to it.

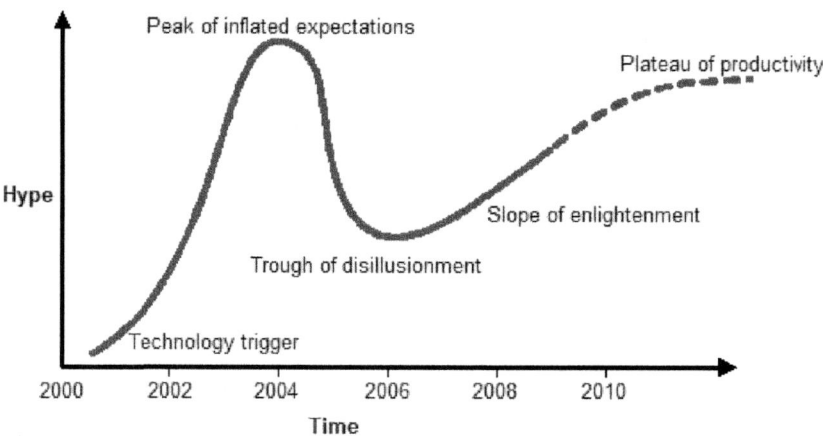

Let's look at each of the major phases in the figure.

S. Katz et al. (Eds.): Transactions on AOSD VIII, LNCS 6580, pp. 108–115, 2011.
© Manning Publications 2009

Technology Trigger

In this phase, a new technology appears on the horizon with a promise to solve a set of problems. It may be an announcement of a new product or an actual release of a product. Either way, it may generate some buzz and attract developers towards it.

For AOP, the technology trigger occurred with AspectJ 1.0 release in 2002 followed by a more serious 1.1 release in 2003 (earlier releases, although interesting, didn't receive much attention). GregorKiczales and his team, while working at Xerox Palo Alto Research Center (PARC), developed the AOP concepts backed by the AspectJ language. Many technologists could immediately understand the potential for AspectJ, especially for enterprise applications. Aspect-oriented programming using AspectJ was seen as a way to modularize some of the common crosscutting concerns—transaction management, security, caching, concurrency control, and lest we forget, tracing.

For many technologies, especially with substantially new ideas and potential to solve complex problems, the next phase follows.

Peak of Inflated Expectations

In this phase, the technology gains much hype (warranted or otherwise). Everyone wants to know about it, everyone has an opinion of it, but few people use it in real applications. A few adventurous (or reckless) developers (or early adopters) try it. If the technology fits the problem well, and you have good understanding of it, adopting technology during this phase can give you a competitive advantage. It's fascinating to be associated with a technology in this phase. People perceive you as "cool."

For AOP, the peak occurred around 2004. I enjoyed the attention I received as well as the response to the first edition of AspectJ in Action (thank you!). Many smaller companies and a few larger ones used AspectJ in a few projects. During this time, most developers working on AspectJ and AspectJ Development Tools (AJDT) were from IBM. This significant investment from IBM helped AspectJ gain solid footing.

But the lack of mass adoption made using the technology, an adventure. Fortunately for AspectJ the peak wasn't high due to expectation management by AspectJ evangelists. For example, GregorKiczales, the father of AOP, portrayed AspectJ as the "15% solution" (http://www.ddj.com/architect/184414845): he argues that in a typical project, you'll use AspectJ for about 15% of your coding. Think about it. When was the last time the creator of a language quoted such a small number for his own language? This expectation management led to a smaller peak in the hype cycle and, fortunately, a shorter fall in the next phase.

Trough of Disillusionment

In this phase, the technology starts to lose the attention it once received. It becomes one of many things vying for attention. In this phase, many early adopters continue to use the technology creatively to gain a competitive advantage. Others begin to look at it with a skeptical eye. The technology sees serious and innovative competition from newer solutions that address part of the same problem space. Interestingly, many of these competing technologies are going through the "peak of inflated expectation" phase. On one extreme, these new technologies can drive the existing one into oblivion (which isn't necessarily a bad thing—if the technology couldn't take on a competition, oblivion is a respectful resting place). On the other side, competition can shake the technology and force it to innovate further.

For AOP, the trough occurred around 2006. In addition to the naturally expected trough that follows a peak, Java 5 also proved to be disruptive to implementing other features needed in making AspectJ an easily acceptable technology—compiler and weaver speed, tools integration, and so on. Although the core AJDT committers kept developing the technology, much more dedicated effort was needed. Furthermore, many users perceived the adoption of AspectJ as a big step due to the requirement of using a brand-new syntax and the need to use a special compiler at the beginning of a project. Eclipse, the main supported IDE for AspectJ, was advancing at a rapid pace, leaving a large gap between its Java support and AspectJ support.

Enterprise Java Beans (EJB) provided serious competition. Through a framework-centric approach, you could implement crosscutting functionality such as transaction management and security in a modular fashion. More serious competition came from dynamic languages such as Ruby and Groovy and associated frameworks such as Rails and Grails. The metaprogramming model available in these technologies provided an alternative solution to modularize crosscutting concerns.

On the tooling side, all new languages suffer from the lack of maturity (although most new language proponents would argue otherwise). In reality, tools always lag behind language creation. I still remember using Emacs with Java for several years after disappointing experiences with many IDEs. But this didn't cause us early Java adopters to discard the language for the lack of tools. A judicious decision requires that you weigh the benefits of the language against the handicaps introduced by immature or nonexisting tools. For AspectJ, the tools side—especially IDEs—has been a weakness, especially if you expected its support to match that of Java.

AspectJ took on all these challenges to enter the next—and most useful—phase.

Slope of Enlightenment

This phase results from multiple factors such as changes in the technology to meet real-world requirements, maturing of the technology due to sustained field testing, finding the right context for the technology to make an impact, and disillusionment about other technologies once considered as alternatives. The technology also starts to be used to solve problems in the context of focused application areas.

The slope of enlightenment started for AOP right after its trough. Adrian Colyer, the AspectJ lead, left IBM to join SpringSource. Soon, I joined SpringSource, and I've been contributing to Spring AspectJ integration as a committer. Later, Andy Clement, a lead AspectJ developer, also left IBM to join SpringSource. Recently, Andrew Eisenberg joined SpringSource and is working on improving AspectJ-related tools. Currently, AspectJ is a SpringSource portfolio project and enjoys its sponsorship. All these factors helped bring together Spring and AspectJ and afford sustained development.

During my consulting engagements, I see signs of AspectJ being in this phase. Developers no longer fear it for its perceived complexity but rather show curiosity about exploring the benefit it offers and eagerly want to use AspectJ.

Let's look at the underlying factors that caused AspectJ to enter this phase.

Response to User Needs

AspectJ followed a path to enlightenment (pardon the pun) by simplifying its adoption. New syntax and weaving models (in part due to merger with AspectWerkz—a project led by Jonas Bonér and AlexandreVasseur) removed some of the bumpiest patches on the path. The new syntax choices delayed the use of the weaver as far as executing the application (and, used with Spring, eliminated the weaver altogether). Load-time weaving allowed the introduction of AspectJ without much fuss. Java 5 also made a huge difference with the introduction of annotations. Annotations allow a simple collaboration point between developers of the main-line business logic and developers of aspects. Annotations alleviate the difficulty of writing good pointcuts to a large degree by enabling course-grained pointcuts that identify fine-grained join points in the main-line code.

The promise of good tooling—especially the possibility of visualizing the interaction between aspects and classes—has been an important differentiator from similar technologies (such as metaprogramming). Although AspectJ's support for Eclipse has always been reasonable, it was never as good as that for Java. Part of the problem was fast innovation in the underlying Eclipse JDT, which kept raising user expectations.

Furthermore, compilation speed and memory requirement have been less than optimal. Overall, there was a gap between potential and reality when it came to tooling. Lately, the AspectJ and AJDT teams have performed some amazing feats in optimizing the compilation process and IDE integration. The changes in the latest AJDT, where the JDT is woven with AspectJ functionality (using AspectJ itself) make development within Eclipse a pleasant and productive experience. With all these changes, any issues with tooling are a thing of past.

Spring AOP also needed to respond to user needs. Although proxy-based AOP lowered the adoption barrier compared to AspectJ's byte-code based AOP, Spring's programming model wasn't inviting. Aspects written using it were type-unsafe and verbose. As a result, most developers limited themselves to the aspects shipped as part of Spring and other frameworks. Spring responded by adopting the AspectJ programming model with a proxy-based implementation. This new possibility lets you use a subset of the AspectJ syntax without the need for a special compiler or weaver. This significantly reduced the barrier to writing custom aspects to meet the specific needs of an application. Here, too, annotation-based pointcuts helped remove whatever was left of the barrier to its adoption. Currently, Spring considers AspectJ to be its preferred programming model and has relegated the old model to a transitionary technology status.

Spring's adoption of AspectJ also provided AspectJ a much needed context to grow.

Focused Context: The Spring Factor

Languages grow within a certain context. C grew in the context of operating system programming, C++ grew in context of UI programming, Java grew in the context of servlets (leading it to be the favored server-side language), and Ruby grew in the context of Rails. AspectJ lacked such a context. It has been used in real-time programming, UI programming, and server-side programming. As a result, there has been a dissipated effort to make AOP, a mainstream technology. The Spring Frame-work has changed it all. It provided the right context—enterprise applications—for AOP to gain prominence.

AOP was already an integral part of Spring, helping with concerns such as transaction management, security, and monitoring. By using an elegant programming model offered by AspectJ, it paved the way for mass adoption.

Availability of a Gradual Adoption Path

The adoption of a new technology, especially with significantly new concepts such as AOP, is never easy. You need a path that allows a gradual introduction of the technology. Before AspectJ 5 and Spring AOP, the adoption path for AOP was steep.

Spring's proxy-based AOP with AspectJ syntax is a great way to start with AOP. It yields immediate benefits and provides experience with AOP. Spring even provides a few pre-built aspects to get you started. During this phase, you can start writing simple aspects based on the @AspectJ syntax applied using proxy-based AOP. Later, you can use byte-code-based weaving along with or as a replacement for the proxy-based AOP. Here, you can have several smaller steps available to manage risk. Initially, you can use aspects such as tracing and monitoring for development. Because you don't need to commit to using these aspects in production, there is little risk in trying them. With these aspects, load-time weaving is a great help; you don't need to modify your build system or use a special IDE, making the addition of aspects a much simpler task.

Next, you can begin using policy enforcement aspects. You can get feedback provided by the aspects about any policy violations while remaining uncommitted to their production use. In this phase, you can start using AJDT for immediate feedback right inside the IDE. During this process, you can vastly simplify the writing of the aspects using custom annotations—something you couldn't do before AspectJ 5. By this stage, you should be comfortable with the patterns and practices of AOP. This is the point at which you can make a judicious decision based on real experience.

New Jvm Languages

In the last few years, practitioners have distinguished between Java the platform and Java the language. There is a growing recognition that Java the language isn't sufficient for productivity even considering the vast number of tools available for it. You need to choose some other language to gain a competitive advantage. At the same time, there is growing faith in the other part of Java the platform. With all the innovations in the VM as well as the overall platform (OSGi, mature libraries, IDEs), it's compelling to use the Java platform for many projects. Combining these factors has led to innovative new languages such as Groovy, JRuby, Scala, and Clojure on the Java platform. Today, it's not a shock to hear of a project using one of these new languages. As a result, the fear of new languages has gone down substantially. The use of multiple languages within the same project is also common. One of the negatives of AspectJ—that it's a new language—is no longer the case.

Even on the methodology front, there is a growing sense that OOP may have run its course. For today's complex problems, we need more power. We need to use OOP with something else: metaprogramming, functional programming, or aspect-oriented programming. Furthermore, you may use several additional methodologies along with OOP. For example, you may use Java with Scala to take the functional approach along with AspectJ to deal with crosscutting concerns. This Polyglot Programming (http://www.polyglotprogramming.com) approach uses multiple languages in the same application and is steadily gaining traction. AspectJ may have to adopt its join point model, which exclusively targets the Java language, to fit into the polyglot programming scenario. Fun times may lie ahead!

Acceptance of Annotations

Selecting the required crosscutting points is one of the most critical and difficult tasks in writing aspects. Relying only on naming convention, type hierarchy, and package structure takes you quite a way. But in many case, defining a robust pointcut poses some difficulty. With the introduction of annotations in Java 5, AspectJ provides an easy and transparent way to select the join points you want. With annotations in play, aspect developers can expect class developers to mark program elements with annotations. It makes both camps happy—aspect developers can write simple pointcuts that can select program elements based on annotations they carry. On the other hand, class developers control the application of crosscutting functionality, because they choose what to annotate. The result is simplified and robust adoption of AOP.

Disillusionment from the Alternative Technologies

The EJB framework appeared to provide a solution to modularizing crosscutting concerns. But most developers realize that the approach it offers is too heavyweight.

Various interceptor-based technologies promise to be alternatives to AOP. For example, EJB3 introduces interceptors as a new mechanism, a concept similar to AOP's advice—a definite step in the right direction, but lacking the join point model, which lies at the core of AOP.

Dynamic languages provide an alternative to AOP. But even with Groovy and Ruby, AOP has a place. Dynamic languages, despite the buzz surrounding them, are still new. As these languages mature and are used more seriously in enterprise applications, I expect AOP to gain prominence. After all, not many people thought anything was lacking in the Java programming language 10 years back! Interestingly, due to the availability of metaprogramming in dynamic languages, implementing AOP is easy.

For AspectJ, this phase is ongoing. It will be interesting to see how it unfolds.

Plateau of Productivity

This is a boring phase, where there is little hype. The technology is no longer cool and on the leading or bleeding edge. It starts to appear on resumes and job applications in a substantial way. The technology fulfills its promise of improved productivity, and developers use it for the problems where it's known to really work. Although it's boring to those who are looking for a shot of excitement, this phase is the most appropriate for mass adoption. This phase often includes interesting innovations, but they aren't a hallmark of the phase. Instead, the focus is on best (and worst) practices based on real experience in the technology's adoption and problem-specific premade solutions (libraries).

This is where the Java language is today. AOP and AspectJ should reach this level in a few years.

Where is AOP Being Used?

We can address the question of how real AOP is by looking at where it's being used. Let's see what kind of applications use AOP.

Enterprise Applications

Enterprise applications need to address many crosscutting functionalities: transaction management, security, auditing, service-level agreement, monitoring, concurrency control, improving application availability, error handling, and so on. Many enterprise applications use AOP to implement these functionalities.

Virtually every project that uses Spring uses AOP. Many applications start with pre-written aspects supplied with Spring (primarily transaction management and security). But due to the @AspectJ syntax, writing custom aspects is becoming a common task. After reaching the limits of Spring AOP, many applications move toward AspectJ weaving. The typical trigger point for this change is crosscutting of domain objects or other forms of deeper crosscutting functionalities. At that time, it's common to start with the @AspectJ syntax (which is used with Spring's proxy-based AOP) along with the load-time weaver. Of course, applications that don't use Spring often use AspectJ weaving from the beginning.

The industry sectors in which AspectJ is used in production (with proxy-based and bytecode-based AOP) range from financial companies (banking, trading, hedge funds) and health care to various web sites (e-commerce, customer care, content providers, and so on). If you're implementing enterprise applications and using AOP, you're in good company.

Web and Application Servers

The open source SpringSource dm Server (http://www.springsource.com/products/dmserver) supports developing enterprise application based on OSGi. It uses AspectJ to implement various crosscutting functionalities, such as First Failure Data Capture (FFDC), context collection, tracing, and policy enforcement. The SpringSource tc Server (http://www.springsource.com/products/tcserver) uses AspectJ to implement monitoring of deployed applications. You can expect a lot more functionality to be implemented using AspectJ in both these products.

Application Frameworks

Application frameworks can use AOP effectively to target specific crosscutting functionalities while keeping their structure modularized. As discussed earlier, Spring provides crosscutting solutions such as transaction management and security through aspects. Furthermore, Spring includes aspects for injecting dependencies into domain objects. Frameworks that use AspectJ as their foundation have started to appear as well.

Spring Roo (http://www.springsource.org/roo), an open-source, lightweight, and customizable framework that includes interactive and IDE-based tooling to enable rapid delivery of high performance enterprise Java applications is gaining strong popularity in the Java community. It uses a round-tripping code generator along with AspectJ byte-code weaving to keep the generated code, separate from user-written code. By judiciously combining annotations with AspectJ's static and dynamic crosscutting, it offers a significant boost in developer productivity without tying the application to Spring Roo. Another AspectJ-based project—Magma (http://cwiki.apache.org/labs/magma.html)—is an Apache lab project that simplifies development of Java web applications. It internally uses AspectJ and exposes it to power users to improve developer productivity and produce maintain-able software.

Monitoring Tools

AspectJ makes implementing a flexible monitoring scheme a breeze. Therefore, many tools use AspectJ as the underlying technology. Glassbox (http://www.glassbox.com), an open source product, offers ready-to-use aspects and tools to help you get started with application-level monitoring and pinpoint potential bottlenecks. Another open source product, Perf4J (http://perf4j.codehaus.org), uses annotations along with AspectJ weaving to monitor applications. Yet another open source tool, Contract4J (http://contract4j.org), uses AspectJ to monitor contract violations. Several commercial products also use AspectJ to implement monitoring solutions. Spring Insight as a part of SpringSource tc Server (http://www.springsource.com/products/tcserver) focuses on application-level monitoring and collecting useful context targeting Spring-based applications. It also includes functionality such as alerting and trend analysis to let you take corrective actions. JXInsight (http://www.jinspired.com/products/jxinsight) monitors applications to provide insight into potential performance bottlenecks. It uses AspectJ-based probes to weave into various technologies. MaintainJ (http://maintainj.com) uses aspects to monitor system execution and generates sequence diagrams.

Compiler and IDE Integration

AspectJ itself uses AspectJ to extend the JDT complier to support AspectJ constructs. AJDT uses AspectJ weaving through OSGi-based weaving service implemented by the Equinox Aspect project (http://www.eclipse.org/equinox/incubator/aspects) to better integrate with the JDT in Eclipse. This recent change enabled AJDT to provide a much better user experience. ScalaIDE for Eclipse also followed the same route to provide a better experience for Scala developers.

I hope this discussion has helped put AOP and AspectJ in perspective. Rather than being a niche product, AspectJ has long been considered a standard tool in the developer toolbox.

Tackling the Challenges of Integrating 3rd Party Software Using AspectJ

Uwe Hohenstein and Michael C. Jaeger

Siemens AG, Corporate Technology CT T DE IT 1,
Otto-Hahn-Ring.6, D-80200 München, Germany
{Uwe.Hohenstein,Michael.C.Jaeger}@siemens.com

Abstract. This article reports on the usage of aspect-orientation in an industrial project, which means that aspects are an active part of a real software product. Moreover, aspect-orientation, in particular the language AspectJ, is used to overcome several critical problems. Those problems are well motivated and discussed in detail. Some of them are hard to solve with conventional programming techniques whereas an AspectJ-based solution is very straightforward. Since some of the reported problems are not really of crosscutting nature, the solutions might be questionable. This leads to a discussion about the "political correctness" of this approach. Furthermore, the paper explains why and how the project management has been convinced to use AspectJ.

Keywords: Aspect-orientation, AspectJ, O/R persistence framework, Hibernate, JPA, persistence, industrial application, case study.

1 Introduction

The evolution of software development techniques has been driven by the need to achieve a better separation of crosscutting concerns (CCCs). CCCs are those functionalities that are typically spread across several places in the source code. They often lead to lower programming productivity, poor quality and traceability, and lower degree of code reuse [9]. Aspect-orientation (AO) is a technology that helps to develop software in a more modular manner. AO is a promising solution for a better code structure and provides systematic means for effective modularization of CCCs by avoiding scattering of code [9].

Recent research on aspect-orientation has shown its usefulness in various application fields. For example, [19,29] use AO to separate concurrency control and failure handling code in a distributed system. The work on patterns and AO by Hannemann and Kiczales [13] identifies several crosscutting concerns in the GoF patterns [10] and extracts them into aspects. Garcia et al. [37] extend this work by assessing the GoF implementations with regard to well-known software engineering metrics such as separation of concerns, coupling, cohesion, and size. Some features of a middleware platform are refactored into aspects by Zhang and Jacobsen [33]. Burke also uses AO to implement CCCs in middleware projects [4]. Rashid [27] discusses all facets of AO in the context of databases: AO to implement database systems (DBSs) in a more

S. Katz et al. (Eds.): Transactions on AOSD VIII, LNCS 6580, pp. 116–140, 2011.

modular manner, persistence for aspects, and a persistence framework [28]. Hohenstein continues this work on persistence frameworks in another article [14]. Others present a case study called HyperCast; they use common AO methods to improve the software design in [35] and [36].

There are fewer reports on industrial applications. [5,6,24] are some examples that report on experience with AO in industrial settings. According to the classification of Joosen et al. [17], a study of the adoption of aspect-oriented programming within non-academic projects by Duck [8] indicates that the majority of the interviewed developers were "early adopters" of this technology. At the current stage of adoption, venturous developers learn the AO concepts and try to apply them in *non-critical* phases of development projects. This is confirmed by Wiese and Meunier [32] as well, who apply AO for performance monitoring or architectural checks that can be turned off in productive code. This leads to the obstinate myth "AO is good only for logging/tracing" [23]. However, [32] is also an example for real industrial usage as it uses an aspect for caching method invocations. Another example is the use of AspectJ to improve the performance of database applications [15].

Moreover, some tools have been implemented from scratch using AO, which obviously could benefit from AO. AO is used in the Spring framework and the JBoss application server. Some authors ([2] and [11]) report on AspectJ-based tools for monitoring performance, using and clearly taking benefit from AO techniques. Certainly, the implementers are far beyond the early adopter stage.

Most of this work uses AO programming to handle typical CCCs by developing software in an aspect-oriented manner from design to implementation, thereby increasing software modularity, achieving a better separation of crosscutting concerns, or avoiding code tangling and scattering [25].

This paper presents a large industrial project that uses AspectJ [22] in a different way. The project itself was nearly finished and the main focus of our work was to stabilize the software platform and to improve the overall performance. AO was not considered during software development, but came into play when we had to solve some hard and critical real-world problems that occurred suddenly in the project and were not or at least hard to solve with conventional techniques. These issues occurred late in the development cycle and endangered the product delivery. In order to cope with them, we found and applied solutions using AO. AO helped us to provide simple and straightforward solutions quickly, thus saving development time and efforts. In particular, we implemented aspects to address the challenges of integrating 3rd party software to be able to manage the concerns of integration in a maintainable manner. Hence, the paper presents several real-world examples from a large industrial project to underline the well-known advantages of AO such as adding functionality, tracing, and changing behavior without touching code explicitly. All aspects are part of the product.

The project we are referring to has been developed by a business unit of the Siemens AG [30]. The developed product is a service-oriented telecommunication platform. It is supposed to be an open service platform for the deployment and provision of communication services. Section 2 presents the overall architecture of this platform.

Before we discuss the severe problems we were faced with in this project, we give a short introduction into aspect-oriented programming (AOP) in Section 3, in particular into the language AspectJ [22], as far as it is necessary to understand how we use AspectJ in the project.

The following Sections 4 to 6 motivate and discuss the problems and the aspect-oriented solutions in detail in order to give a better understanding about the complexity of the addressed problems. The following sections will present issues from all corners of a software project, structured by the following characteristics:

Section 4 is concerned with correcting the functionality of 3rd party libraries. We discuss how to enable streaming of large query results by means of an aspect in order to improve query performance. This problem cannot be fixed easily with established object-oriented techniques.

In Section 5, we discuss how to use aspects for adding new important functionality to 3rd party libraries in a modular way, e.g., adding optimizer hints to Hibernate queries or introducing some missing functionality in OpenJPA.

That AO is good for tracing is demonstrated in Section 6. We use AspectJ to detect the root cause of several problems. A problem-specific tracing becomes very easy and reduces the usually overwhelming logging output to only the relevant parts. Moreover, we set up a performance and resource monitoring environment.

In Section 7, we summarize our lessons learned. Although we find AspectJ easy to use, we want to present some problems we had using AspectJ. Since AO in general and AspectJ in particular might not always be a welcome visitor in industrial projects, we discuss how we succeeded in bringing AO into the project.

Sometimes it seems to us that we take advantage of the power of AO too much: We increase our programming productivity, the quality, traceability, or the degree of code reuse, which is the primary purpose of AOP. But sometimes, we use AO to avoid source code modifications to 3rd party libraries for various reasons. Most importantly, the motivation is to avoid complete rebuilds of those components, which is often a complex process and which would be required at every update of the 3rd party component. We justify our approach in Section 8 by discussing alternative solutions, which turn out to be more complex.

Finally, the conclusion in Section 9 summarizes this discussion and presents future ideas.

2   The Application Case

The application case we want to report on is a telecommunication platform called Symphonia [30] developed by Siemens Enterprise Communications (SEN). Symphonia is an open service platform for the deployment and provision of communication services following the SOA paradigm (service-oriented architecture). Examples for such services are the capturing of user presence, the management of calling domains, notifications, administration functionality for the underlying switch technology, and so forth. One business case is to sell these services for the integration in groupware and other applications along with the Siemens private branch exchange (PBX) hardware.

The software platform has been implemented in Java and uses an OSGi container. OSGi was preferred to EJB Application Servers because of its smaller size and focused functional extent. Small footprint was considered primarily important for the application in the telecommunication domain. In order to establish an infrastructure for the provision of services, custom built or common off-the-shelf components (depending on the availability) were added. They implement the discovery and registration of services among containers on different computers, a high-performance messaging infrastructure and other functionality. The complete software product involves about 170 projects in Eclipse.

One fundamental service of the SOA platform is the *persistence subsystem*. About 20 projects use the persistence subsystem and manage a data model of their own for storing specific information such as contact lists or domain settings in a relational database system. Figure 1 gives a deeper insight into the persistence architecture required for the remainder of this paper.

Each of the tiers access the functionality provided by the tier below. Any service or component that requires persistence, generally uses a *wrapping template*. This is indicated by the first arrow in this figure. A direct access to lower layers (see dashed lines) is possible but not desired.

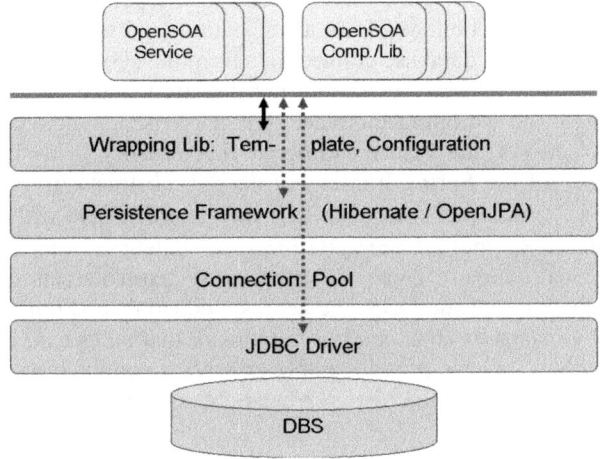

Fig. 1. Architecture of Persistence Subsystem

The wrapping template wraps an object-relational (O/R) persistence framework. The project uses an O/R framework for implementing the persistence layer of our communication platform for two reasons: first, O/R frameworks enable us to run the platform on several relational DBSs, in particular solidDB, MySQL, and PostgreSQL. Second, we benefit from the higher, object-oriented level of database programming. Generally, a persistence framework makes programming easier by offering an object-oriented API to store and retrieve the data of Java objects in relational tables without knowing about underlying tables and SQL. The persistence framework translates those object-oriented accesses into SQL. Even queries are expressed in an object-oriented SQL and refer to Java classes (instead of tables) and associations (instead of joins over foreign keys).

In the beginning, the Hibernate O/R framework [12] by Red Hat Inc was used. However, in summer 2006, the owner of Hibernate, Red Hat, was accused of violating a patent on O/R frameworks in the United States. This patent infringement claim seemed to be a problem of Red Hat only at a first glance. However, every software product with Hibernate inside is affected as well, if the product is shipped to the United States. Any redistribution of Hibernate implies the role of a supplier. Hence, using the Hibernate framework as a component, our communications platform was indirectly affected by this patent claim. To avoid the risk of a patent infringement, the project management decided to replace Hibernate with another persistence framework. An additional business issue was the licensing model of Hibernate. The GNU Lesser General Public License (LGPL) is not fully compatible with agreements that SEN has with its business partners. As a consequence, the project management decided to replace LGPL software in general. These two reasons were the drivers for the effort to replace Hibernate. As a substitute, we chose OpenJPA, because it is an open source adoption of the Java Persistence API (JPA). And it is distributed by the Apache Software Foundation, which suits particular interests better than the licensing model of Hibernate. However, this caused some problems.

Both O/R frameworks use JDBC to communicate with the DBS. However, a connection pool is set between the JDBC driver and the persistence framework. Thus, database connections are obtained from a connection pool such as DBCP or c3p0, and the pool obtains concrete database connections from the JDBC driver.

As already mentioned, services should not directly use the persistence framework or JDBC. Instead, the wrapping template should be used. It standardizes the use of Hibernate or OpenJPA and offers additional functionality in a similar way as the JDBC abstraction of the Spring framework does. It abstracts from concepts such as OpenJPA's `EntityManagerFactory` (in principle a database with a schema and an associated connection pool), `EntityManager` (a database connection) and persistence units (logical database name). The wrapping template sets up the framework correctly with the URL of the DBS, the access credentials and other settings. It eases programming by means of an execution framework that takes care of connection and transaction handling. In case of recoverable errors, exceptions returned by the persistence framework or by the JDBC driver are caught and a retry is initiated, e.g., in case of concurrency conflicts.

3   Aspect-Oriented Programming in AspectJ

Aspect-orientation (AO) comes up with new languages that employ special constructs to separate crosscutting concerns. This separation allows for a better modularization, thereby avoiding the well-known symptoms of non-modularization such as code tangling and code scattering [25].

The most popular AO language is certainly AspectJ [22]. Special extensions to Java enable developers to separate the definition of crosscutting concerns. Programming with AspectJ is essentially like using Java and extended with new *aspects*. The main purpose of an aspect is to affect the dynamic structure of a program by changing the program flow. An aspect can intercept certain points of the program flow, called *join points*. Examples of join points are method and constructor calls or executions, attribute accesses, and exception handling. Join points are syntactically specified by means of *pointcuts*. Pointcuts identify join points in the program flow by means of a signature expression. For example, a method specification can determine exactly one method by describing the complete signature including `private`, `final`, `static`, return and parameter types etc. Or wildcards can be used to select several methods of several classes by `* MyClass*.get*(.., String)`. A "`*`" in names denotes any character sequence, hence, `get*` means any method that starts with "get". A type "`*`" denotes any type. Parameter types can be fixed or left open (`..`). Once join points are captured, *advices* specify weaving rules involving those joint points, such as taking a certain action before or after the join points.

The following is an example for an AspectJ aspect:

```
aspect MyAspect {
  internal variables and methods;
  pointcut myPC() : execution(*MyClass*.get*(..));
  before() : myPC() { do something before join points of myPC }
}
```

This aspect has a `before` advice that adds logic before executing those methods that are captured by the pointcut `myPC`. An aspect is similar to a Java class from a syntactic point of view. An aspect can declare attributes and methods; it can also extend another aspect in the same way classes can extend other classes.

As AspectJ is a new language, it requires its own compiler. Usually, the AJDT plug-in will be installed in Eclipse. However, a new compiler requires changes in the build process, which is often not desired, like in the context of our project. Then, using Java-5 annotations is an alternative:

```
@Aspect
class MyAspect {
  internal variables and methods;
  @Before("execution(* MyClass*.get*(..))")
  public void myPC() { do something before join point }
}
```

Hence, aspect code can be written in pure Java; this was important for us, because we could rely on standard Eclipse with an ordinary Java compiler, without AJDT plug-in for AspectJ compilation etc.

An annotation `@Aspect` lets a Java class `MyAspect` become an aspect. We refer to such a class as an *@Aspect class* in the following. If a method is annotated with `@Before`, `@After` etc., it becomes an advice that is executed before or after join points, respectively. These annotations specify pointcuts as a string.

In order to use these annotations, the AspectJ runtime JAR is required in the classpath. To activate the aspect, we also have to start the JVM (e.g., in Eclipse or an OSGi container) with an `-javaagent` argument referring to the AspectJ weaver. Annotations are then evaluated and become active, because a so-called *load-time weaving* takes place: aspect weaving occurs whenever a matching class is loaded.

A file aop.xml in a META-INF directory restricts a given aspect to specific classes.

This is only a very brief overview of AspectJ and load-time weaving. Concrete examples will be discussed in the next sections.

4 AOP for Correcting Functionality

The first category of issues where we applied AOP is concerned with correcting the functionality of 3rd party libraries. In this case, the interaction between an object-relational persistence framework and an underlying JDBC driver did not allow for streaming large query results which is important to improve query performance. With a simple aspect, we enabled streaming.

Object-relational (O/R) persistence frameworks such as Hibernate [12] or JPA tools [16] allow application programmers to store and retrieve Java objects in relational tables without knowing about underlying tables and SQL. An example demonstrates how to execute a query in the Hibernate Query Language (HQL) and how to process the result in Java:

```
Query hql = session.createQuery
                    ("SELECT p FROM MyPersistentClass p WHERE ...");
List<MyPersistentClass> result
                    = (List<MyPersistentClass>) hql.list();
for (MyPersistentClass p : hql.list()) {
    ... process object p ...
}
```

HQL is similar to relational SQL, however, it is an object-oriented SQL in the sense that it refers to Java classes (instead of tables) and associations (instead of joins over foreign keys). The HQL query is a string, which is passed to a createQuery method: this query selects all those objects of the class MyPersistentClass that satisfy a certain condition. createQuery returns a Query object hql, which can be executed with list(); the result is a Java list of MyPersistentClass objects. Consequently, it is possible to iterate over the list with a Java for-loop, fetching object by object. No table structures, no records and no relational SQL become visible.

It is important to know what happens internally. Hibernate transforms the HQL query into SQL and passes the SQL query to the underlying JDBC driver. The result is then computed within the database server. Usually the JDBC driver can be asked to return record by record. However, Hibernate asks the JDBC driver to get the *complete* result in order to fill the result list. Then Hibernate converts each record into an object and puts it into the result. Consequently, there is no lazy materialization, which would compose result objects just when being accessed in the for-loop; the complete result is materialized as a Java list at once.

Hibernate keeps the result in a cache. When a query returns millions of objects, such a huge result set can easily exceed the cache of Hibernate and the JVM will throw an out-of-memory exception. In fact, there are only a few cases where the complete result is really needed. Usually, some data of the result is displayed in a GUI, and whenever the user is scrolling down, the next bulk of the result list will be displayed. Maybe the complete result will be accessed bit by bit, but nobody will use the complete result at once.

This problem is aggravated in our project by the fact that we use a container-based environment with OSGi: there are a lot of services deployed so that several service requests can run queries in parallel. Hence, out-of-memory exceptions are very likely.

A better approach to handle those scenarios is to use streaming with a scrollable result. Hibernate provides a special `ScrollableResults` class to this end:

```
Query hql = session.createQuery
                  ("SELECT p FROM MyPersistentClass p WHERE ...");
ScrollableResults result = hql.scroll(ScrollMode.FORWARD_ONLY);
while (result.next()) {
  MyPersistentClass p = (MyPersistentClass) result.get(0);
  session.evict(p); ...
}
```

Here, the HQL query is executed with a `scroll` method, which returns a `ScrollableResults` object. A scrollable result means that the result is fetched object by object. Using `results.get(0)`, the while-loop processes single database objects; Hibernate internally fetches the next record and converts it into an object. Result objects that are no longer needed, for instance, because they have already been displayed, can be evicted from the Hibernate cache with `evict()`, e.g., when the next bulk of data is displayed. This reduces memory consumption drastically and avoids out-of-memory exceptions. This works fine for MySQL and PostgreSQL. But the main DBS we have to support is solidDB. Unfortunately, using `ScrollableResults` with solidDB raises the following exception: `org.hibernate.AssertionFailure: scrollable result sets are not enabled`. What is the reason for the exception? Using AspectJ for tracing (cf. Section 6.1), we detected that Hibernate asks the solidDB JDBC driver whether it supports such a scrollable behavior – and solidDB answers no. This is in fact surprising, as scrollable result sets are supported by the solidDB DBS, but obviously solidDB does not know itself. How can we convince solidDB to be able to deliver scrollable results?

The idea is to let solidDB answer yes when being asked for scrollable result sets – as already mentioned, those are indeed supported. However, modifying source code is not possible since the code for the solidDB JDBC driver is not available.

An AO solution is here feasible because it allows us to change the behavior of existing JAR files, even of 3rd party tools. Fortunately, AspectJ is not frightened off by non-existing source code. An `@Around` advice can change the behavior in the following way:

```
@Aspect
public class StreamingAspect {
  @Around("execution(boolean solid.jdbc.SolidDatabaseMetaData
                              .supportsResultSetType(..))")
  public boolean answerYes() { return true; }
}
```

As already mentioned, we use AspectJ annotations instead of the AspectJ language. The annotation `@Aspect` makes a Java class `StreamingAspect` be an aspect. The annotation `@Around` defines an advice to be executed at join points. `@Around` includes a pointcut as a string to determine the relevant join points. Here, it is any execution of a method `supportsResultSetType` belonging to class `solid.jdbc.Solid DatabaseMetaData` returning a `boolean`; the parameters are irrelevant due to "`..`".

The advice is implemented in the method `answerYes` annotated with `@Around`. It defines the logic to be executed at each join point. This advice traps the execution of exactly one method `SolidDatabaseMetaData.SupportsResultSetType` and changes its behavior by simply answering true. The original logic of `supportsResultSetType` is no longer executed.

These are simple changes done in a couple of minutes. Thanks to this very simple aspect, streaming is now working for solidDB, and out-of-memory exceptions are gone.

5 AOP for Adding Functionality

The next category applies aspects for adding new important functionality to 3rd party libraries in a modular way such as adding optimizer hints to Hibernate queries or introducing missing functionality in the persistence framework OpenJPA.

5.1 Query Optimization

If a database system is used in an application, it is almost the most important factor for the application's performance. In particular, relational database applications often suffer from bad performance. This is somehow the fault of relational database systems: SQL is designed to allow for an easy access to databases by providing powerful query capabilities. Hence, users are tempted to formulate complex SQL statements, joining several tables and filtering records with complex conditions. Internally, a DBS's query optimizer creates an execution plan for each query. If the optimizer does a good job, queries will be executed fast, otherwise the performance will suffer. Unfortunately, the optimizer of the solidDB DBS, which we are using in our project, has some problems with complex queries.

One solution to overcome this problem of bad query optimization is to force the optimizer to use certain strategies specified by vendor-specific optimizer hints. These are some special comments or pragmas in SQL to tell the optimizer what to do: using a special index, performing a special join strategy etc. Inserting these optimizer hints is a manual task, which has to be done for all complex queries.

To force the solidDB optimizer, hints, surrounded by `--(*` ... `*)--`, can be used in relational SQL, e.g., to use an index:

```
SELECT
--(* vendor(SOLID),product(Engine),option(hint)
     INDEX IndexToBeUsed *)--
FROM MyTable ...
```

This is applicable to JDBC programming where SQL statements are composed and executed directly. But every persistence framework introduces a layer upon JDBC. In Hibernate, queries are expressed in an object-oriented HQL, which is internally translated into SQL:

```
Query qu = session.createQuery
                ("SELECT p FROM MyPersistentClass p WHERE ...");
```

The question now is how to pass optimizer hints through Hibernate. One could embed hints in HQL as in SQL `"SELECT <hint> p FROM MyPersistentClass p ..."`. But this does not work: Hibernate's HQL parser does not understand the proprietary solidDB optimizer hint (or any other) and issues an error:

```
org.hibernate.hql.ast.QuerySyntaxException: unexpected token: *
near line 2, column 4 [SELECT
--(* vendor(SOLID), product(Engine), option(hint) ...
```

Furthermore, `createQuery` has no additional parameters that allow passing any optimizer hint in addition to the HQL query.

One possibility is certainly to use JDBC with SQL instead of HQL. However, then we are losing the higher level of abstraction of HQL, which results in additional programming. This means in particular that we have to do Hibernate's work, namely to convert database records into Java objects and relationships manually. Anyway, inserting hints is a manual task that must be done for every critical query.

A better approach is to have a centralized "add appropriate hint" component. Our basic idea is to intercept JDBC operations, to check the type of query (SELECT, INSERT, UPDATE ...), and to determine the base table to be queried or modified. Using this information, we can decide for critical statements what strategy to use, e.g., to take a special index for a certain large table, and to add an appropriate optimizer hint.

Intercepting JDBC in order to check every SQL statement is indeed crosscutting and can easily be done with AspectJ. Any JDBC method that possesses a query `String` parameter, the SQL statement to be executed, is relevant.

```
@Before("(call(* java.sql.Connection.prepare*(String,..))
       || call(* java.sql.Statement+.execute*(String))   )
       && args(query)")
public Object addHint(JoinPoint jp, String query)
       throws Throwable {
  Object[] args = jp.getArgs();
  // analyze query and determine index to be used:
  if (query.contains("select") && query.contains("MyTable")) {
    String hint = "SELECT\n
        --(* vendor(SOLID),product(Engine),option(hint)\n"
    + "-- INDEX MyIndex *)--\n";
    args[0] = query.replace("select", hint);
  }
}
```

We need a `@Before` advice, because we are checking the issued SQL statement before the execution takes place: we have to modify the SQL statement by adding the optimizer hint, i.e., changing the parameter value. The pointcut of `addHint` intercepts all relevant calls: `Connection`-methods that start with `prepare` and methods of class `Statement` or any subclass (`Statement+`) that start with `execute`; all those methods have a `String` parameter that contains the query to be executed or prepared. Thanks to `args(query)`, we can analyze whether the `String` parameter `query` contains an SQL statement, what kind of statement this is, and which tables are involved.

Having extracted the type of operation and the table from the SQL string, the advice can determine whether to support the optimizer with a hint. This part has only been sketched in the code out above. The advice adds an adequate hint into the SQL string and replaces the old `String` parameter value with the new one by simply assigning a new SQL statement – including the hint – to the first parameter `args[0]`.

We applied this aspect to a sample query:

```
SELECT com
FROM Contact c JOIN c.communications com
WHERE c.lastName = '...'
AND com.normalizedValue LIKE '...%'
```

This query looks for contacts with a specific last name, provided they have an associated communication with a normalized value, which is compared with a wildcard string "…%". This query is not really complex; it uses the relationship `communications` between the `Contact` and `Communication` classes. However, the execution is slow and takes 493 ms (as average of 10 executions) for 200.000 contacts.

Using an index on the `Communication` table turned out to be useful. Hence, the aspect checks for this critical SELECT statement and adds a corresponding hint. The aspect helps to speed up the execution from 493 ms to 48 ms for this particular query.

The aspect as presented here is tailored to one critical query the execution of which it intercepts. However, this is part of a more general, central query optimization aspect: Whenever a query turned out to be too slow and had to be speeded up by an optimizer hint, the query is added to this aspect.

5.2   Lack of Key Generation Concept in OpenJPA

As already mentioned, we were forced to migrate from Hibernate to OpenJPA because of a patent infringement claim against Red Hat, the vendor of Hibernate. Although the migration seems to be straightforward at a first glance, severe problems arose that were not easy to detect. These issues occurred late in development and endangered the success of the overall migration.

One problem we want to discuss is the mapping from Java classes to database tables, in particular the key generation. An O/R framework requires mapping information on how to map classes onto database tables, attributes to table columns, associations to foreign keys etc. This can either be done by means of XML mapping files or Java-5 annotations in the entity classes. Our project uses XML mapping files. The following Hibernate mapping relates a class `MyClass` (`<class>`) to a table `MyTable` (`table=…`), fields id and p2 to table columns `pk` and `c2` (`<property>`) respectively.

```
<class name="MyClass" table="MyTable">
  <id name="id" column="pk">
    <generator class="sequence"/>
  </id>
  <property name="p2" column="c2"/>
</class>
```

Thereby, `<id>` defines a key field that uniquely identifies objects in a class; the corresponding column `pk` is used as a database primary key.

In fact, the mapping specification in OpenJPA looks different; a file `orm.xml` specifies mappings with a different syntax. One fundamental difference is the presence of various alternatives for providing `<id>` values. Hibernate offers a strategy named `native` that uses mechanisms of the underlying DBS, either a `sequence` generator (e.g., for solidDB) or an auto-`increment` column (e.g., for MySQL).

OpenJPA has an `auto` strategy that lets OpenJPA decide what to do, but in contrast to the `native` concept, OpenJPA uses a table for maintaining high/low values instead of taking sequences or auto-increment columns.

Since the project must support several DBSs, especially MySQL, solidDB, and PostgreSQL, and since the deployment should be independent of the DBS, an abstract strategy is required. If we consider the `auto` strategy of OpenJPA, this indeed abstracts from the DBS, but it is not appropriate for us: database installations already exist at customers, i.e., databases contain keys generated by either sequences or auto-increment columns. For these, the probability is high that `auto` generates already existing values. Hence, value clashes are likely.

One solution is certainly to maintain three XML mapping files, one for each DBS with the supported strategy. A simple model-driven approach that generates DBS-specific variants with `sequence` or `identity`, respectively, could help here. This was regarded as an inappropriate solution as it causes a deployment problem. OpenJPA expects the mapping file in a JAR. The overall project strategy is to have only a single deployment JAR: all parameters that might vary from one installation to another, such as the database URL, user and password, must be placed outside the deployed JAR file. This is because only parts of the JDK are installed on the target machine and unzip/zipping of JAR files is not available to exchange parts such as mapping files. Hence, the resulting installation procedure would now need to handle several JAR files for deployment, one for each DBS.

The issues with providing the mapping files for deployment becomes even worse, since some useful OpenJPA features are not available in XML mappings, but only by annotations, e.g., the "delete-orphan" cascade. On the one hand, implementing delete-orphan behavior manually, i.e., deleting objects explicitly whenever they become parentless, can be very cumbersome since cascades go over several levels in the object model. On the other hand, using the delete-orphan option with annotations means that also several code variants have to be maintained, since the mapping is part of the source code. Hence, both proposals require massive changes in the deployment infrastructure.

The basic idea to remedy the lack of key generation is to accept both strategies `sequence` and `identity`, but to change the internal OpenJPA behavior in such a way that it uses the available strategy. Hence, if `identity` has been chosen, but if the DBS does not supply auto-increment columns, then let OpenJPA internally switch to the `sequence` strategy. This is much easier than adding a new `native` strategy for mapping specifications and/or annotations, which requires a corresponding modification of the XML parser, the analysis of annotations, the use of this kind of meta-data to derive SQL operations adequately etc.

Changing the OpenJPA behavior to handle `identity` appropriately according to the type of DBS is not easy. Of course, the source code of OpenJPA is available and can be changed, but the code changes affect different parts and have to exchange new information between otherwise unrelated classes. It is much easier to use the following aspect:

```
@Aspect
public class KeyGenerationAspect {
  private String db = null;
  private static final int STRATEGY_SEQUENCE = 2;
  private static final int STRATEGY_IDENTITY = 3;
  @Before("execution(* org.apache.openjpa.persistence
        .PersistenceProviderImpl.createEntityManagerFactory(..))
          && args(.., p)")
  public void determineDBS(final Properties p) {
    String str = p.getProperty("openjpa.ConnectionProperties");
    if (str != null) {
      if (str.contains("Solid"))
        db = "SOLID";
      else if (str.contains("mysql"))
        db = "MYSQL";
      else if (str.contains("postgresql"))
        db = "POSTGRES";
  }

  @Around("call(* org.apache.openjpa.meta.FieldMetaData
                    .getValueStrategy(..))
          && !within(com.siemens.ct.aspects.*)")
  public Object useAppropriateStrategy(final JoinPoint jp) {
    FieldMetaData fmd = (FieldMetaData) jp.getTarget();
    int strat = fmd.getValueStrategy();
    if (db == null)
      LOG.error("DB was not determined");
    else if (db.equals("SOLID") && strat == STRATEGY_IDENTITY) {
      fmd.setValueSequenceName("system");
      return STRATEGY_SEQUENCE;
    } ... // similar for "MYSQL" etc.
    return strat;
  }
}
```

KeyGenerationAspect is an @Aspect class with two advices: the first one determineDBS determines the DBS and the second one useAppropriateStrategy changes the strategy if necessary. Both exchange information about the DBS in use by means of a local variable db according to Laddad's "Wormhole Pattern" [22].

Since the method determineDBS is annotated with @Before, it defines an advice to be executed before those join points that are specified by the pointcut string: any execution of the method PersistenceProviderImpl.createEntityManager-Factory with a Properties parameter. Although "(..)" means any parameters, the args(..,p) clause requires at least a Properties parameter and binds a variable p to that parameter. The variable also occurs in the method signature and allows accessing the value inside the advice: thus, p.getProperty ("openjpa.ConnectionProperties") yields the connection properties so that we can extract the type of DBS. The result is stored in an internal variable db.

The `useAppropriateStrategy` advice uses this information about the DBS to switch from strategy `identity` to `sequence` in case of solidDB. Hence, the aspect can simply be used to share and exchange information even if different parts of code, even of different JARs, are intercepted. The technical problem how to determine the type of DBS is solved in an easy way.

The `@Around` advice `useAppropriateStrategy` intercepts any call of `Field-MetaData.getValueStrategy`, which yields the original strategy, and can now decide when to switch the strategy.

The parameter `JoinPoint jp` gives access to context information about the join point, especially the target object on which the method is invoked (`jp.getTarget()`). This is a `FieldMetaData` object in this case, which allows determining the current strategy with `getValueStrategy()`. Due to `@Around`, the original logic is replaced. Instead of returning the original strategy, e.g., `identity`, we can switch to `sequence` for solidDB and set the sequence name to the system sequence.

Note that `!within(com.siemens.ct.aspects.*)` is necessary to eliminate recursions: whenever `getValueStrategy` is called, the call is implicitly changed to calling the `@Around` method, which performs `strat=fmd.getValueStrategy()` inside. `!within` prevents this call from being intercepted again, resulting in a stack overflow error.

6   AOP for Tracing and Monitoring

The last category confirms the well-known statement that AOP is good for logging and tracing [23]. In fact, aspects allow for some specific tracing and logging by yielding only the relevant information about specific problems.

6.1   Advanced Tracing

In Section 4, we found an AO solution to solve the streaming problem for solidDB – after having understood what went wrong. But the question remains how to find the reason for the exception, i.e., why the exception occurs and where to correct the problem and how to detect the relevant method `SolidDatabaseMetaData.supportsResultSetType()` that has to be corrected. Of course, the stacktrace gives us a first hint:

```
org.hibernate.AssertionFailure: scrollable result sets are not
enabled
at org.hibernate.jdbc.AbstractBatcher.getPreparedStatement
(AbstractBatcher.java:467)
at …
```

Checking the Hibernate code, line 467 in the class `AbstractBatcher` refers to the statement written in bold face below:

```
private PreparedStatement getPreparedStatement(
   final Connection conn, String sql, boolean scrollable, ...)
        throws SQLException {
```

```
if (scrollable && !factory.getSettings() &&
    isScrollableResultSetsEnabled()) {
  throw new AssertionFailure
                ("scrollable result sets are not enabled");
}
...
return result;
}
```

We found that the exception is raised because isScrollableResultSets-
Enabled() returns false. The implementation of this method is simple:

```
public boolean isScrollableResultSetsEnabled() {
  return scrollableResultSetsEnabled;
}
```

Now, we must know who sets the internal field scrollableResultSetsEnabled
to false and where. Well, there is a corresponding setter void setScrollable-
ResultSetsEnabled(boolean b), which is called at several places, for instance
in

```
SettingsFactory Settings.buildSettings(Properties props) {
  ...
  setScrollableResultSetsEnabled(useScrollableResultSets);
  ...
}
```

This refers to another internal field useScrollableResultSet. It turned out to be
tedious to check the dynamic control flow that way.

Since we use a 3ʳᵈ party logger tool, we can increase the log level. But then, we obtain a full trace of method calls, i.e., a lot of information, which mostly is not relevant
to solve the issue.

Debugging, as another alternative, is tedious and works only if the source code is
available, and there is no source code for the solidDB JDBC driver. Moreover, several
dynamic method invocations interrupt the execution flow: Hibernate has a pluggable
connection pool and loads dynamically the one that has been configured. And the
connection pool dynamically invokes the JDBC driver for the selected DBS. Crossing
dynamic method invocations with a debugger is cumbersome.

We want to show how AO allows for an easier, quicker, and better controlled tracing of the dynamic control flow than any other approach. Indeed, there is no need for
code changes when adding tracing or logging statements. An aspect can select any
method that returns a boolean, one of those is the one we are looking for. Even
more, an advice can restrict the methods to those that return false:

```
@AfterReturning(pointcut="call(boolean *.*(..)))",
               returning="ret")
public void findProblem(boolean ret, final JoinPoint jp) {
  if (!ret) {
    System.out.println("* " + jp.getSignature()
                    + "\n-> " + jp.getSourceLocation());
  }
}
```

Due to @AfterReturning the advice is executed after returning from a method. The findProblem pointcut let us detect any invocation (i.e., *.*(..)) of a boolean method. returning="ret" binds a variable ret to the returned value so that we can check for ret==false. The method possesses a corresponding parameter boolean ret that yields access to the return value. The parameter JoinPoint jp gives access to context information about the join point, particularly the intercepted method and its location by means of jp.getSignature() and jp.getSourceLocation().

We obtain about 15 matches including methods such as equals, isNotEmpty, isEmpty, contains, isLazy, isQuoted etc. which are obviously irrelevant. However, we can take out those methods quite easily by checking for irrelevant signatures:

```
String method = ((MethodSignature) jp.getSignature()).getName();
if (!ret && !method.equals("isEmpty")
          && ignore other trivial boolean methods) {
   System.out.println("* " + jp.getSignature()
                    + "\n-> " + jp.getSourceLocation());
}
```

The output is now better arranged:

```
* boolean org.hibernate.mapping.Collection.isInverse()
-> HbmBinder.java:2472
* boolean org.hibernate.mapping.Collection.isOneToMany()
-> HbmBinder.java:2365
* boolean org.hibernate.mapping.KeyValue.isNullable()
-> HbmBinder.java:2472
* boolean org.hibernate.mapping.PersistentClass.isJoinedSubclass()
-> Configuration.java:1259
* boolean java.sql.DatabaseMetaData.supportsResultSetType(int)
-> SettingsFactory.java:92
* boolean java.sql.DatabaseMetaData.dataDefinitionIgnoredInTransact
ions()
-> SettingsFactory.java:95
* boolean org.hibernate.cache.CacheProvider.isMinimalPutsEnabledByD
efault()
-> SettingsFactory.java:247
```

In this trace, supportsResultSetType matches the problem of scrollable result sets best. With the help of the aspect, we found the critical method in a few minutes.

6.2 Advanced Monitoring

We had some performance problems in the project that required different kinds of monitoring. The first problem was about performance monitoring. We used AO similar to [32] in order to monitor the execution times at various layers by issuing warnings if certain thresholds are passed. Other tools such as glassbox [2] serve the same purpose. However, they require some configuration effort and provide general performance output. In contrast, we preferred an ad-hoc AO-based monitoring dedicated to individual problems.

Moreover, we used monitoring to track down issues with database connections. We detected that sometimes about 400 database connections are used at the same time. However, it was unclear which service consumes such a high number of connections. In fact, the DBS provides information about currently used connections, but only administered for database accounts. This does not help to detect critical, badly implemented services since all use the same database account.

To solve the problem, AspectJ helped us to detect services that are bypassing our wrapping template, e.g., setting up a connection pool wrongly or requesting connections directly via JDBC and maybe forgetting to close the connection.

Moreover, we could monitor whenever a connection is requested and released; the difference determines the number of currently active connections. The major monitoring task is to relate any information to a persistence unit in OpenJPA, which is equivalent to a service as each service has a persistence unit of its own. Generally, the developer of a service should implicitly obtain connections by using the wrapping template. This corresponds to a *logical* acquisition of connections since not always real physical JDBC connections are requested thanks to pooling. The goal of monitoring is then to get information about any *physical* open/close connection activity in order to keep track of the number of currently used connections. This means that the JDBC driver (here shown for solidDB) needs to be intercepted the source code of which is not available. But the following aspect supports monitoring:

```
@Aspect
public class ConnectionMonitorAspect {
  @AfterReturning(pointcut ="execution(Connection
                            solid.jdbc.SolidDriver.connect(..))",
                  returning = "ret")
  public void monitorOpenJDBC(final Connection ret) {
    if (monitoringIsEnabled) {
      String unit = determineFunctionalUnit();
      SolidConnection conn = (SolidConnection) ret;
      theStatistics.notifyJDBCConnectionObtained(unit, conn);
    }
  }
}
```

Due to @AfterReturning, the advice is executed after returning from any execution (execution) of a method SolidDriver.connect with any parameters (..) returning a Connection. The logic of the monitorOpenJDBC method is executed after being returned. In other words, this advice monitors whenever a connection is opened. It determines the functional unit and uses the hashCode to identify the connection.

Closing a connection via JDBC is monitored similarly by using a pointcut. @Before("execution(* solid.jdbc.SolidConnection.close(..))")

Using theStatistics.notifyJDBCConnectionObtained, the gathered information about opening or closing a connection and its functional unit is sent to a logging component that collects this information to determine the number of currently open connections for each service. Moreover, it keeps track of the maximum value. This information helped us to determine critical services w.r.t. the number of obtained connections. Moreover, the gathered information enabled us to configure the connection pool correctly, e.g., tuning its minimal and maximal size and eviction parameters.

Additional advices allow for monitoring certain kinds of misusages. For example, it is monitored whenever an EntityManagerFactory is created by bypassing our wrapper template (creation should not be done explicitly, but implicitly in the template). This means that an additional connection pool would be created for the same service, doubling the number of connections. The corresponding pointcut is:

```
@Before("execution(* *..*.createEntityManagerFactory
                    (String, java.util.Map)) && args(str,map)")
```

Another pointcut detects any direct usage of a JDBC connection beside the connection pool:

```
@Pointcut("execution(* org.apache.commons.dbcp.*.*(..))")
public void withinDbcp() {}

@AfterReturning(pointcut =
                "execution(* solid.jdbc.SolidDriver.connect(..))
                 && !cflow(withinDbcp)",
                returning = "ret")
```

If the programmer connects to the DBS using JDBC, thus bypassing the entire infrastructure, he could easily forget to release a connection. This would lead to an increase in connection usage.

In both cases, an advice will issue a warning and thus help us to detect the misuse of JDBC connections inspecting the log file output.

7 Lessons Learned

It is important to note that our telecommunication platform has not been developed in an aspect-oriented manner. Hence, we cannot provide any general lessons on AO software development. Anyway, there are still some interesting observations.

7.1 General Lessons

The first lesson is not really an experience, but rather a confirmation of our approach: integrating or replacing 3rd party tools, there is no need to worry about potential or suddenly arising problems, e.g., during the replacement of Hibernate with OpenJPA. Even if hard problems occur unexpectedly, aspect-orientation is a very powerful mechanism to overcome them.

Moreover, we experienced one major benefit of AOP in our case study: saving development time. We were able to provide solutions for hard problems in a couple of minutes. Particularly, we could confirm the usefulness of AOP for tracing: at first, we started analyzing problems in the conventional way: static code analysis, debugging, and increasing the debug level, but such a procedure turned out to be very time consuming. For example, migrating from Hibernate to OpenJPA, we were faced with the problem that our application could not connect to the database with a so-called *dual-node* URL of the form jdbc:solid://node1:1315,node2:1315 /myusr/mypw. Such a URL specifies two servers, one on node1 and another on node2, the databases of both being synchronized. If one solidDB server crashes, the secondary, silently takes over the work immediately. We spent several hours to find the reason why the application cannot connect – without success. With AspectJ, we could trace what happens to the URL by intercepting any execution of any method with a String parameter and check whether the string contains a solidDB URL. If it does, an advice prints out that URL. We detected in a couple of minutes that the URL has been truncated by OpenJPA to `jdbc:solid://node1:1315` thus disabling the dual-server operations with OpenJPA.

7.2 Lessons about AspectJ Load-Time Weaving and the Build Process

We intended to use load-time weaving (cf. Section 3), however, we immediately ran into problems with OSGi class loading. If AspectJ should be applied to code running in an OSGi container, then special extensions are necessary. For example, a special *Equinox Aspects* implementation exists for the Equinox OSGi container, which is however not portable to other OSGi implementations. That is why we decided not to use Equinox Aspects.

Instead, we chose another approach using pre-compilation. This requires the AspectJ command line compiler `iajc`. Then, there is no need to change the build infrastructure. We can take the "aspect" class and compile it into a JAR file with an ordinary Java compiler. Then, the aspect's JAR can be applied to classes or existing (3rd party) JARs such as Hibernate or JDBC drivers at compile-time. The newly produced JAR contains the original one including aspect weaving and can then further be used instead of the original one in the build process. An external `iajc` taskdef exists for Apache ant in order to make these steps easier [34]. The result is a new JAR, e.g., myhibernate.jar, which has to be used instead of the original one. Please note, building the new JAR file requires only a single build file and a single additional build step.

The advantages are obvious: at first, integration into an external build process, for example by using a tool like CruiseControl [38] with daily builds and overnight test reports, does not pose any problems and can be done by exchanging the JAR files. Second, scaling problems with AspectJ for large projects such as long compile-times, as reported by [32], are avoided. And finally, no knowledge about the source code and build process is required for all the modifications to a 3rd party tool JAR file. If a tool is maven-based, it can now easily be integrated in our ant-based build infrastructure.

Using this approach, we detected some strange effects, which are specific to the pre-compilation process. When we used an execution pointcut, we obtained some strange AspectJ `iajc` compilation errors sometimes:

```
[iajc] [Xlint:cantFindTypeAffectingJPMatch]
[iajc] (no source information available)
[iajc] ...\openjpa-1.1.0.jar [error] can't determine implemented
interfaces of missing type javax.jms.ExceptionListener
[iajc]    when    matching    pointcut    (execution((execution(*
solid.jdbc.SolidConnection+.close( ..))))
[iajc] when matching shadow method-execution
(void org.apache.openjpa.event.JMSRemoteCommitProvider.close())
[iajc]    when    weaving    type    org.apache.openjpa.event.
JMSRemoteCommitProvider
[iajc] when weaving classes
[iajc] when weaving
[iajc] when batch building with classpath:...
```

This error message is confusing because the pointcut itself does neither contain nor match the mentioned `ExceptionListener` or `JMSRemoteCommitProvider`. A simple solution is to add an unnecessary "`&& within(MyClass)`" for any class `MyClass` captured by the execution pointcut. This `within` clause is useless from a join point perspective, but lets the messages disappear. Moreover, adding the clause improves the compilation times.

This kind of error occurred more frequently for call pointcuts, which was a reason for preferring execution pointcuts whenever possible.

Anyhow, execution pointcuts are also simpler to use in our pre-compilation approach modifying external libraries. Since an execution pointcut intercepts at the callee side, it is clear which JAR is modified and must become part of an outjar: the JAR that contains the join points. In case of call pointcuts, it is not that easy, particularly, because Hibernate and OpenJPA are calling a connection pool, available in another JAR, which in turn invokes JDBC drivers. Hence, having a call pointcut on the JDBC driver could affect Hibernate, OpenJPA, or the connection pool JARs. This must be treated more carefully.

Moreover, in some cases a `cflow` pointcut would be useful for us to restrict the stacktrace. For example, we wanted to intercept the creation of a new JDBC connection, however, only if it is acquired in case of an exhausted connection pool. We had problems to use `cflow`, not because of syntactical points but technical AspectJ compilation problems. Strangely, the same `cflow` pointcut worked fine in Eclipse with AJDT.

7.3 Lessons about AspectJ

The usage of AspectJ is quite straightforward and easy. In our opinion, even the pointcut syntax of AspectJ is not too complex to be applied correctly. Moreover, in contrast to [18,26], we are satisfied with the power of the AspectJ language.

However, we detected further points that caused us some trouble. The first issue is about around call advices. At the very beginning, we sometimes overlooked that `proceed()` is intercepted, too. This is a typical beginner's error which caused an infinite recursion and led to a `StackOverflowError`. However, the problem could easily be detected and then corrected by `!within(MyAspect)`. The problem mainly arose when switching from `execution` to `call` pointcuts because execution pointcuts are safe in this respect.

7.4 Convincing Project Management

We have some good news for the AO community: within our company, most software developers are not afraid of AspectJ or complex pointcut syntax. When they become familiar with AO, they want to use it and they find useful cases where to apply and to gain benefit from it. This is somehow in contrast to what is often perceived by AO research.

However, there is also some bad news: several of our project managers are not always keen on using AO or having AspectJ in their running projects. Using the approach of Ron Bodkin [3] and others [21] to guide single developers who want to get familiar with AO in several steps is a good idea. But even if a critical mass of developers can be convinced of AO, they are often not able to influence decisions of their management. In particular, our project managers are afraid of having uncontrollable behavior if several developers use aspect-oriented programming. Further fears are concerned with long compilation times and the need to change the infrastructure such as the build process, especially continuous builds and daily overnight testing [31].

Moreover and more important, most running projects are concerned with hard problems to solve – now. Hence, there is currently only little interest in CCCs, the problems they could cause (unless they are starting to cause real trouble), modularization, and flexibility. Those points seem to be not concrete enough: our managers cannot see or measure these things in terms of time and money. They are only interested in how much money flexibility or modularity could save, which is hard to estimate.

The important question now is: how could we then convince our project management of using the AO solution? Why were we able to introduce AspectJ?

Of course, we had a lucky situation that we had to find solutions for critical problems in a short time, which imposed a lot of pressure. Moreover, there was a lack of adequate alternative solutions to overcome the problems. The only alternative seems to be patching source code. But then the source code of 3rd party tools must be available and furthermore the build process must be known in order to rebuild the library; even if this were possible, it would have been much more effort to understand how to handle it. Hence, managers agreed to try the AO solutions.

Anyway, AspectJ in its "originally intended" form would be still not accepted in the project because the infrastructure would have to change a lot: AspectJ requires a special compiler, for instance given by the Eclipse AJDT plug-in. AspectJ must also be integrated in the automatic build process with CruiseControl [38] and daily overnight tests. This is an absolute must in most industrial projects!

Hence, it is very important that we use aspects that are implemented as ordinary Java classes; aspects, pointcuts, and advices are specified as annotations: a Java class becomes an aspect annotating it with @Aspect. This requires only an AspectJ runtime environment, i.e., aspectjrt.jar. Moreover, using explicit compilation simplifies the build process. This gave us the sanction to use AspectJ, and our project management was happy with the result.

7.5 Downsides

Any new technology has also some downsides. In case of AOP, comprehension and maintainability are often cited criteria. Concerning comprehension, we did not detect any problems. On the one hand, we only had a small number of aspects. On the other hand, the aspects intercepted 3rd party libraries, i.e., the behavior of aspects was manageable and did not really affect programmer's code. Anyway, it happened that developers did not take into account the aspect behavior when analyzing problems.

Interestingly enough, the point of maintainability turned out to be an advantage. The aspects have been defined once and work forever since then. This might be surprising since we exchanged the solidDB JDBC driver twice and switched from OpenJPA version 0.9.7 to 1.1.0, but did not touch our aspects; they are stable and still work correctly with the newer versions. All the alternative solutions, we are mentioning in the next section would have caused a rebuild of 3rd party tools.

That is, pointcut fragility is not a problem, mainly due to stable and partially stan-dardized interfaces. Anyway, we introduced test output to check whether advices were really executed.

8 Alternative Solutions

Most of the problems we discussed are mainly caused by 3rd party tools that were buggy or did not behave the way we wanted. Of course, we could have replaced those tools – and indeed we did in case of Hibernate – but this would be a time-consuming and expensive action.

What are the possible solutions to solve the above problems? There is no easy work around such as wrapping OpenJPA or JDBC methods, because the tool's inter-nal behavior must be changed.

We can certainly ask the tool vendor, e.g., solidDB to change its JDBC driver. However, we have to pay for such a change, and even more, this change has to be done for each future version we intend to use. Our AO solution is more stable in this respect in spite of discussions about pointcut fragility!

For patches of Hibernate or OpenJPA, the open source community could provide solutions. However, the problem affects the interaction between Hibernate or OpenJPA and the rather specific solidDB DBS. We require solidDB-specific patches to the Hi-bernate/OpenJPA source code, but solidDB is not officially supported by Hibernate and OpenJPA. We did report solidDB specific issues to the OpenJPA project, but we did not expect support that matches the schedule of our project management. Moreo-ver, waiting for external solutions would have caused a significant delay.

Patching source code is possible, if the code is accessible. This is not always the case, e.g., the sources of the solidDB JDBC driver are not publicly available. In case of Hi-bernate or OpenJPA, the source code is available. Hence, we can patch the sources to solve some problems. But a deeper understanding of the complete source code is neces-sary, because several logical parts are involved. For example, to add a new `native` key generation concept to OpenJPA with Hibernate's behavior, the XML parser for map-ping files, the handling of annotations, storing and using meta-data, interpreting the meta-data to perform database operations etc. has to be changed. The functionality is spread over several unrelated classes. In addition, the code must be changed in such a way that changes apply only for solidDB, but not for other DBSs. The O/R framework knows the JDBC driver and can derive the used DBS. However, this information is needed in a different class. Hence, we have to let unrelated classes exchange this kind of information, which means the change cannot be done locally. Again, any code change must be repeated when switching to a new version of the 3rd party tool.

Furthermore, changing source code implies that the 3rd party JAR must be re-built with our changes, which means the build process must be known in order to produce a new JAR file. For some 3rd party projects, integration of sub projects into our ant-based build system might be an easy task, for example with an ant-based build project that provides a single ant target for providing the complete JAR file. But considering other projects that use Maven, the integration effort can be more cumbersome.

Obviously, aspect-oriented programming with AspectJ provides simpler solutions.

9 Conclusions

In this paper, we presented some applications of aspect-orientation (AO), more precisely of the AspectJ language [22], in an industrial project. AO is not just applied for "harmless" architectural checks, performance monitoring [32], and other concerns that can be switched off during productive operation. Aspects are really part of the product. AO is even more used to solve some critical problems for which a conventional solution is hard to find. Indeed, AspectJ provides easy and quick solutions, because of its possibility to affect the behavior of existing code. Hence, it turned out that AspectJ has a strong potential to be extremely useful in industrial projects. Especially, using tracing to detect the reason for problems, turned out to be of excellent benefit in terms of saving time.

The common usage of AspectJ is to apply aspects to Java classes, mostly using the AJDT plugin for AspectJ compilation in Eclipse projects. It is often overlooked that aspects can be applied to existing JARs as well, even to 3rd party tools: indeed, to solve our problems, we applied aspects to 3rd party tools, more precisely JARs, such as persistence frameworks or JDBC drivers, in order to add functionality or to correct some "strange" behavior, which were massive blocking points in our project. The essential value of our AO approach is a new method for addressing the challenges of integrating 3rd party software, keeping the existing code untouched and being able to manage the concerns of integration in a maintainable manner. Moreover, there is a lack of adequate alternative solutions. AO helped us to find and apply solutions in short time, thus saving development time and money.

To achieve our goals, we preferred an explicit AspectJ compilation step to load-time weaving or the AJDT Eclipse plug-in since our overall OSGi environment was very complex. This approach was demanded by the project management in order to avoid unpredictable problems combining AO and OSGi. Moreover, integration into an external build process with CruiseControl [38] was quite simple by exchanging JAR files. This was important for us, because we could rely on standard Eclipse with an ordinary Java compiler – without AJDT plug-in for AspectJ compilation etc.

In future work, we try to use AO programming in other areas within the project. For example, we are currently investigating whether AO is an alternative to a model-driven approach, which is currently using XML input and XSLT transformations to produce Java code. Using AO instead seems to be an interesting alternative.

References

1. Proc. of 2nd Int. Conf. on Aspect-Oriented Software Development, Boston (2003)
2. Bodkin, R.: AOP@Work: Performance monitoring with AspectJ,
    http://www.128.ibm.com/developerworks/java/library/
    j-aopwork10/index.html

3. Bodkin, R.: AOP@Work: Next Steps with Aspects,
   http://www.128.ibm.com/developerworks/java/
   library/j-aopwork-16
4. Burke, B.: Implementing Middleware Using AOP. In: Proc. 4th Conf. on Aspect-Oriented
   Software Development, AOSD 2005, Chicago. ACM Press, New York (2005)
5. Bodkin, R., Furlong, J.: Gathering Feedback on User Behaviour using AspectJ. In: [7]
6. Colyer, A., Clement, A.: Large-scale AOSD for Middleware. In: Proc. 3rd Conf. on
   Aspect-Oriented Software Development, AOSD 2004, Lancaster. ACM Press, New York
   (2004)
7. Chapman, M., Vasseur, A., Kniesel, G. (eds.): Proc. of Industry Track 3rd Conf. on
   Aspect-Oriented Software Development, AOSD 2006. ACM Press, Bonn (2006)
8. Duck, A.: Implementation of AOP in Non-Academic Projects. In: [7]
9. Elrad, T., Filman, R., Bader, A. (eds.): Theme Section on Aspect-Oriented Programming.
   CACM 44(10) (2001)
10. Gamma, E., Helm, R., Johnson, R., Vlissides, J.: Design Patterns – Elements of Reusable
    Object-Oriented Software. Addison-Wesley, Reading (1995)
11. Govindraj, K., Narayanan, S., et al.: On Using AOP for Application Performance Man-
    agement. In: [7]
12. Hibernate Reference Documentation,
    http://www.hibernate.org/hib_docs/v3/reference/en/html
13. Hannemann, J., Kiczales, G.: Design Pattern Implementation in Java and AspectJ. In: Proc.
    of the 17th Annual ACM Conference on Object-Oriented Programming, Systems, Lan-
    guages, and Applications, OOPSLA 2002, Seattle (2002)
14. Hohenstein, U.: Using Aspect-Orientation to Add Persistency to Applications. In: Proc. of
    Datenbanksysteme in Business, Technologie und Web (BTW), Karlsruhe (2005)
15. Hohenstein, U.: Using Aspect-Orientation to Manage Database Statistics. In: [7]
16. Java Persistence API,
    http://java.sun.com/javaee/technologies/persistence.jsp
17. Joosen, W., Sanen, F., Truyen, E.: Dissemination of AOSD expertise – Support documen-
    tation. AOSD-Europe Project Deliverable No.: AOSD-Europe-KUL–8 (March 2006)
18. Kästner, C., Apel, S., Batory, D.: A Case Study Implementing Features Using AspectJ. In:
    Proc. Int. Software Product Line Conference (SPLC), Kyoto, IEEE Computer Society, Los
    Alamitos (2007)
19. Kienzle, J., Guerraoui, R.: AOP: Does It Make Sense? The Case of Concurrency and Fail-
    ures. In: Deng, T. (ed.) ECOOP 2002. LNCS, vol. 2374, p. 37. Springer, Heidelberg
    (2002)
20. Kienzle, J., Gélineau, S.: AO Challenge – Implementing the ACID Properties for Transac-
    tional Attributes. In: Masuhara, H., Rashid, A. (eds.) Proc of 5th Int Conf on Aspect-
    Oriented Software Development, Bonn, Germany (2006)
21. Kiczales, G.: Adopting AOP. In: Proc. 4th Conf. on Aspect-Oriented Software Develop-
    ment, AOSD 2005. ACM Press, Chicago (2005)
22. Laddad, R.: AspectJ in Action: Practical Aspect-Oriented Programming, 2nd edn. Man-
    ning, Greenwich (2008)
23. Laddad, R.: AOP@Work: Myths about AOP,
    http://www.128.ibm.com/developerworks/java/
    library/j-aopwork15
24. Lesiecki, N.: Applying AspectJ to J2EE Application Development; IEEE Software (Janu-
    ary/February 2006)

25. Murphy, G., Walker, A.R., Robillard, M.: Separating Features in Source Code: An Exploratory Study. In: Proc. of 23rd Int. Conf. on Software Engineering 2001 (2001)
26. Ostermann, K., Mezini, M., Bockisch, C.: Expressive Pointcuts for Increased Modularity. In: Gao, X.-X. (ed.) ECOOP 2005. LNCS, vol. 3586, pp. 214–240. Springer, Heidelberg (2005)
27. Rashid, A.: Aspect-Oriented Database Systems. Springer, Heidelberg (2004)
28. Rashid, A., Chitchyan, R.: Persistence as an Aspect. In: Aksit, M. (ed.) 2nd Int. Conf. on Aspect-Oriented Software Development, AOSD 2003, Boston. ACM Press, New York (2003)
29. Soares, S., Borba, P.: Implementing Modular and Reusable Aspect-Oriented Concurrency Control with AspectJ. In: WASP 2005, Uberlândia, Brazil (2005)
30. Strunk, W.: The Symphonia Product-Line. In: Java and Object-Oriented (JAOO) Conference 2007, Arhus, Denmark (2007)
31. Wiese, D., Hohenstein, U., Meunier, R.: How to Convince Industry of Aspect-Orientation? In: 6th Int. Conf. on Aspect-Oriented Software Development, AOSD 2007, Vancouver. ACM Press, New York (2007)
32. Wiese, D., Meunier, R.: Large Scale Application of AOP in the Healthcare Domain: A Case Study. In: 7th Int. Conf. on Aspect-Oriented Software Development, AOSD, Brussels (2008)
33. Zhang, C., Jacobsen, H.-A.: Quantifying Aspects in Middleware Platforms. In: [1]
34. AspectJ Project Page: "AspectJ Ant Tasks",
    `http://www.eclipse.org/aspectj/doc/released/`
    `devguide/antTasks.html`
35. Sullivan, K., Griswold, W., Song, Y., Cai, Y., Shonle, M., Tewari, N., Rajan, H.: Information hiding interfaces for aspect-oriented design. In: ESEC/SIGSOFT FSE 2005 (2005)
36. Griswold, W., Sullivan, K., Song, Y., Shonle, M., Tewari, N., Cai, Y., Rajan, H.: Modular Software Design with Crosscutting Interfaces. IEEE Software 23(1) (January/February 2006)
37. Garcia, A., Sant'Anna, C., Figueiredo, E., Kulesza, U., de Lucena, C.J.P., von Staa, A.: Modularizing design patterns with aspects: A quantitative study. In: Rashid, A., Liu, Y. (eds.) Transactions on Aspect-Oriented Software Development I. LNCS, vol. 3880, pp. 36–74. Springer, Heidelberg (2006)
38. CruiseControl, `http://cruisecontrol.sourceforge.net/`

PUMA: An Aspect-Oriented Code Analysis and Manipulation Framework for C and C++*

Matthias Urban[1], Daniel Lohmann[2], and Olaf Spinczyk[3]

[1] Pure-Systems GmbH, Magdeburg, Germany
matthias.urban@pure-systems.com
[2] Friedrich-Alexander-University Erlangen-Nuremberg, Germany
Computer Science 4 – Distributed Systems and Operating Systems
daniel.lohmann@informatik.uni-erlangen.de
[3] Technische Universität Dortmund, Germany
Computer Science 12 – Embedded System Software
olaf.spinczyk@tu-dortmund.de

Abstract. PUMA is a framework for the development of applications that analyze and optionally transform C or C++ source code. It supports all standard ISO C and C++ language features as well as many language extensions of the GNU Compiler Collection and Microsoft Visual C++. Aspects played an important role during the design and implementation of the framework. It is written in the AspectC++ language. By employing AOSD concepts we gained clean separation of concerns and, thereby, very good configurability and extensibility. All these −ilities are of vital importance for our project, because the available manpower for maintenance tasks is limited. This paper describes the tools, which we used for the development, the principles behind the design of PUMA, and its implementation. Even though criticized during the last few years, our experiences show that aspect technology has clear benefits for the development of complex industrial applications.

1 Introduction

PUMA is a framework that facilitates the development of applications that parse, analyze, and optionally transform C or C++ source code. It has been developed by pure-systems GmbH, a company located in Magdeburg, Germany, and is used for client-specific solutions. For instance, one recent PUMA-based project was a mutation testing tool for SystemC code [25]. SystemC is used to describe hardware structures in a high-level language. Technically, SystemC is a C++ library and the description of the hardware structures is in fact C++ code that uses the library. By automatically injecting faulty code into the SystemC code at arbitrary locations, hardware failures can be simulated. With PUMA, the development of this tool could be simplified significantly.

Even though PUMA is a very powerful framework, which is being used in commercial projects, it is also available for free under the GPL license. This is remarkable, because as far as we know there are no other open source parsers for C++ available that

---

* This work was partly supported by the German Research Council (DFG) under grant no. SCHR 603/4, SP 968/2-1, and SP 968/4-1.

S. Katz et al. (Eds.): Transactions on AOSD VIII, LNCS 6580, pp. 141–162, 2011.

are as feature complete as PUMA. Another (non-commercial) application of PUMA is the AspectC++ [22] aspect weaver ac++. AspectC++ is an aspect-oriented extension of C++ and at the same time the implementation language of PUMA. The main focus of this article is to describe how AspectC++ has been applied for the development of PUMA and what are the benefits that we account to our aspect-oriented development approach.

Figure 1 gives an overview of the features, which PUMA provides for its applications. As several features are configurable, we regard PUMA not as a single framework but as a product line of frameworks. The graphical notation that is used in the figure is a *feature diagram*, which is a concept that is used to describe the variable and common properties of a family of related software products [3]. A detailed explanation is given in the caption of the figure.

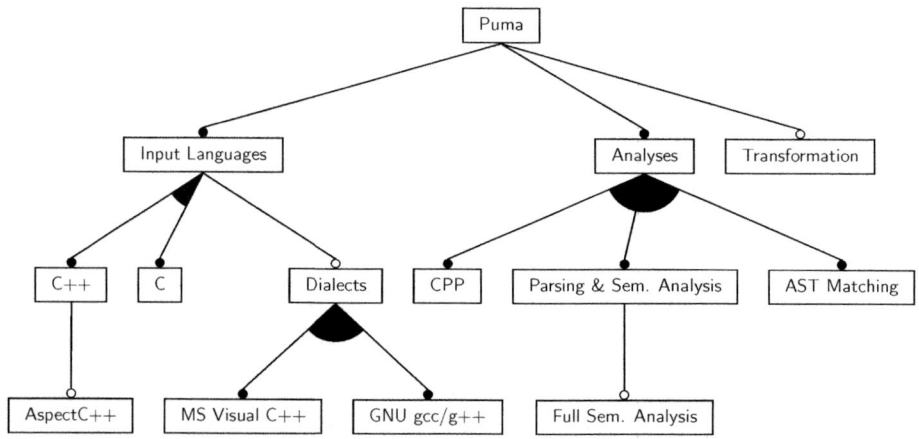

Fig. 1. PUMA's feature model: Supported input languages are C and C++. AspectC++ is an optional extension of C++. PUMA also optionally supports the two language dialects of the Microsoft Visual C++ compiler and GNU gcc/g++. The source code analyses consist of preprocessing (CPP) and parsing the code. The parser already performs most of the semantic analysis. Additional semantic analyses are provided as an optional subfeature. AST Matching is a mechanism to compile syntax tree patterns, which can be matched against the output syntax tree of the parser. For applications that want to perform source-to-source transformations an optional feature Transformation is provided.

The source code of the PUMA framework is available as a part of the AspectC++ weaver ac++. It's latest version can be anonymously downloaded via subversion from the URL https://svn.aspectc.org/repos/Puma/trunk. The most challenging part of the implementation is the tremendously complex syntax and semantics of C++. In order to test the maturity of PUMA's C and C++ parsers, we regularly feed them with the gcc resp. g++ test suite. Table 1 shows the current status of these tests. The tests for which PUMA was expected to fail are those with wrong test code that should be rejected with an error message. These cases are less critical than the cases where PUMA was expected to parse the test code but failed (452/389). This means that valid source code was not accepted. However, a more detailed look at these particular test cases shows that in most of these cases *very specific* GNU gcc/g++ language extensions, such as attributes or pragmas for less frequently used CPU types, are involved, which have not yet been implemented in PUMA. In practice, this doesn't mean a severe restriction, as most of these features are rarely needed. For instance, PUMA parses the latest STL header files easily.

Table 1. Results of parsing the GNU gcc and g++ test suites with PUMA

total no. of **gcc** tests	6385	total no. of **g++** tests	6025
expected to pass but failed	452	expected to pass but failed	389
expected to fail but passed	373	expected to fail but passed	958

Crosscutting Concerns in C and C++ parsers

With about 83.000 lines of code PUMA is a complex piece of software. It is impossible to describe the role of aspect orientation in all of its subsystems. Therefore, the remainder of this article will concentrate on the construction of PUMA *parsers*. This is the most interesting and challenging part. Code transformations and AST matching will not be covered.

A parser has to accomplish various tasks at the same time. Primarily it has to read tokens (such as identifiers, keywords, or operator symbols) from an input stream and match them against a set of grammar rules. The rules can either be represented by tables or by source code. In most cases parsers with tables are generated and otherwise hand-written. The GNU gcc/g++ parser is a huge piece of hand-written C Code. The grammar rules are expressed by C functions, which call each other. Besides this, there are many other concerns:

- Language extensions: Objective-C and OpenMP (implemented by conditional code)
- Construction of syntax tree nodes
- "Tentative Parsing" (speculative parsing and backtracking)
- Connection to the semantic analysis
- Error handling
- Specific lookahead for optimization of the parse process

All these concerns are an integral part of the C/C++ grammar. The code is tangled, which probably makes it difficult to maintain and especially extend the parser. This could be done better by using aspect technology. Furthermore, there is no re-use even though parts of the C++ grammar are very similar to the C grammar.

Requirements

For PUMA, a different design had to be chosen. We have to deal with various language extensions such as AspectC++, GNU and MS Visual C++, and a number of different C and C++ standards (C99, C++1x, etc.). Additionally, PUMA is intended to support client-specific language extension. Therefore, the design must focus on extensibility as a key feature. Here is a list of our requirements:

- Maintainability and extensibility with minimal effort, even in the case of unantici-pated extensions
- Cope with the complexity of the supported languages as well as their dialects and extensions
- Configurability according to the application's demands
- Openness for other languages than C and C++ in the future

Over the years we have learned that these goals could never be reached without very clean separation of concerns. Therefore, we found that aspect orientation is very promis-ing for the design and implementation of the framework.

As PUMA is not intended to become a front-end for a compiler, performance is an important issue, but not important enough to dominate design decisions.

Contributions of this Paper

This article is primarily intended for developers and managers in the industry, who want to learn more about the benefits and possible problems of using aspect technology in real world application scenarios, but also for members of the AOSD community, who are interested in aspect-oriented design principles and the maturity of the AspectC++ language. In summary the contribution of the article is as follows:

- It will be shown that aspects are indeed helpful for the design of complex software systems, especially for the construction of a parser. The main benefits are separation of concerns, extensibility, and configurability.
- We will present design principles and AspectC++ idioms that turned out to be use-ful and that were already successfully applied in another domain's.
- As PUMA is the largest AspectC++ application we are aware of, the article also shows that the language, the aspect weaver, and the IDE are ready for real-world applications.

Outline

The paper is organized as follows: In the next section, we briefly present the AspectC++ language and the set of tools, which we used for the implementation of PUMA. Section 3 explains the design principles behind the system. They are the result of several years of work with AspectC++ in the domain of aspect-oriented operating systems and soft-ware product-lines for embedded systems. In section 4 and 5 we introduce step-by-step the design and implementation of the PUMA parser. This illustrates how we achieved clean separation of concerns. One of our key design goals was extensibility with min-imal effort even if the extensions are unanticipated. Section 6 shows whether this goal has been reached. Based on the necessary modifications for a new C++1X feature, we evaluate PUMA's extensibility. The overall pros and cons of applying aspect technology are discussed in section 7. Section 8 provides an overview of related work. Finally, the paper is briefly summarized in section 9.

2   Toolkit

2.1   The AspectC++ Language

AspectC++ [22] is the implementation language of PUMA. It is an aspect-oriented extension of C++, which at the beginning aimed to mimic the syntax and semantics of the well-known AspectJ language [6]. Later it was extended in order to combine aspect-oriented programming with generic and generative programming in C++ [15]. In recent past, it was even extended to support dynamic aspect weaving [24]. However, the aspects that are used for PUMA are purely static.

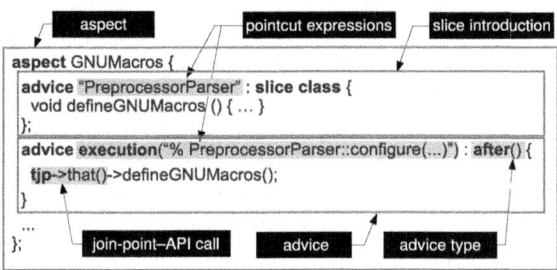

Fig. 2. The AspectC++ syntax

Figure 2 illustrates the most important elements of the AspectC++ syntax. The aspect GNUMacros implements an extension of the PUMA preprocessor parser. For this purpose, it *introduces* a *slice* of additional elements (the member function defineGNUMacros) into the class PreprocessorParser and gives a piece of *advice* to call the introduced function *after* each *execution* of the preprocessor parser member function configure. The targets of the introduction and of the execution advice are given by *pointcut expressions*.

In AspectC++, pointcut expressions are built from *match expressions* and *pointcut functions*. The match expression "PreprocessorParser", for instance, returns a pointcut containing just the class PreprocessorParser. Match expressions can also be fed into pointcut functions to yield pointcuts that represent events in the control flow of the running program, such as the event where some function is about to be *called* (call() advice), *executed* (execution() advice as in figure 2) or an object instance is about to be *constructed* (construction() advice) or *destructed* (destruction() advice). In most cases, the join points for a given pointcut can be derived statically by the aspect weaver so that the respective advice is also inserted statically at compile time without any run-time overhead.

The execution pointcut in the example is used to specify some *after* advice – that is, additional behavior to be triggered after the event occurrence. Other types of advice include *before* advice (speaks for itself) and *around* advice (replaces the original behavior associated with the event occurrence).

Inside the advice body, the type and pointer JoinPoint *tjp provide an interface to the event context. The aspect developer can use this *join-point API* to retrieve (and partly modify) contextual information associated with the event, such as the arguments or return value of the intercepted function call (`tjp->arg(i)`, `tjp->result()`). The `tjp->that()` API-call in Figure 2 returns the `this` pointer of the affected object instance, which is used here to call the member function `defineGNUMacros` (which in this case was introduced by the aspect itself).

2.2   Tool Support

Aspect Weaver: `ac++`

An implementation of the AspectC++ language is available from `http://www.aspectc.org/` for free under the GPL license. It is a static aspect weaver called `ac++`, which is based on the PUMA framework. There are binary packages for Linux, Windows, Solaris, and MacOS and the latest source code is available via subversion.

ac++ makes use of PUMA's code transformation feature, i.e. it is implemented as a source-to-source transformation, which has AspectC++ as its input language and ISO C++ as output language. The resulting source code can be compiled with any ISO C++ compliant compiler. To make this more convenient for `g++` users, the `ac++` and `g++` invocations are wrapped by an additional tool called `ag++`. This makes it fairly easy to integrate aspect weaving into existing makefiles. Debian and Ubuntu Linux users can alternatively install AspectC++ from their standard package repository.

For MS Visual Studio users there is an AspectC++-Add-In[1], which integrates aspect weaving into the build process transparently. For the compilation of PUMA we are using both alternatively, GNU g++ or MS Visual Studio.

Integrated Development Environment: ACDT

An important factor for the development of PUMA are effective tools for join-point traceability. From the viewpoint of an aspect developer, the set of join points offered by some class implementation constitutes an interface. However, these interfaces are "implicit at best" [23]; a simple refactoring, such as renaming a method, might silently change the set of join points and thereby break some aspect. To prevent such situations, we are using the Eclipse-based AspectC++ Development Toolkit (ACDT[2]), which provides a join-point–set delta analysis (very helpful after updating from the repository) and visualizes code that is affected by aspects. Thereby, unwanted side effects of code changes can be detected relatively, easily. The ACDT also includes an aspect-aware debugger.

Automatic Build and Test System: Akut

For the development of a software product line such as PUMA, it is generally recommended to establish a continuous integration process [4]. This is necessary, because

---

[1] The AspectC++-Add-In for MS Visual Studio is commercial software that can be purchased at `http://www.pure-systems.com/`. However, there are plans to turn the Add-In into an open source project in the near future. Commercial support will still be available.

[2] `http://acdt.aspectc.org/`

developers can hardly test the product line in all configurations manually. For PUMA and AspectC++ we use a self-made build and test system called Akut, which is based on CruiseControl[3]. The resulting binaries and test results (including the GNU gcc/g++ test suite) can be inspected at `http://akut.aspectc.org`.

Toolkit Summary

For the development of PUMA an aspect-oriented programming language as well as fully-featured tool support are available. At a first glance AspectC++ looks very similar to AspectJ. However, a closer look reveals that AspectC++ differs as much from AspectJ as C++ from Java. There is a strong focus on static typing and compile time introspection. This is sometimes less convenient, as Java's runtime reflection mechanism is more powerful. However, the big advantages are better performance and error detection at compile time [15].

3   Design Methodology

During the last eight years we have developed aspect-oriented software product-lines with AspectC++ for various purposes. Our application domains were operating systems [19,16] and application product-lines for highly resource-constrained embedded systems [18]. Over the years there evolved a design methodology that will now be briefly presented (for more details see [14]).

3.1 Principles

The basic idea behind this development approach is the strict separation of concerns in the *implementation*. Each implementation unit provides exactly one feature; its mere presence or absence in the configured source tree decides on the inclusion of the particular feature into the resulting system variant.

Technically, this comes down to a strict decoupling of policies and mechanisms by using aspects as the primary composition technique: Mechanisms are glued together and extended by aspects; they support aspects by ensuring that all relevant internal control-flow transitions are available as unambiguous and statically evaluable join points.

We learned from this that the exposure of all relevant gluing and extension points as statically evaluable and unambiguous join points has to be understood as a primary design goal from the very beginning. The key premise for such *aspect awareness* is a component structure that makes it possible to influence the composition and shape of components as well as all run-time control flows that run through them by aspects. This led to the following design principles for PUMA:

The principle of loose coupling. Make sure that aspects can hook into all facets of the static and dynamic *integration* of system components.
The principle of visible transitions. Make sure that aspects can hook into all control flows that run through the system. All control-flow transitions into, out of, and

---

[3] `http://cruisecontrol.sourceforge.net/`

within the system should be influenceable by aspects. For this they have to be represented on the join-point level as statically evaluable, unambiguous join points.

The principle of minimal extensions. Make sure that aspects can extend all features provided by the system on a fine granularity. System components and system abstractions should be fine-grained, sparse, and extensible by aspects.

Aspect awareness, as described by these principles, means that we moderate the AOP ideal of obliviousness, which is generally considered by the AOP community as a defining characteristic of AOP [5]. PUMA's system components and abstractions are *not* totally oblivious to aspects – they are supposed to provide explicit support for aspects and even depend on them for their integration.

3.2 Role and Types of Classes and Aspects

The relationship between aspects and classes is asymmetrical in most AOP languages including AspectC++: Aspects augment classes, but not vice versa. This gives rise to the question as to which features are best to be implemented as classes and which as aspects and how both should be applied to meet the above design principles.

The general rule we came up with in the development of PUMA and other systems is to provide some feature as a class if – and only if – it represents a *distinguishable instantiable concept* of the system. Provided as classes are:

1. **System Components**, which are instantiated on behalf of PUMA and manage its run-time state (such as the UnitManager, which maintains a list of opened and scanned source code files in PUM).
2. **System Abstractions**, which are instantiated on behalf of the application and represent a system object (such as the C or C++ parser).

However, the classes for system components and system abstractions are sparse and to be further "filled" by *extension slices*. The main purpose of these classes is to provide a distinct scope with unambiguous join points for the aspects (that is, *visible transitions*).

All other features are implemented as aspects. During the development of PUMA we came up with three idiomatic roles of aspects:

1. **Extension Aspects** add additional features to a system abstraction or component (*minimal extensions*), such as extending the preprocessor by GNU compiler-specific predefined macros. This example was shown in Figure 2.
2. **Policy Aspects** "glue" otherwise unrelated system abstractions or components together to implement some policy (*loose coupling*). For instance, handling syntax errors during the parse process can very well be handled by glueing the component that generates error messages with the appropriate rules of the grammar by a policy aspect. This example will be explained in Section 4.
3. **Upcall Aspects** bind behavior defined by higher layers to events produced in lower layers of the system, such as intercepting the execution of the preprocessor configure function by the higher-level GNU extension (again Figure 2).

One aspect in the implementation can fulfill multiple roles. The effect of *extension aspects* typically becomes visible in the API of the affected system component or abstraction. *Policy aspects*, in contrast, lead to a different system behavior. We will see examples for extension and policy aspects in the following section. *Upcall aspects* do not contribute directly to a design principle, but have a more technical purpose: they exploit advice-based binding and the fact that AspectC++ inlines advice code at the respective join point for flexible, yet very efficient upcalls.

4 Separation of Concerns

In this section we will incrementally describe the design and implementation of the Puma C and C++ parsers, following the design principles of the previous section. The design process led to clean separation of concerns.

4.1 C and C++ Syntax

The syntax of C and C++ is precisely defined in the respective ISO standards [9,10]. For most other programming languages one would start writing a parser by using a parser generator such as yacc [11] or antlr [21]. However, taking a generated parser would prohibit the possibility to use AspectC++ for weaving orthogonal concerns or configurable extensions into the syntax rules. Furthermore, most other C++ parsers are hand written, because the parsing process is very complex and dependent on a semantic analysis, which has to be performed in parallel, and optimized by specialized look-ahead functions. Therefore, we decided to express the rules of the C and C++ grammar in plain C++ code. The result is a recursive-decent parser. Because many of the syntax rules of C are also used in C++ with only minor extensions, we decided to avoid redundancy and, thus, expressed the C and C++ syntax as classes with an inheritance relation. According to Section 3.2 their role is to be system components. The initial design is sketched in Figure 3.

By this design, the grammars of C and C++ (Figure 3 right) can almost literally be translated into C++ code (left). The base class `Syntax` provides the interface to the scanner via the `token()` function and convenience functions such as `list()`, which calls a specific rule in a loop and checks whether a specific token is used as a separator. All implementations of grammar rules are `virtual` functions in order to allow a derived grammar implementation to override the rule. This is done for `literal()` in our simplified example grammar. All functions return a `bool` value that is `true` if the input token stream matches the implemented rule and `false` otherwise. In the example, calling `expr()` for the input stream **ID + (ID + ID)** would yield `true`, while, for instance, **(+ ID)** would yield `false`. For an instance of `CCSyntax` **(TRUE)** would be a valid input stream, because of the overridden `literal()` function, while a `CSyntax` instance would reject it.

We regard this initial design as ideal, because it naturally expresses the relations between the different grammar rules as well as between the C and C++ syntax at large. However, it is not *aspect-aware* in the sense that not all relevant events are accessible

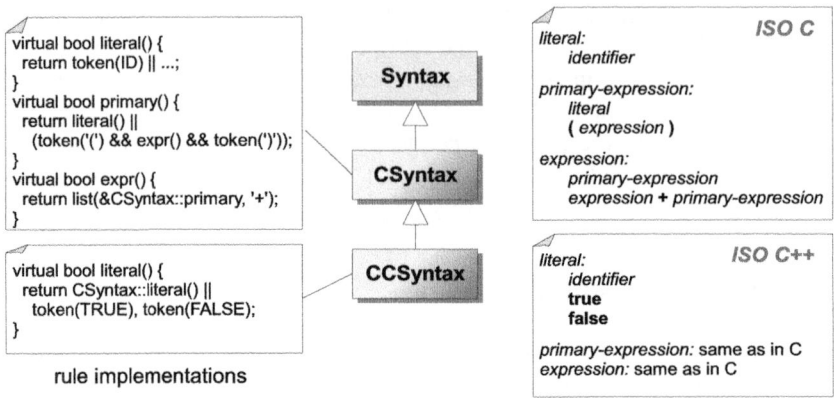

rule implementations

Fig. 3. Initial design of the C and C++ syntax in PUMA. The source code fragments and the corresponding grammar rules are simplified for the sake of comprehensibility.

for aspects in an *unambiguous* manner. There are four kinds of relevant events in the control flow during the execution of the grammar rule implementations:

1. execution of a grammar rule (before/after "parse")
2. invocation of another grammar rule (before/after "check")
3. invocation of a base class grammar rule without dynamic dispatch (before/after "base check")
4. the dynamic dispatch (before/after "dispatch")

The ambiguity problem with the presented initial implementation is that the dynamic dispatch and the execution and invocation of the grammar rules are not properly separated. For instance, the AspectC++ pointcut expression call("bool CSyntax::literal()") would match the call within CSyntax::primary() as well as the call within CCSyntax::literal(), even though the first call leads to a dynamic dispatch while the latter does not. Therefore, in our real implementation each grammar rule was represented differently. An excerpt of this aspect-aware implementation is shown in Figure 4. The disadvantage of this implementation is that some more source code has to be written. However, this is *the only* disadvantage. It is purely mechanic work and was done quickly. Thanks to function inling the C++ compiler generates the same machine code as with the initial implementation. The advantages are that:

- function calls that perform a dynamic dispatch are only located in check() functions. There is no longer an ambiguity of join-points.
- each grammar rule now has an associated type. We will soon show that this is extremely useful for the implementation of the remaining parser concerns as aspects.

Based on the homogeneous structure of the implementation and the unambiguous join-points we can define a number of pointcuts as members of the Syntax class. This is shown in Figure 5. The pointcuts can be regarded as an explicit representation of an interface for aspects, which need to be activated when events occur that are related to the execution of the syntax rules.

```
1    struct CSyntax : public Syntax {
2      struct Literal {
3        static bool check (CSyntax &s) { return s.literal(); }
4        static bool parse (CSyntax &s) { return s.token(ID); }
5      };
6      virtual bool literal() { return Literal::parse(*this); }
7
8      struct Primary {
9        static bool check (CSyntax &s) { return s.primary(); }
10       static bool parse (CSyntax &s) {
11         return Literal::check(s) ||
12                (s.token('(') && Expr::check(s) && s.token(')'));
13       }
14     };
15     virtual bool primary() { return Primary::parse(*this); }
16
17     // ... struct Expr not shown here
18   };
19
20   class CCSyntax : public CSyntax {
21     struct Literal : public CSyntax::Literal {
22       static bool parse (CCSyntax &s) {
23         return CSyntax::Literal::parse(s) || s.token(TRUE) || s.token(FALSE);
24       }
25     };
26     virtual bool literal() { return Literal::parse(*this); }
27   };
```

Fig. 4. Aspect-aware implementation of the grammar rules

4.2   Backtracking and Scanner State

You might have noticed that the simple parser described so far only works correctly if the token() function does not consume the current token in cases where it does *not* match its argument and if the grammar is LL(1), which means that one token lookahead is sufficient to decide which production of a grammar rule is the right one. For C and C++, the latter precondition does not hold. Therefore, the parser has to deal with backtracking, which means that the state of the scanner has to be saved when a rule is entered and restored afterwards if the result is false. Otherwise an alternative rule would not be tried with the same input tokens as the first rule, which failed.

```
1    class Syntax {
2      // ...
3      pointcut parse_fct ()  = "bool %::%::parse(%)";
4      pointcut check_fct ()  = "bool %::%::check(%)";
5      pointcut in_syntax ()  = within(derived("Syntax"));
6      // rule_exec: execution of a parse function
7      pointcut rule_exec () = execution(parse_fct()) && in_syntax();
8      // rule_call: call of a parse function after a dynamic dispatch
9      pointcut rule_call () = call(parse_fct()) && in_syntax() && !within("%::...::%");
10     // rule_check: a rule checks a sub-rule (before dynamic dispatch)
11     pointcut rule_check () = execution(check_fct()) && in_syntax();
12   };
```

Fig. 5. An interface for aspects based on named pointcut definitions

Because of the aspect-aware system structure (Figure 3) and the aspect interface (Figure 5), this can be expressed easily as an aspect in AspectC++ (see Figure 6). The aspect SyntaxState is a *policy aspect*, because it connects the syntax rules with the functions to save and restore the parser state and decides under which circumstances this should happen. For instance, a more sophisticated implementation of this policy could avoid to retrieve and copy the parser state if it hasn't changed since the last time it was saved. As the aspect only relies on the aspect interface pointcut Syntax::rule_call(), it is automatically open for future extensions, namely aspects that extend the syntax classes by additional rules.

```
1    aspect SyntaxState {
2      // intercept all calls of rules (after dynamic dispatch)
3      advice Syntax::rule_call() : around () {
4        Syntax &s = *tjp ->arg<0>();   // get the 0th argument, i.e. the CSyntax object
5        Syntax::State state;            // create a local variable to store the state
6        s.get_state(state);             // save the current state of the parser
7        tjp ->proceed();                // perform the intercepted call
8        if (!*tjp ->result())           // check whether the result is false
9          s.set_state(stat);            // restore the state
10     }
11   };
```

Fig. 6. Backtracking support implemented as an aspect: The current parser state is automatically saved and restored if necessary. Because the aspect does not use more information than the name of the type State, which is looked up in the scope of the syntax class, the content of the State object could be extended by other aspects.

The SyntaxState aspect is very closely connected with the syntax classes. Other aspects and classes regard the syntax classes and the SyntaxState aspects as a union. Therefore, it could be regarded as *local* aspect. Nevertheless, it implements a highly crosscutting concern. In the C and C++ syntax it matches 104 and 118 grammar rules respectively.

4.3   Error Handling

Up to this point the parser is already able to tell whether a given token sequence matches the grammar rules. If the parser detects an error, the root syntax rule will return false and the application can print a syntax error. However, users expect more precise error messages than this and also don't want the parser to stop checking the code when the first syntactic problem shows up. Usually this problem is solved in recursive decent parsers by a so-called *panic mode*. This means that for certain grammar rules there is a check whether parsing failed. If it did, a corresponding error message is issued, tokens are skipped until it is likely that parsing can continue without errors, and the process is resumed as if the rule hadn't failed. This is illustrated in a very simplified manner in Figure 7.

The main argument for separating the error handling from the implementation of the grammar rules is configurability. In some projects we can assume that the source code that we have to analyze is syntactically correct. In other projects the error handling has

```
1   aspect SyntaxErrors {
2     advice call("bool CSyntax::Primary::parse(%)" ||
3            bool CCSyntax::Primary::parse(%)") : after () {
4       if (!*tjp->result()) {                    // check if result was false
5         err() << "invalid expression" << endl;  // print an error message
6         tjp->that()->panic();                    // skip some tokens
7         *tjp->result() = true;                   // change the result to 'true'
8       }
9     }
10  };
```

Fig. 7. Very simple error handling policy aspect

to be more or less sophisticated. By separating the error handling,P this *policy* became configurable without having to bloat the syntax classes with conditional error handling code.

4.4 Control Flow Tracing

Generating control flow traces is a task where aspect technology is particularly good at. It is an orthogonal concern and better be implemented by a separated module in a declarative manner. The power of quantification becomes obvious in the case of tracing. For a parser implementation, this is very helpful during the development phase. While in non-aspect-oriented implementations the tracing code bloats the implementations of the syntax rules, this is completely separated in PUMA.

4.5 Syntax Tree Construction

PUMA supports arbitrary code analysis tasks. Therefore, the output of the parser has to be more than just `true` or `false`. A syntax tree has to be constructed on-the-fly. In PUMA this feature is implemented by the two *extension aspects* `CBuilder` and `CCBuilder` in combination with an *upcall aspect* `Builder`. The extension aspects introduce a function called `build()` into all classes that represent grammar rules. The implementation of these functions is different for each rule, because PUMA uses different C++ classes to represent the syntax tree nodes. If we wanted to change this in order to perform the syntax tree construction with a more generic aspect, this would merely require to replace the `CBuilder` and `CCBuilder` extension aspects. Figure 8 gives an overview of this design.

The `Builder` aspect is fully generic. It could even be used with syntax implementations of other languages than C or C++. It only depends on the assumption that each class that represents a grammar rule contains a static member function `build()`. This function is called after each successful run of the corresponding `parse()` function. The builder slices are higher-level code in the sense that they are aware of the implementation of the syntax classes, but not vice versa. Therefore, the `Builder` aspect falls into the *upcall aspect* category. The `build()` functions are introduced by the two *extension aspects* `CBuilder` and `CCBuilder`. If the `build()` function returns a syntax tree and not `NULL`, a pointer to this tree is pushed onto a stack, which has been introduced by the `Builder` aspect into the `Syntax` class. At the same time the syntax trees that were pushed onto the stack by successfully parsed sub-rules are removed from the stack.

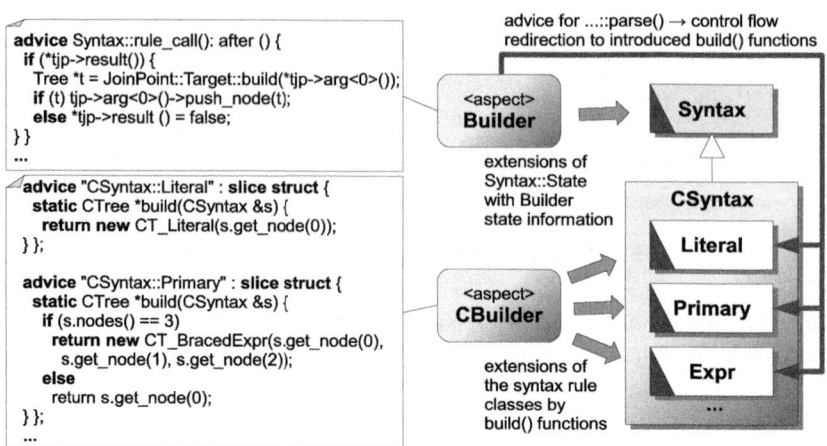

Fig. 8. Aspects for syntax tree construction

In addition to the code fragments shown in Figure 8, the Builder aspect has to make sure that new syntax tree nodes are correctly destroyed in the case of backtracking. This means that there is an interaction between the aspects `SyntaxState` and `Builder`. The `Builder` aspect is aware of `SyntaxState` but not vice versa. Both aspects define after-advice for the pointcut `Syntax::rule_call()`. In order to make sure that two aspects, which affect the same join-points, have their advice code run in a well-defined order, AspectC++ provides so-called *order-advice*. Here the `Builder` has to make sure that its after advice code is run before the after advice of the `SyntaxState` aspect. According to the AspectC++ semantics this means that the `SyntaxState` aspect has to have a higher *precedence*. This is achieved in the following way:

```
advice Syntax::rule_call() : order("SyntaxState", "Builder");
```

4.6   Semantic Analysis

Because the C and C++ grammar are ambiguous, parsing is not possible without performing a semantic analysis on-the-fly. For example, the parser sometimes cannot distinguish between a declaration and an expression statement without knowing whether an identifier token represents a type or an object. In the standardized grammar this problem becomes obvious, for instance, in the *typedef-name* rule:

A.1 Keywords   **[gram.key]**
New context-dependent keywords are introduced into a program by typedef (7.1.3), namespace (7.3.1), class (clause 9), enumeration (7.2), and template (clause 14) declarations.

typedef-name:
    identifier
...

It means that whenever a type is defined, its name as well as information about its scope has to be saved in a database of semantic information. When the rule *typedef-name* is parsed, it has to be checked whether an identifier comes next on the token stream and a name lookup for this identifier has to be performed. If it is found and if it is a typedef, the rule should return `true` and `false` otherwise.

There are many more of these interactions between the syntactic and semantic analysis in C and C++. Therefore, in non-aspect-oriented parser implementations both concerns are tangled. In order to avoid bi-directional dependencies between system components, we decided to separate the syntactic and semantic analysis and connect them by a *policy aspect*.

4.7 Optimization

A major difference between the PUMA parser and the GNU gcc/g++ is the optimization of the parse process. The GNU parsers are implemented in an optimized way. For instance, they perform a look-ahead of several tokens in order to chose the right production within a grammar rule. Therefore, the grammar implementation is bloated with code for this purpose. Even worse, in many cases simple look-ahead is not possible and the parser has to be switched into a "tentative" parsing mode. This means a speculative execution of parser rules. If it turns out that the chosen production was the wrong one, backtracking has to take place.

In the design of the PUMA parser, optimization by look-ahead is regarded as a concern that has to be separated from the underlying grammar implementation. Speculative execution of rules and the possible need for backtracking is the default for all rules. A separate optimization aspect can improve the parser performance by introducing look-ahead at various points in the grammar. The optimization aspect consists of two parts: A generic optimization for all rules, which is based on the calculation of the "first set", i.e. the set of possible first tokens for each rule, and specific optimization with arbitrary look-ahead. For instance, a significant improvement can be achieved if function declarations and function definitions can be distinguished early.

The implementation of the generic look-ahead is very similar to the `Builder` implementation: Each grammar rule type is extended by an individual `lookahead()` function. Furthermore, the `CSyntax` class and the `CCSyntax` class are extended by a token set attribute for each of these rules. Virtual initialization functions are added to the syntax classes, which construct the first sets before the first parser run.

4.8 Summary

This section gave some insights into the aspect-oriented design and implementation of the PUMA parser. Seven concerns that are tangled in the implementation of other C and C++ parsers could be completely separated. We believe that we have found a number of very good use cases for aspect technology. An indicator for the maintainability improvements is shown in Table 2. It compares the size of the source code files in lines of code, which implement the syntax rules, of GNU gcc/g++ and PUMA. The PUMA files are significantly smaller and, thus, much better to understand than the corresponding GNU C/C++ files. In contrast to GNU gcc/g++ PUMA is aimed to be configurable. For instance, it should be able to remove error handling or use a completely different kind of syntax tree classes. By the level of modularization that we have achieved, all this is feasible now.

A drawback of the design is that the control flow through the different modules is not obvious. It has been extremely helpful that the ACDT is able to visualize where aspects affect other components and how modifications on the aspect code change the set of matched join-points.

Table 2. Source code size comparison between the PUMA and the GNU C/C++ syntax rules

LOCs	GNU gcc/g++		PUMA	
C	c-parser.c	8676	CSyntax.cc	1786
C++	cpp-parser.cc	22964	CCSyntax.cc	2802

5   Configurability and Extensibility

The feature model in Figure 1 shows that there are a number of optional features provided by the PUMA framework. Ideally each of these features should be implemented by a single module. This make it much easier to statically configure whether a feature should be enabled. We achieved this goal for all optional features.

Most of them are implemented by means of object orientation. For instance, the "full semantic analysis" is designed according to the visitor design pattern [7]. The visitor can be instantiated by the application if a detailed analysis, which goes beyond the analysis that is performed on-the-fly during the parse process, is required. The C and C++ parsers form an inheritance hierarchy as described in the previous section. This means that the application is free to instantiate any parser on demand.

Some of the optional features are implemented by aspects or groups of aspects. For instance, the GNU and the MS Visual C++ extensions belong to this category. Both language dialects crosscut the C as well as the C++ level. The aspect-aware design of the system components and system abstractions simplifies to write these extensions a lot. For instance, it is very easy to introduce new rules into the syntax, because the name of the syntax classes is well-known and stable. Furthermore, individual syntax rules can be extended easily, because they directly represent the rules from the C/C++ standard documents. The names of the `parse()`, `build()`, `check()`, and `lookahead()` member functions of the nested classes that represent syntax rules all follow the same conventions. Therefore, their behavior can be changed easily. At the moment the GNU extension aspect code has 1420 lines of code. This does not include all GNU-specific C and C++ extensions, yet, but the most important ones, which are necessary to parse the header files of the GNU C and C++ standard libraries. The Visual C++ extension consists of 711 lines of aspect code in total. Its status is the same as the status of the GNU extension: It is not totally complete, but functional for the relevant use cases.

For the AspectC++ language extension the decision, whether it should become an aspect or a subclass of the C++ parser, was difficult. If a language inherits several syntactic and semantic rules from another language it is the natural choice to implement the parsers by using inheritance. AspectC++ extends C++ and every valid C++ program is also a valid AspectC++ program. These are arguments for deriving the AspectC++ parser from the C++ parser. On the other hand, we wanted to be open for the development of an aspect-oriented C dialect in the future. With an AspectC++ extension aspect this would be easier. The reason is illustrated in Figure 9. It shows that a single aspect can extend or modify the C and C++ language at the same time. All modification's done on the C level are automatically propagated to the C++ level, because the modifications are inherited.

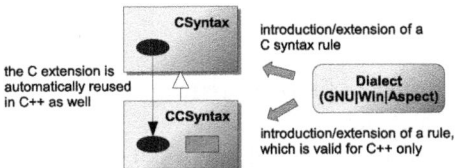

Fig. 9. Relation of the C and C++ parser classes with aspects, which implement language dialects

PUMA supports different "feature binding times" for the language dialects. They can be statically enabled or disabled by changing a single Makefile variable. For instance, most of our commercial customers are not interested in the AspectC++ extension of PUMA. Therefore, it can be disabled by this mechanism and consumes no resources at all. Besides this, all dialects can be enabled or disabled at runtime. Therefore, each of these aspects analyses the command line parameters of the application. Special options such as `--gnu` or `--gnu-<some-specific-extension>` are introduced into the command line parser. If any of these options was entered on the command line, an internal variable will be set accordingly. This variable can also be modified by the application code directly. The advice code of the dialect aspects is written in a way that it only affects the parser if the corresponding variable indicates that the feature is enabled.

6   C++1X Static Assertions: An Unanticipated Extension

This section will describe one particular extension in detail, which could not be foreseen, when PUMA was designed. It is the brand new 'static assertion' feature [13], which is likely to become part of the upcoming C++ standard "C++1X". Therefore, we regard the time needed for integrating this feature as a valid indicator that our design really meets our expectations, namely easy extensibility. Static assertions have the following syntax:

```
static_assert ( constant-expression, error-message ) ;
```

The constant expression argument is evaluated at compile time. If the static assert is located within a template and if the argument depends on a template parameter, the evaluation is postponed until the template is being instantiated. The error message is issued by the compiler if the constant expression is `false`. It is a very useful new language feature, which has the potential to make template libraries much better usable in the future.

C++1X language features are described by members of the standardization commit-tee in separate documents. These documents contain an introduction about the moti-vation for the new feature as well as a section on "proposed wording". This part lists the necessary changes to the current C++ standard in order to describe the new fea-ture properly. When we implemented the static assertion feature it turned out that we could almost literally translate this document into aspect code. The code consists of the following parts[4]:

Part	LOCs
new syntax tree class for static assertions	102
new syntax rule (slice)	77
function for the semantic analysis (slice)	100
builder function for syntax tree creation (slice)	73
policy aspect for binding connecting the new code, including the analysis of command line options and enable/disable functions	112

Only the necessary definition of a new keyword `static_assert` could not be im-plemented by an aspect. The reason is that the scanner, which is integrated in PUMA, uses a generator. Its input files are not written in C++ and, thus, are not accessible by aspects.

The feature proposal for static assertions also contains an interesting statement about the estimate time for the integration of this feature into an existing compiler:

> *"A compiler writer could certainly implement this feature, as specified, in two or three days ..."*

Our integration into PUMA took us only a single day including tests, documentation, and some additional effort, which was needed, because it was the first C++1X feature that we integrated. Even though this case study is very promising, we are aware that the integration of *all* C++1X features will nevertheless be a tremendous effort. In the GNU g++ project the integration of C++1X is still an ongoing process. However, we are very optimistic that it will be a lot easier for us, because of the aspect-oriented design. This is also absolutely necessary from the business perspective, because we would never be able to spend as much manpower into PUMA as is working on the GNU g++ project.

7   Discussion

7.1   Integration versus Separation

A general question, which arises with C++1X, is whether extensions should be im-plemented as separate aspects and slices or whether they should be directly integrated

---

[4] The LOCs include all comments (GPL headers as well as text fragments copied from the feature proposal).

into the system components and abstractions. Typically there is no benefit from quantification when extensions are to be implemented. Therefore, one might argue that an integration is less confusing for people trying to understand the system behavior. However, we believe that whenever an extension corresponds to an optional (configurable) feature, the separate and modularized implementation is the better choice. For C++1X we assume that it will have to be configurable for at least 5-10 years, because there will be a significant code base, which cannot be parsed with a C++1X parser.

7.2   Design Methodology

Software design is a difficult task, which require a lot of experience. Therefore, it is very helpful if there are patterns or idioms, which a developer can adopt. The design methodology, which we presented in Section 3, is an attempt into this direction. The same principles where applied in other domains as well. We therefore believe that they are general enough to also provide other developers with some guidance.

One of the key contributions of the design methodology is that we treat obliviousness for extensibility. Our experience is that it is not realistic to believe that arbitrary code can be extended by aspects. The design has to be aspect-aware. This means that the system abstractions and components should provide interfaces for aspects – but not for a specific aspect. For legacy code, this sometimes means a significant cost for refactoring.

7.3   AspectC++ Language Deficiencies

Our implementation of language AspectC++ is work in progress. The combination of AOP with generic and generative programming is still a research topic. During the development of PUMA we found several language problems, which will hopefully lead to an improvement of the language as well as a better design of PUMA. One of the deficiencies is the need for nested classes within CSyntax and CCSyntax that represent grammar rules. The `parse()`, `build()`, `lookahead()`, and `check()` functions are related. However, aspects can only exploit this relationship, e.g. calling the corresponding `build()` function after the execution of `parse()`, if they are all members of a common class. In the future we will investigate whether an annotation mechanism as in AspectJ [12] might solve this problem.

7.4   Other Issues

Feature interactions are a general problem of software development. Aspect-oriented programming is not the reason for this problem. It is an inherent property of certain features. Our experience is that aspects *help* to identify and understand these interactions. For instance, when two aspects affect the same join-points, the aspect weaver can warn the developer[5] and ask him to specify the correct order of advice execution explicitly.

Another issue that is sometimes raised is the problem that aspects that are written in AspectC++ rely on C++ templates in order to be generic. The consequences are not only that the developers have to deal with the non-intuitive template Syntax. Templates also carry the risk of code bloating. We have intensively studied the code size implications

---

[5] The AspectC++ weaver doesn't do that, yet.

of our design methodology and AspectC++ in other projects [17,16,18]. There was no indication that the code size grows by more than 1%. We believe that this is the case, because C++ are aware of the code bloating problem and avoid it.

8 Related Work

PUMA exploits AOP for the development of a parser. De Moor et al. had the same goal when they wrote a paper on "Aspect-Oriented Compilers" in 1999 [20]. However, while we concentrate on the parser front-end, de Moor's paper focusses on the semantic analysis with attribute grammars and the translation. A second piece of general work on this topic describes a few AspectJ idioms for compiler construction [26]. This work also assumes that there is already a syntax tree. The focus of this paper is on visitors such as an `UnparseVisitor`.

Another related approach is the design of aspect-oriented compiler construction systems called JustAdd [8]. In contrast to our design, which is centered around the grammar rules, which regard as very stable, JustAdd is centered around the syntax tree classes. It also supports to write different aspects that operate on the syntax tree such as name analysis, type checking, and code generation. Into a different direction goes the very popular C++-based parser generator *spirit*[6] . It uses C++ template metaprogramming to generate the parser. Although the grammar rules are written in C++, the description language looks like a DSL. There is no C++ grammar implementation for *spirit*, yet.

A commercial counterpart to PUMA is the DMS by Semantic Designs [2,1]. This is a generic code transformation system, which supports a number of target languages including C and C++. However, the DMS is not open source and not many details about the parsing process are known.

9 Summary and Conclusions

For the development of PUMA Aspect-Oriented Software Development and AspectC++ have worked well. Even though C++ is one of the most complex programming languages at all, the parser is still manageable. We achieved our key goals, which are configurability and extensibility. Both properties are needed to develop client-specific code analysis tools in very short time. Compared to GNU gcc/g++ the source code is quite small. The design is open for various kinds of extensions and even an unanticipated extension could be implemented quickly. Thus, we are confidant that PUMA is well prepared for the upcoming requirements.

Concerning the future of PUMA we are very optimistic. It is the best open source C++ code analysis and transformation framework that we are aware of. At the moment the project is still a bid hidden (the source code is part of AspectC++), but in the future we plan to promote it more actively. The features of the new C++1X have to be integrated as soon as the standard is officially published. Until this time we will continue to work on C++1X, starting with the features that are most likely to become part of the standard. If time and money allows it, we would also like to evolve the AspectC++ language based on the lessons learned from PUMA.

---

[6] http://spirit.sourceforge.net/

References

1. Akers, R.L., Baxter, I.D., Mehlich, M., Ellis, B.J., Luecke, K.R.: Reengineering C++ component models via automatic program transformation. In: WCRE 2005: Proceedings of the 12th Working Conference on Reverse Engineering, pp. 13–22. IEEE Computer Society, Washington, DC, USA (2005)
2. Baxter, I.D.: Design maintenance systems. Communications of the ACM 35(4), 73–89 (1992)
3. Czarnecki, K., Eisenecker, U.W.: Generative Programming. Methods, Tools and Applications. Addison-Wesley, Reading (2000)
4. Duvall, P., Matyas, S., Glover, A.: Continuous integration: improving software quality and reducing risk. Addison-Wesley Professional, Reading (2007)
5. Filman, R.E., Friedman, D.P.: Aspect-oriented programming is quantification and obliviousness. In: Workshop on Advanced SoC (OOPSLA 2000) (October 2000)
6. Gal, A., Schröder-Preikschat, W., Spinczyk, O.: AspectC++: Language proposal and prototype implementation. In: Proceedings of the OOPSLA 2001 Workshop on Advanced Separation of Concerns in Object-Oriented Systems, Tampa, Florida (October 2001)
7. Gamma, E., Helm, R., Johnson, R., Vlissides, J.: Design Patterns: Elements of Reusable Object-Oriented Software. Addison-Wesley, Reading (1995)
8. Hedin, G., Magnusson, E.: Jastadd: an aspect-oriented compiler construction system. Science of Computer Programming 47(1), 37–58 (2003)
9. The British Standards Institute. The C++ Standard (Incorporating Technical Corrigendum No. 1), 2 edn. John Wiley & Sons, Inc., Chichester (2003); Printed version of the ISO/IEC 14882:2003 standard
10. ISO. The ANSI C standard (C99). Technical Report WG14 N1124, ISO/IEC (1999)
11. Johnson, S.C., Sethi, R.: Yacc: a parser generator. pp. 347–374 (1990)
12. Kiczales, G., Hilsdale, E., Hugunin, J., Kersten, M., Palm, J., Griswold, W.G.: An Overview of AspectJ. In: Lindskov Knudsen, J. (ed.) ECOOP 2001. LNCS, vol. 2072, pp. 327–353. Springer, Heidelberg (2001)
13. Klarer, R., Maddock, J., Dawes, B., Hinnant, H.: Proposal to add static assertions to the core language (revision 3). Technical Report SC22/WG21/N1720, ISO/IEC (October 2004)
14. Lohmann, D.: Aspect Awareness in the Development of Configurable System Software. PhD thesis, Friedrich-Alexander University Erlangen-Nuremberg (2009)
15. Lohmann, D., Blaschke, G., Spinczyk, O.: Generic Advice: On the Combination of AOP with Generative Programming in AspectC++. In: Karsai, G., Visser, E. (eds.) GPCE 2004. LNCS, vol. 3286, pp. 55–74. Springer, Heidelberg (2004)
16. Lohmann, D., Hofer, W., Schröder-Preikschat, W., Streicher, J., Spinczyk, O.: CiAO: An aspect-oriented operating-system family for resource-constrained embedded systems. In: Proceedings of the 2009 USENIX Annual Technical Conference, pp. 215–228. USENIX Association, Berkeley (2009)
17. Lohmann, D., Scheler, F., Tartler, R., Spinczyk, O., Schröder-Preikschat, W.: A quantitative analysis of aspects in the eCos kernel. In: Proceedings of the EuroSys 2006 Conference (EuroSys 2006), pp. 191–204. ACM Press, New York (2006)
18. Lohmann, D., Spinczyk, O., Schröder-Preikschat, W.: Lean and Efficient System Software Product Lines: Where Aspects Beat Objects. In: Rashid, A., Liu, Y. (eds.) Transactions on Aspect-Oriented Software Development II. LNCS, vol. 4242, pp. 227–255. Springer, Heidelberg (2006)
19. Mahrenholz, D., Spinczyk, O., Gal, A., Schröder-Preikschat, W.: An aspect-orientied implementation of interrupt synchronization in the PURE operating system family. In: Proceedings of the 5th ECOOP Workshop on Object Orientation and Operating Systems (ECOOP-OOOSWS 2002), Malaga, Spanien, pp. 49–54 (June 2002)

20. de Moor, O., Peyton-Jones, S., Van Wyk, E.: Aspect-Oriented Compilers. In: Busch, C. (ed.) GCSE 1999. LNCS, vol. 1799, pp. 121–133. Springer, Heidelberg (2000)
21. Parr, T.: The Definitive ANTLR Reference: Building Domain-Specific Languages. Pragmatic Bookshelf (2007)
22. Spinczyk, O., Lohmann, D.: The design and implementation of AspectC++. Knowledge-Based Systems, Special Issue on Techniques to Produce Intelligent Secure Software 20(7), 636–651 (2007)
23. Steimann, F.: The paradoxical success of aspect-oriented programming. In: Proceedings of the 21st ACM Conference on Object-Oriented Programming, Systems, Languages, and Applications (OOPSLA 2006), pp. 481–497. ACM Press, New York (2006)
24. Tartler, R., Lohmann, D., Schröder-Preikschat, W., Spinczyk, O.: Dynamic AspectC++: Generic advice at any time. In: Fujita, H., Marík, V. (eds.) The 8th International Conference on Software Methodologies, Tools and Techniques, Frontiers in Artificial Intelligence and Applications, Prag, Czech Republic, pp. 165–186. IOS Press, Amsterdam (2009)
25. The Design Automation Standards Committee of the IEEE Computer Society. IEEE Standard 1666-2005: SystemC. IEEE (2005)
26. Wu, X., Bryant, B.R., Gray, J., Roychoudhury, S., Mernik, M.: Separation of concerns in compiler development using aspect-orientation. In: SAC 2006: Proceedings of the 2006 ACM Symposium on Applied Computing, pp. 1585–1590. ACM, New York (2006)

Building a Digital Publishing Platform Using AOSD
Experiences and Lessons Learned

Dimitri Van Landuyt, Steven Op de beeck,
Eddy Truyen, and Pierre Verbaeten

DistriNet, Katholieke Universiteit Leuven
Celestijnenlaan 200A
B-3001 Leuven, Belgium
{dimitri.vanlanduyt,steven.opdebeeck,
eddy.truyen,pierre.verbaeten}@cs.kuleuven.be

Abstract. This paper presents the results of applying aspect-oriented methods and techniques during the construction of a demonstrator of an industry-grade digital publishing platform. In a rapidly evolving publishing landscape, publishing companies will have a competitive advantage in the long run if their supporting software infrastructure can sustain evolution. In this paper, we show how a component-based software architecture is refactored using AOSD techniques, and how this leads to an improved variability and evolvability of the publishing infrastructure by enabling invasive features to be introduced easily and dynamically. Finally, we provide an in-depth analysis of our main experiences and lessons learned during development of this demonstrator, in terms of three of the industrial acceptance criteria of a programming paradigm: its expressivity, its efficiency, and compatibility. The strength of this demonstrator lies in the fact that it presents a realistic, and high-effort case study, which is the result of collaboration with real-world industrial actors in the news publishing field.

1 Introduction

To demonstrate the benefits of Aspect-Oriented Software Development (AOSD) to industry, the AOSD-Europe project [1] has presented several demonstrators of successful applications of AOSD in real-life software systems. The final demonstrator is about the application of AOSD during the development of a digital publishing system.

Over the last four years, our research group has built up an expertise in various application domains including e-media, e-government and e-health, hereby actively collaborating in research projects with industrial partners from these respective domains. In the projects on e-media [2,3,4,5], we have cooperated extensively with our industry publishing partner Concentra. Results of this cooperation are the description of the requirements for digital publishing, and the documentation of a component-based software architecture that is strongly based

S. Katz et al. (Eds.): Transactions on AOSD VIII, LNCS 6580, pp. 163–195, 2011.

on Concentra's software infrastructure [6]. This architecture has support for the basic functionalities of digital publishing. For the demonstrator, we focused our efforts on news delivery and advertising towards the consumer. Other concerns that would be addressed in a full fledged publishing system, like the journalist's workflow, news aggregation, and integration with third party services, were considered out of scope.

The goal of the digital publishing demonstrator is to show that an aspect-oriented architecture is better equipped to deal with unanticipated change by leveraging aspects as optional features. It will also show how aspect-orientation can increase the variability of these optional features from requirements to runtime. Secondly, the demonstrator shows the implementation and deployment of the system using an industry-class aspect-oriented middleware platform: the JBoss application server, in combination with JBoss AOP [7].

The *fil rouge* of the demonstrator is an evolution scenario that mimicks a real-world shift in digital publishing. We started from a classical component-based infrastructure, which we then refactored, in terms of requirements and architecture, to an infrastructure that applies aspect-orientation. Finally, we performed a realistic evolution scenario that extends this AO infrastructure with more advanced digital publishing functionalities, such as offering the media consumer personalized or mobile content.

The demonstrator has been developed by a team of three PhD students and one senior researcher who have approximately spent a total of 2 man years on the completion of the project. The resulting implementation consists of around 45 thousand lines of code.

Expressivity, efficiency, and compatibility are three important criteria for industrial acceptance that indicate a paradigms potential, some of its costs and ease of integration [8]. As such, we touch on these criteria throughout the paper.

Section 2 motivates this work. It provides more details on the domain of digital publishing, and the problems that impede its transition into the future of publishing. It explains why we believe that AOSD can help publishers tackle some of the problems. Then, Section 3 shows how we tailored our development process to support the desired evolvability, from requirements to deployment. It describes how we designed, implemented, and deployed our aspect-oriented publishing architecture. As such, it touches upon the expressivity criterion as it discusses various AO-modeling techniques, traceability to implementation and the applications of variability. Consequently, Section 4 presents a quantitative evaluation of the evolvability claims of our AO architecture. It addresses the efficiency criterion in a performance evaluation of dynamic aspect-oriented composition, where we compare a functionally equivalent AO and OO implementation. Then, we present our experiences and lessons learned from developing this demonstrator in Section 5. We address the compatibility criterion, more specifically in terms of existing tool-support. Also, we revisit the other two criteria and discuss additional lessons learned that might be valuable from an industry perspective. Finally, Section 6 concludes the paper.

2   Motivation

The news publishing domain has evolved drastically over the last decade. In Section 2.1, we discuss these evolutions and the challenges they pose on classical news publishers. Then, in Section 2.2, we argue why aspect-oriented software development (AOSD) is a suitable paradigm to cope with these evolutions.

2.1   Trends and Evolutions in News Publishing

Ever since the introduction of the Internet in common households —and with it, the availability of on-line news portals— the way in which news is produced and distributed has been changing significantly [9]. The business landscape of publishing has been evolving drastically towards a more competitive environment, and more recent trends, including user-generated content (blogs, wikis, etc) [10] and social networks, contribute to this even further. A lot of new and unexpected players emerged in the domain, such as the Google News service [11] which aggregates news content from thousands of publishers and bundles this content into one product. This has put a lot of pressure on the traditional publishing companies to evolve into more competitive news offerings.

There has been a trend towards *digital publishing platforms* that support multiple bundled service offerings depending on the targeted group of customers. A digital publishing platform offers news in different media formats and sizes, to be delivered through different telecommunication channels, and to be displayed on different end user terminals and devices. In this way, the daily (either printed or on-line) newspaper is complemented with an aggregation of differentiated services. These services may also offer personalized content and advertisements, tailored to the interests of individual customers, their location, situation and behavior.

Although it may not be clear yet whether this kind of flexible service offering represents the future of news publishing, it is certain that publishing companies will gain a competitive advantage if their ICT infrastructure can rapidly evolve towards supporting these new kinds of offerings.

Over the last five years, we have collaborated closely with a traditional news publisher, Concentra media, in a number of research projects on digital news and e-media [2,3,4,5]. One of the results of these projects is a fully documented component-based software architecture [6] that matches closely the publishing platform in use by Concentra. Figure 1 depicts the high-level system deployment of this publishing platform. Below, we highlight the diverse complexities dealt with in this platform:

- The top-left side of the figure depicts the different output channels. The publishing platform delivers news (i) to mobile users connecting *on the move* using a mobile device (through a telecom infrastructure), (ii) to home users that connect through the publisher website, and (iii) by means of the classical delivery mechanisms of printing and physical delivery of the newspaper.

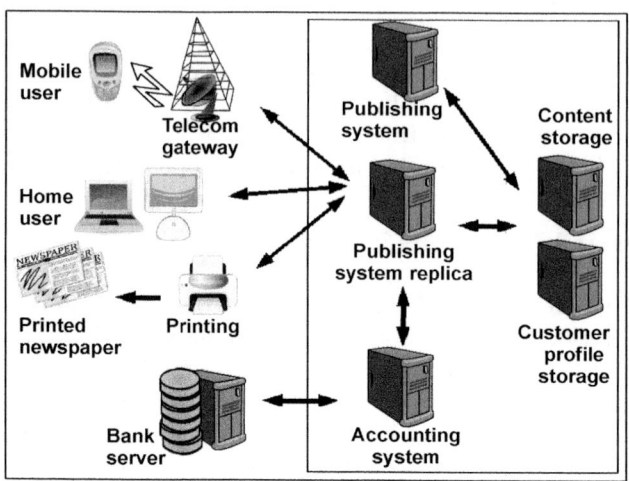

Fig. 1. Deployment view of a typical digital publishing platform

- At the center of the figure, the publishing server is presented, together with a replica for availability, fault-tolerance, and performance. These nodes consist of the actual news services offered by the publisher.
- At the bottom side of the figure, the accounting system is shown, connecting the publishing servers to financial institutions (e.g. bank servers) to request payment.
- At the right-hand side of the figure, two separate back-end servers are represented, one for each of the main types of data. The news content consists of articles, advertisements, advertisement reservations, and their meta-data (tags, etc). The user profile information consists of all customer information, together with user interests that are both statical (defined by the user himself) and dynamical (inferred by the publishing system).

As a result of assessing the impact of the many evolutions in the publishing domain on this component-based architecture, we have experienced several problems which are mostly related to limited evolvability and variability. New features which were not anticipated during the initial architecture could not be added in a modular manner because their introduction required invasive changes across multiple components of the system. Furthermore, publishers want to implement and deploy new features in a way that doesn't interrupt existing services. In addition, they want to be able to sell these features as separate services (or as part of service bundles) that can be enabled on a per-user basis. This kind of deploy-and run-time variability is currently not supported in the publishing system. It would require further heavy modification of the current infrastructure and the supporting deployment frameworks to develop a custom frame that supports variability.

2.2   Rationale for an Aspect-Oriented News Publishing Platform

In this demonstrator, we show how aspect-oriented software development (AOSD) can be adopted to address these problems. The main rationale for developing the demonstrator using AOSD is that we expect the flexibility and dynamism of aspect-oriented composition mechanisms to achieve the desired levels of evolvability and variability.

Evolvability. The development scenario of the demonstrator mimics the development activities that a classical publishing company (like Concentra) would have to perform if it adopted AOSD.

To implement and deploy a digital publishing platform in a realistic setting, we have to take into account that the existing ICT infrastructures of publishing companies have grown and evolved over the years. It would be unrealistic to assume that we can start from scratch. Various concerns in current publishing systems (such as authentication, user profiling, verification, rights management, feedback, etc.) were implemented in different iteration over the course of time. Moreover, a lot of these concerns are known to cut across the existing workflow of the publishing company. Evolving these crosscutting concerns is a very complex matter because it requires invasive changes to multiple software components of the existing ICT infrastructure. These intrusive modifications have set back the overall quality and maintainability of the publishing infrastructure.

Therefore, the existing component-based publishing infrastructure is first refactored, from its requirements to architecture, all the way down to deployment, into an infrastructure that uses aspect-oriented concepts and techniques. Then, we perform software evolution on this publishing system, based on an evolution scenario that mimics the real-world challenges outlined above in Section 2.1. In Section 4, we show that the resulting architecture is better equipped to deal with software evolution, when compared to its non-AO counterpart.

Variability. The demonstrator also shows that the application of AOSD allows complex, domain-specific features such as *user tracking* and *personalization* to be implemented separately and deployed into the system dynamically. The constructed AO-architecture leverages aspects as modular service extensions that represent specific features. This adds a real business value for the publisher, as it enables him to adapt his business strategy in a more responsive manner to market changes, and shorten the time to deliver new and competitive features. For example, consider one instance of the publishing system in which a specific distinction is made between *regular* and *premium* users. By default, each user is a regular user, but users can pay an additional monthly fee to become premium users. The regular user by default does not enjoy a personalized news service, while the premium user does (as he pays for the *personalization* feature). By providing *personalization* and *accounting* as features that are loosely coupled in the publishing platform, such policies can be instated, adapted, or disabled easily at run-time. Section 3.4 provides a more technical description of how AO techniques (including dynamic AOP) enable this run-time variability.

3   Developing Using AOSD

This section discusses the adopted software development process to produce the digital publishing demonstrator. We show how the evolution scenario affects the requirements and architecture, by discussing the most important changes that were introduced. This is illustrated in terms of actual artifacts that apply aspect-oriented modeling techniques. The changes include the identification and separation of crosscutting concerns during requirements, and the introduction of the first-level entity for capturing AO-composition in architecture. We also show how a new (crosscutting) requirement, *user tracking*, is introduced into the requirements and aspect-oriented architecture.

Figure 2 outlines this section. The first column lists the main activities of the software development life-cycle. The various artifacts created in each development stage are outlined in the second column of the figure as sets of bulleted lists. The third column presents the traceability relations between these artifacts: it documents the mapping between the artifacts across the phases of the software development life-cycle. During development, we documented the traceability relations between the artifacts manually as a part of the development management.

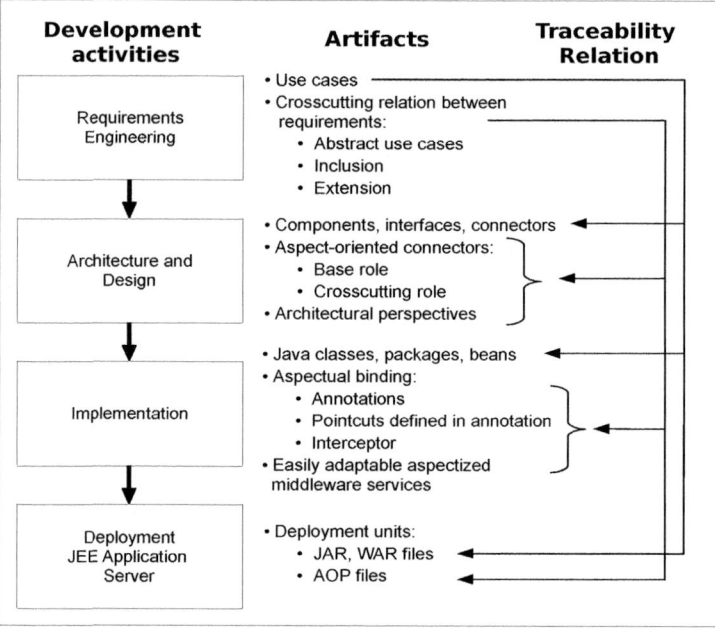

Fig. 2. Overview of the development process for the digital publishing demonstrator

This section starts with a high-level overview of the requirements space and describes how we have addressed and described crosscutting requirements. Subsequently, Section 3.2 gives an overview of how we created the aspect-oriented architecture. Section 3.3 details how we implemented aspect-oriented composition in JBoss AOP. Finally, Section 3.4 discusses deployment of JBoss applications with a focus on the dynamic nature.

Availability of source materials. The full documentation, including requirements, architecture design, various models, source code of the implementation, build scripts, deployment and installation instructions, is publicly available on the project's website [12].

3.1   Requirements Engineering

As a result of close cooperation with our industry publishing partner, Concentra, the requirements of the existing digital publishing system were already described as use cases [13,14]. For practical reasons, we selected a subset of these use cases for the demonstrator (as discussed in Section 1).

We present the approach we applied to identify crosscutting concerns and separate them from the requirement descriptions.

Identification of crosscutting concerns. To investigate the nature of the identified concerns, we have manually created a *concern diffusion* matrix that maps use cases to concerns. This matrix indicates per use case and per concern whether the use case is affected by the concern. A concern that affects a large number of the use cases is identified as a crosscutting concern. We list the important crosscutting concerns that were identified:

1. **Security:** Unauthenticated users or authenticated users with insufficient privileges must be denied some actions, like changing the meta-information of advertisements, or reading articles without having subscribed.
2. **Accounting:** The accounting concern covers the financial aspects of the system. Indeed, the publisher wants to be paid for publishing an advertisement. Also, the media consumers are billed for using the news services based on their usage.
3. **User tracking:** For the publisher, it is crucial to keep track of his target audience, and to have an up-to-date view on *what is hot and what is not*. To this end, the user tracking functionality is responsible for keeping track of news consumption behavior in a *view log*, and for inferring user preferences from this information.
4. **Personalization:** One way to reach a large audience is to offer personalized new services, i.e. present only those news items that the media consumers are interested in. The consumer's interests are mainly inferred from his reading behavior (cf. the *user tracking* concern). Also, a result of *personalization* is *direct marketing*: it allows advertisers to target specific segments of media

consumers that are particularly interested in the advertised products and services. Also, the advertiser is offered a more specific view on the market segments in which his advertisements were most successful.

For example, a crosscutting concern like *user tracking* expands a number of the core publishing use cases with additional functionality related to user tracking.

To illustrate, a subset of the entire matrix for the publishing platform is presented in Table 1. This table only shows the use cases related to news delivery.

Table 1. This table presents the mapping from the stakeholders' concerns to the use cases

Use case	security	accounting	user tracking	personalization
subscribe	x	x		
unsubscribe	x	x		
use a service	x		x	
list articles	x		x	x
list articles by category	x		x	x
list articles by tag	x		x	x
read an article	x		x	

This table allows us to identify *crosscutting concerns*, i.e. concerns whose description are scattered across multiple use cases. The crosscutting concerns in the demonstrator are *security* and *accounting*, which are considered non-functional, and *user tracking* and *personalization*, which are considered functional since they are a part of the publishing domain and help realize important features.

Separation of crosscutting concerns. The identified crosscutting concerns are then represented modularly by remodularizing the set of uses cases. Figure 3 illustrates how this is done for the *user tracking* concern: a separate use case *send viewing information* is introduced and the standard UML use case *extension* mechanism is used to bind the crosscutting use case to the existing use cases [15]. For each crosscutting concern, multiple of such crosscutting use cases have been introduced.

3.2   Architecture and Design

The original component-based architecture is presented in Figure 4 by means of the component-and-connector (C&C) architectural view [16]. This architecture supports a very basic news publishing infrastructure. It is structured in three tiers, according to the multi-tier architectural pattern. These are the client tier, business tier, and the data tier. Tiers are annotated in Figure 4 by grouping the components together in columns, above which the tier names are placed.

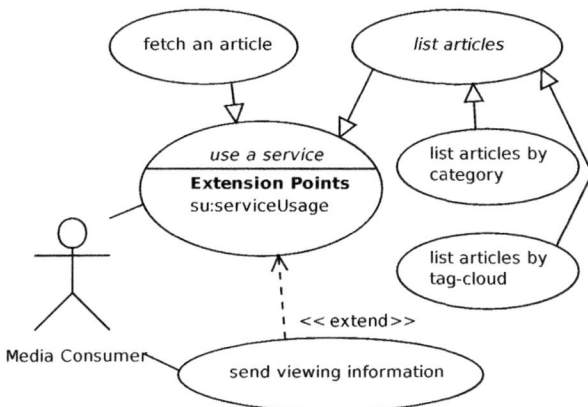

Fig. 3. Use case diagram that presents several use cases offered to the media consumer. The *send viewing information* use case is a crosscutting requirement.

Even in this core architecture, *authentication, authorization*, and *accounting* are crosscutting concerns. The problem with the way of representing crosscutting concerns in Figure 4 is that the composition of the `Authentication &` `Authorization` component with the rest of the system is represented as a vague collection of dependencies. As such the semantics of the composition is not captured as a first-class entity but must be manually extracted from the diagram by iterating over all dependencies that are directed towards the `Authentication` `& Authorization` component.

To solve this issue, we employed an approach for modeling aspects in architectural views, called AO-ADL [17]. This approach does not distinguish a specialized component element for representing aspectual behavior, but introduces a specific aspect-oriented connector for representing aspect-oriented composition logic as first-class entity. This way, aspect-oriented composition exists alongside traditional composition which involves matching *provided* and *required* component interfaces.

Both, a graphical notation (see Figure 5) and a more detailed notation (XML-based) are available. The graphical notation gives a good structural overview of the overall AO architecture, while the textual notation is used in a tool for modeling [18] and transforming aspect-oriented connectors.

To document composition logic in architectural description, we use a notation as in Listing 1. It is AO-ADL, but it uses indentation and shorter keywords to increase readability (instead of XML). The *base role* in Listing 1 aggregates all join points that represent the base in the AO-composition. The main difference with the pointcut in typical joint point models, is that a *base role* is defined and maintained together with the base module it belongs to. The `service usage` base role aggregates all operations in the news interface that are concerned with the —in publishing terms— usage of a service. The *aspectual connector* in Listing 2

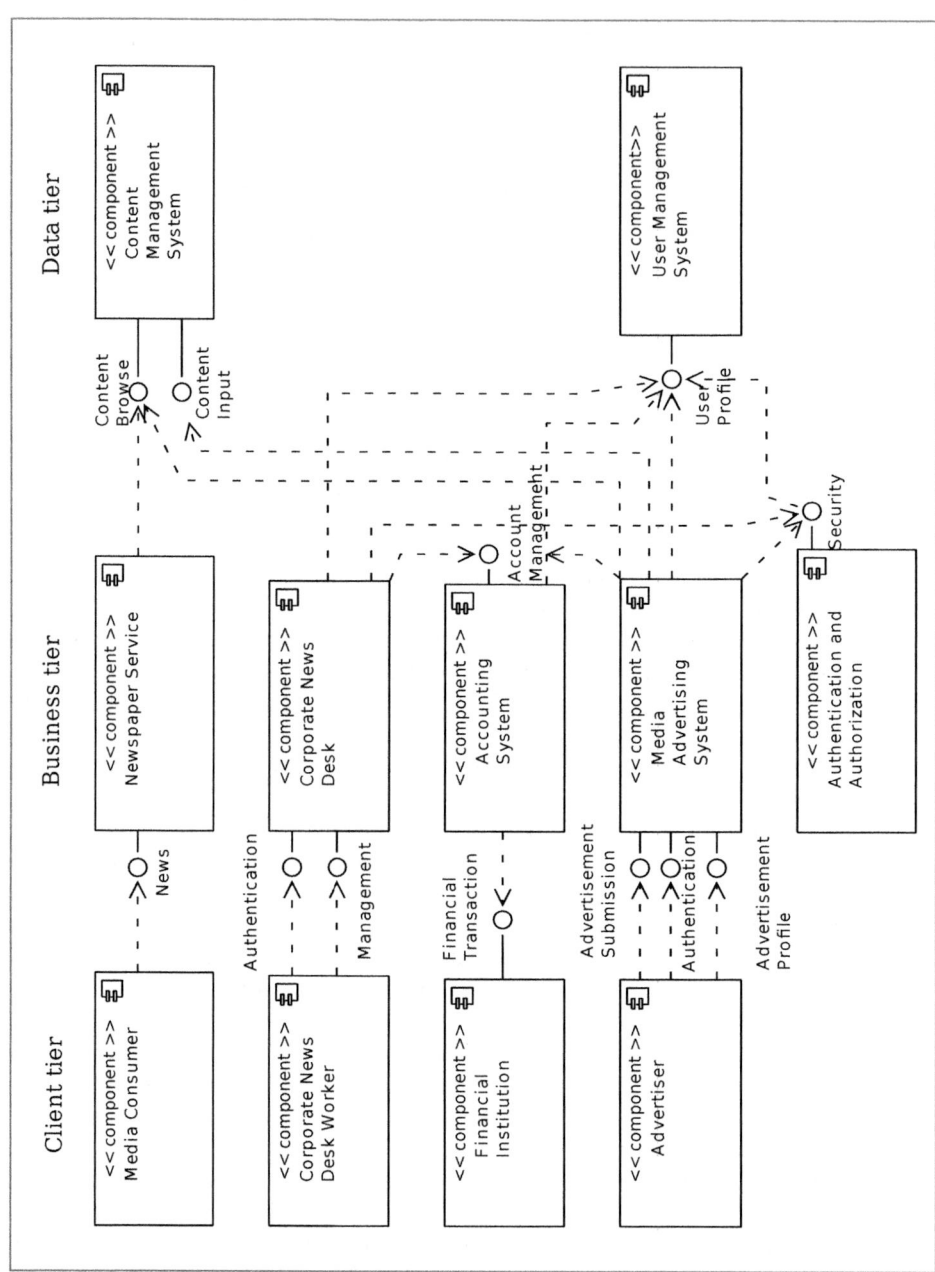

Fig. 4. Component-and-connector view of the original architecture

composes *crosscutting role*, that points to an advising operation `consultTag(..)`, with the *base role* `service` usage. Meaning, every time, after a call to one of the service usage methods with a parameter of type `Tag` (`Category` is-a `Tag`), the usage of this tag will be tracked and stored in that user's profile.

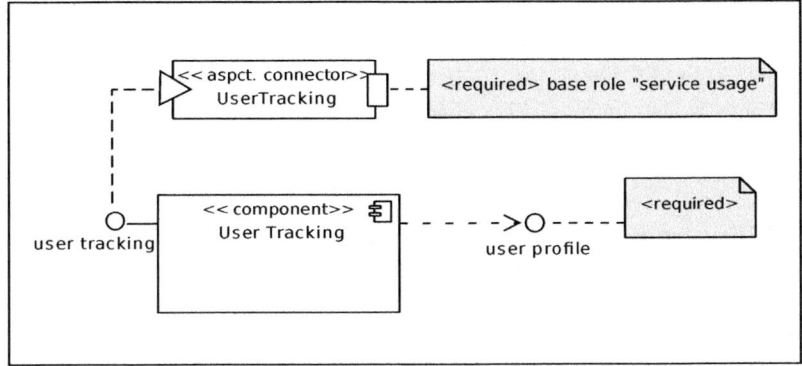

Fig. 5. User tracking perspective of the digital publishing infrastructure

baseRole: "service usage"
    component: "Newspaper Service"
        interface: "news"
            operation: "listArticlesForTag (Tag ?tag)"
            operation: "getSubCategories (Category ?tag)"
            operation: "listArticlesForCategory (Category ?tag)"
            operation: "fetchArticle (ContentID ?contentId)"
            # ...

Listing 1. Part of the `service` usage base role

aspectualConnector: "UserTracking"

    crosscuttingRole: "user tracking: tag listing"
        interface: "user tracking"
            operation: "void consultedTag (int ?tag)"

    crosscut :
        sequence: after returning
        baseBinding: "service usage"
        crosscuttingBinding : "user tracking: tag listing"

Listing 2. Part of the `user tracking` connector

An overview of the *user tracking* perspective is given in Figure 5. It shows how the crosscutting composition is specified using an AO-connector called `UserTracking`. This connector binds to the *service usage* base role, which is defined in Listing 1.

By representing aspectual connectors as first-class entities, we have a modular unit for defining the semantics of crosscutting compositions. Additionally the AO-ADL notation is used for defining a full architectural specification of the aspect-oriented connectors. The ensued benefits are a clearer representation of crosscutting concerns, their identification, maintenance and evolution. Productivity is also increased because the AO-ADL notation is formal enough to generate the design and implementation of aspect-oriented connectors automatically.

Traceability from architecture to implementation. As will be elaborated later on, aspect-oriented middleware is used for implementing and deploying the software of the digital publishing demonstrator. Current state-of-the-art aspect-oriented middleware platforms support a programming model that is very similar to the aspect-oriented architecture approach for representing aspects and components [19] —in the sense that there is no specialized component for representing aspectual behavior, but there is a specific construct for representing aspect-oriented composition logic as a first-class entity. Because of this similarity, a smooth transition from architecture towards implementation on top of aspect-oriented middleware is enabled — provided that the components of the C&C view are mapped to units of implementation. Specifying this mapping from architectural components to implementation modules is the goal of the module viewpoint [17]. Similarly, smooth deployment of the components is enabled, provided the mapping from architectural components to a particular distributed architecture is specified in the deployment view.

3.3   Implementation

We chose the JBoss middleware platform [7] for implementing and deploying the software of the digital publishing demonstrator because it is one of the more industry-ready aspect-oriented platforms, next to Spring [20]. JBoss is EJB 3.0 compliant. The built-in JBoss AOP framework offers powerful support for implementing aspect-oriented composition logic. More importantly for the publishing demonstrator, its advanced dynamic AOP features enable us to attain the desired degree of run-time variability. We discuss this key advantage of JBoss AOP in Section 3.3. The JBoss application server uses JBoss AOP internally for modularly implementing various services such as transactions and security.

In the demonstrator, all components are implemented in pure Java and aspect-oriented connectors are directly implemented using JBoss AOP aspects. Similar to the architectural level, there is no essential difference between traditional and aspectual components, except that some aspectual components can be implemented by reusing and or customizing pre-packaged aspects found in the JBoss application server such as *security*.

Implementing AO-connectors in JBoss AOP. JBoss AOP offers several ways of implementing an aspect-oriented composition: providing bindings through XML, annotation-driven bindings, specializing an `Interceptor` class and binding that to a pointcut. During development of the demonstrator, we have selected one particular way to define such a composition:

1. An aspect is implemented as a regular java class that is annotated with the JBoss AOP `@Aspect` annotation.
2. The pointcut and advice are specified by annotating a regular method with the JBoss AOP `@Bind()` annotation. This method is then considered to be an advice method. This annotation accepts two arguments: (i) the advice type (before, after or around), and (ii) the pointcut expression. In the demonstrator, the pointcut quantifies over Java annotations placed in the base code, and adds possible constraints on argument types or run-time characteristics that must be met before the pointcut is to become active.
3. An advice method is specified that delegates to another component. In JBoss AOP, this method must have a `@JoinPoint` annotated argument, through which an object representation of the join point is offered to the advice method. To pass other required contextual information to the advice method, other `@Arg`-annotated arguments are passed.

An example of a JBoss AOP aspect is presented in Listing 3. In this example, the class `UserTrackingConnector` is annotated with `@Aspect` indicating that it encapsulates the implementation of the corresponding aspect-oriented connector in the architecture. It offers one method `consultedTag`, which is bound to the pointcut specified in the `@Bind` annotation.

The pointcut matches with the execution of any method that is annotated with the `@ServiceUsage` annotation and has a `Tag` as one of its parameter types. The `@ServiceUsage` annotation is defined by ourselves and derived from the previous development stages: it maps to one of the extension points (see Figure 3) that have been declared in the use case descriptions, and to one of the base roles (see Listing 1) that were declared in the architectural descriptions. The second parameter of the `@Bind` annotation specifies the type of advice, in this case this is `after` advice, meaning that this aspect will be invoked after the execution of the original method.

The advice method `consultedTag` is responsible for directly invoking another component –the `User Tracking` component– which stores this information in the user profile and derives new user interests from this. This is roughly similar to the gang-of-four Adapter design pattern [21]: the matching of the pointcut indicates a certain event in the base, which in turn must be *adapted* to match the component interface that delivers the advice functionality.

The main advantage of this particular pattern to specify aspectual composition is that the source code of regular components does not contain any pointcut and advice declarations. Indeed, if regular component interface methods would serve as advice methods (for example, the `consultedTag()` method offered by the `User Tracking` component), these would have to comply to a certain signature (e.g. having specific advice methods with a `MethodInvocation` or `JoinPoint` parameter). This would obviously hinder the reuse of the components in non-aspectual compositions, where such signature would not make sense. Also, this would increase the degree of invasiveness of AO-specific artifacts to the advising components.

```
@Aspect
public class UserTrackingConnector {
    @Bind(pointcut = "execution(public * news->
        @news.annotations.ServiceUsage(Tag tag)",
            type = AdviceType.AFTER)
    public void consultedTag(@JoinPoint JoinPointBean mjp,
            @Arg Tag tag) {
        getUtBean().consultedTag(tag);
        getUtBean().evaluateInterests();
    }
}
```

Listing 3. A JBoss AOP aspect for *user tracking* that binds to the `@ServiceUsage` annotation

Reusing middleware services: aspects under cover. Traditional container-based middleware platforms are typically equipped with several services that support different non-functional requirements such as *transaction management, asynchronous messaging* and *security* (*authentication* and *authorization*). The implementation of these services in traditional middleware platforms is however often monolithic because there is a high coupling between the services and the middleware container. As a negative consequence, there is often no easy way to adapt the implementation of a particular middleware service. Nor is it possible to remove unneeded services from the container, or install new (third-party) middleware services. For example, in a classical JEE container like the GlassFish application server [22], it is not possible to remove *transaction handling*, even when such functionality is not needed.

This lack of adaptability often limits the reusability of the middleware services. When a certain middleware service does not comply to the exact requirements of the application, the application developer has no option left than to fully implement its own specific requirements on top of the middleware, without being able to reuse parts of the middleware service implementation. Suppose for example that the built-in *authorization* service offers role-based access control, while the application requires also mandatory access control. In an ideal world, the application developer would like to implement the enforcement of the mandatory access control as an incremental replacement of the role-based access control service. However, currently, the application developer must fully implement mandatory access control on top of a "fat" middleware container, which is considered rather useless from a security perspective.

In JBoss' EJB 3.0 application server, such downsides are tackled by using JBoss AOP for implementing the middleware services. In the application server, some mission-critical services such as *transaction management, asynchronous messaging*, and *security* (*authentication* and *authorization*) are composed aspectually to the middleware.

More importantly, the aspect-oriented implementation of the application server exploits the existing standardized annotations that are defined as part of the EJB 3.0 standard. The aspects in the middleware container uses these annotations as stable interface for binding themselves to the application. For example, the role-based access control aspect uses the @RolesAllowed annotation defined in the EJB3 standard. Listing 4 illustrates the standard usage of this annotation by the application developer as specified in the EJB standard. By placing the annotation in the definition of the class, the access control logic to all methods is set to a default, in this case to all users in the "anonymous" or "media consumer" role. For one method —fetching an article— this access control logic is overridden: only authenticated media consumers are allowed to read full articles. This illustrates the ease to customize existing middleware services by reusing aspectual bindings: in this case, the developer only needs to use the right annotation, and should not be aware of the aspects under cover and their complexities.

```
@RolesAllowed (  {"anonymous" ,  "media  consumer"}  )
public  class  NewsBean  implements  News  {
    @RolesAllowed ("media  consumer")
    public  Pair  fetchArticle (ContentItemId  contentId ){  .. }
    public  Category  getCategory (String  cat )  {  .. }
}
```

Listing 4. Illustration of the re-use of standard EJB annotations in the **newspaper service** component

3.4 Deployment and Configuration

Deploying a particular variant of the publishing infrastructure is a matter of selecting the additional aspectual components one wants to add to the base system. Such aspectual components are packaged together with their aspectual connector as separate deployment units.

Deployment involves mapping the different implementation modules to units of deployment. AOSD provides good support for *feature-oriented* decomposition [23,24,25,26,27]. This is elaborated below:

- **Features.** Specific features are represented in the form of aspects. Each aspect is a modular extension to the base architecture, extending the existing base functionalities with crosscutting functionalities.
- **Variation points.** These are certain points in execution where variation —the addition of certain features— is expected. As mentioned above, these

points are represented by plain java annotations in the demonstrator. One example is the `ServiceUsage` annotation. These are points in the base architecture that are exposed to the outside world, and open for extension.

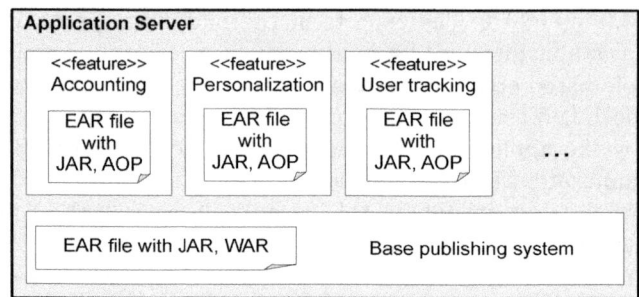

Fig. 6. Feature-based variability in a system on top of JBoss

Table 2. The build process from code unit to deployment unit

Type	Source Folder	Intermediary	Deployment Unit
Component	/componentCode	.jar	
Component interface	/interfaces	.jar	base .ear
Web code	/webcode	.war	
Aspectual component	/componentCode	.jar	
Asp. component interface	/interfaces	.jar	aspect .ear
Aspectual connector	/aop	.aop	
JUnit Test code	/tests	.class	in tmp folder

This has an impact on the way we build our implementation artifacts into deployment units. In order to be able to deploy and undeploy features as a whole, the source code artifacts must be packaged "per feature". The different deployment units (enterprise application package (.ear) files) are presented graphically in figure 6. It represents the base system, in which the crosscutting concerns are optional features such as *user tracking, personalization* and *accounting.* Table 2 shows the logical mapping between source code artifacts and .ear files. All components and web code artifacts related to the base publishing system are packaged in a single .ear file. The features on the other hand are all packaged into separate .ear files such that they can be deployed separately or in a mixed combination. Notice that an aspectual component's code is packaged together with its corresponding aspect-oriented connector. After all, these two artifacts both contribute to the implementation of the feature and therefore should be deployed as one atomic unit.

Either deploy-time or run-time aspect interception techniques can be used for creating customized variants of the publishing platform. How to use these two different interception techniques is described next.

```
<project name="e-publishing: settings" basedir="..">
  <property name="projects" value="diginews shared ,cms,ums,efi ,
    security context ,user credentials ,authentication service ,
    newspaper service ,cnd,mas,ut ,accounting ,cnd presentation ,
    mas presentation ,newspaper presentation ,aspect manager,
    personalization"/>
  [...]
</project>
```

Listing 5. Example of the `settings.xml` file

Deploy-time configuration. In theory, deploying a feature into the system is as simple as dropping the corresponding `.ear` file in a specific `deploy` directory of the JBoss application server. The application server will automatically detect all `.ear` files in this directory and start installing them. In order to make the build and deployment process as easy as possible for the user, we have defined several Ant scripts [28] that handle some of the low-level packaging and deployment details.

These Ant scripts can be found in the `_build` folder of the source code. The `settings.xml` file (see Listing 5) is most relevant for the user. In this file, the `project` variable enumerates the parts of the application that must be deployed. To create a variant of the publishing system at deployment-time, the user must only adapt this variable to the desired set of features.

Run-time (re-)configuration. The JBoss AOP middleware also enables such product variability at run-time; i.e. aspects can be enabled and disabled programmatically based on run-time decisions. To this end, the JBoss AOP libraries include the so-called `Aspect Manager`, which allows the programmer to (1) consult the state of the aspects at run-time, and (2) manipulate the state of the aspects at run-time (e.g. add advice bindings, broaden, narrow or redefine pointcuts of existing advice bindings, disable advice bindings altogether, ...). Figure 7 presents a screenshot of a straightforward web front-end to the JBoss Aspect Manager that was developed for the demonstrator. This front-end allows dynamic customization of the publishing system by disabling or re-enabling the available advice bindings at run-time. This is still an error-prone process that should only be performed by developers who have a good understanding of the overall dependencies between the advice bindings. Indeed, attaining key safety properties when dynamically reconfiguring complex systems is known to be a difficult problem [29,30]: for example, as personalization depends on user tracking, one must be careful not to break this dependency chain by disabling user tracking before personalization, as this would leave the system in an inconsistent state.

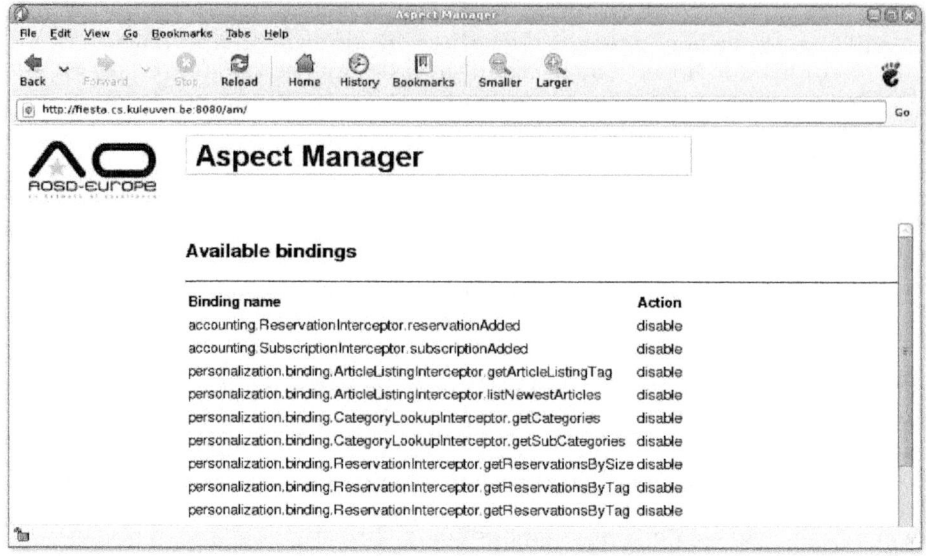

Fig. 7. Screenshot of the Aspect Manager

4 Evaluation

In this section, we compare the AO version of the publishing platform presented in Section 3 to its object-oriented (OO) counterpart.

Figure 8 serves as a reminder of how the demonstrator was developed. First, a classical publishing platform was created from requirements to implementation, which is called version 001 in the figure. Then, this version was refactored into an aspect-oriented variant by separating the crosscutting concerns (version A01 in the figure). Finally, we applied an evolution scenario on this version of the publishing platform, leading to version A02, the demonstrator.

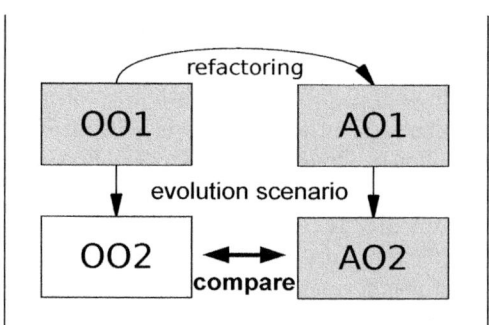

Fig. 8. Overview of the development of the demonstrator showing all intermediate versions

To compare the OO and AO versions of the demonstrator, we applied the same evolution scenario to version 001 of the publishing platform, leading to version 002 which is equivalent to the A02 version. As discussed in Section 2, the evolution scenario mimics recent, real-world evolutions in the domain of (digital) news publishing and includes introducing publishing features such as *user tracking*, *personalization*, and *targeted advertising* (direct marketing).

The first part of the evaluation (Section 4.1) focuses on quantitatively assessing the evolvability of both versions, while the second part (Section 4.2) discusses the results of comparing their performance.

4.1 Quantitative Evolvability Evaluation

The overall goal of this assessment is to compare the impact of the implemented evolution scenario on the OO and AO versions of the publishing platform. For this, we adopt the assessment methodology for *design stability* from [31] and [32]. In essence, this measurement framework offers a two-pronged approach, comprising (i) change impact analysis and (ii) modularity analysis.

Change Impact Analysis. This part of the quantitative evaluation focuses on the absolute impact of the evolution scenario. The underlying principle is that the impact of evolution on the affected architecture and implementation artifacts is an indicator of the effort required to perform that evolution scenario. Three attributes are investigated: (i) size, (ii) change localization, and (iii) modification types.

Size. The size metrics measure the effects of the evolution scenario on software size. These include:

- $\Delta(NoC)$: number of classes added, changed or removed
- $\Delta(NoM)$: number of methods added, changed or removed
- $\Delta(LoC)$: number of lines of code added, changed or removed
- $\Delta(LoC_{base})$: number of lines of code added, changed or removed in base components (i.e. the components affected by a crosscutting concern)
- $\Delta(LoC_{adv})$: number of lines of code added, changed or removed in advicing components (i.e. the components offering advice functionality)

Table 3. Results for size metrics

Metric	Size metrics				
	$\Delta(NoC)$	$\Delta(NoM)$	$\Delta(LoC)$	$\Delta(LoC_{base})$	$\Delta(LoC_{adv})$
OO	98	510	5351	1044	2539
AO	104	502	5122	660	2880

The results for these metrics are shown in Table 3. It shows that in general, evolving the AO version of the publishing platform consistently required less changes than the OO version. More specifically:

- The evolution scenario involved adding, removing or changing 6 more classes in the AO version than in the OO version. This is due to the fact that the aspectual connectors are counted as classes.
- The AO version involved adding, removing, or changing 8 methods less than the OO version, and this despite the fact that the pointcuts and helper methods in the aspectual connectors are also counted.
- Evolving the AO version required the creation, removal, or modification of 229 lines of code less (5% of all lines of code adapted) than in the OO version.

These observations confirm the notion that aspectual compositions help to reduce code duplication and scattering. The code fragments for calling the advicing components directly from within the base components in the OO version is in the AO version replaced with the source code for the aspectual connectors, and the latter represents less lines of code.

Looking specifically at the lines of code related to the components providing advice functionality $(\Delta(LoC_{adv}))$, we can see that the number of lines of code specifically changed for the aspects is larger in the AO case than it is in the OO case (341 lines of code). The specific reason for this is the fact that the aspectual connectors are counted to be part of the advicing components, and thus they are systematically larger than their OO counterparts, which do not provide such connectors. The main advantage is that the lines of code affected by crosscutting concerns in the base components $(\Delta(LoC_{base}))$ are substantially less in the AO version: in total, the difference is 444 lines of code.

Change Localization.   These metrics are used to assess the intrusiveness of the evolution scenario in the architecture. This assessment focuses on comparing the effects of evolution on the component and class interfaces, which are the main mechanism for encapsulation in a component-based and object-oriented setting. The more a component interface is affected, the higher the risk of introducing ripple effects to the clients of that interface. These metrics include:

- $\Delta(NoI)$: number of interfaces added, changed or removed
- $\Delta(Par)$: number of method parameters added, changed or removed
- $\Delta(IS)$: degree of how the overall interface size is affected [33]. Per interface, the interface size is defined as the sum, over all interface operations, of the number of parameters plus the sum of parameters weight. This weight factor depends on the parameters type. The idea behind this metric is to measure the amount of information passing through the interface.

Table 4. Results for change localization metrics

Metric	Change localization metrics		
	$\Delta(NoI)$	$\Delta(Par)$	$\Delta(IS)$
OO	11	3.82	1234
AO	12	2.72	1013

Table 4 presents the results of these metrics. In general, evolving in the AO version of the publishing system consistently involved less changes to the component interfaces than in the OO version. This is manifested particularly in the number of parameters affected by the evolution ($\Delta(Par)$), and the interface size metric ($\Delta(IS)$). In general, evolving the AO version required less parameters to be adapted.

Modification types. Finally, we evaluate the modifications made during evolution at the level of architecture by their invasiveness. We distinguish between:

1. **non-invasive modifications:** these include introducing components, interfaces or interface operations in the architecture. Such modifications are considered to be *non-invasive*, as they do not affect the existing artifacts.
2. **invasive modifications:** these include renaming or removing of components, interfaces or interface operations and operation parameters, as well as changes to operation signatures. There is a risk of architecture-level *ripple effects*, as these modifications potentially affect all other artifacts that depend on them as well. Therefore, they are considered *invasive*, and potentially harmful.

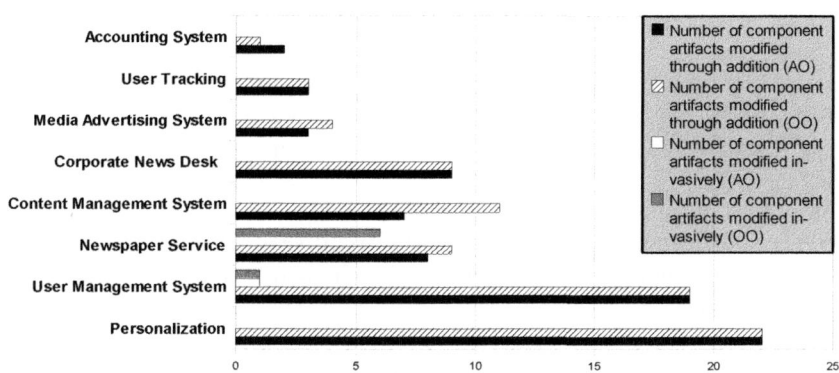

Fig. 9. The percentage of artifacts per component in the OO and AO architectures that were modified in the evolution scenario, per type of modification

Figure 9 shows the amount of architecture-level artifacts per component (interfaces, interface operations, and interface operation parameters) that were modified during the evolution scenario, in both AO and OO architecture. It indicates that the majority of the modifications were of a non-invasive nature, and only a very small fraction of all modifications can be considered invasive and potentially harmful. This is the result of the complementary nature of the evolution scenario: it mostly involved new features and functionalities, and only few adaptations to the functionalities developed in the first iteration.

Nonetheless, comparing the degree of invasive changes between OO and AO, we observe that 8 % of all changes in the OO case are of an invasive nature, while this is only 1 % in the AO case. Again, this confirms the finding that there is less potential for harmful ripple effects in the AO architecture.

Modularity Analysis. This part of the quantitative evaluation investigates the effects of the evolution scenario on software modularity. One of Lehman's software evolution laws [34,35] states that over time, software grows larger and more complex. As modularity is the main tool to address software complexity, we measure this effect by conducting a modularity analysis. More specifically, the goal is to investigate whether or not the modularity of the AO architecture is impacted differently by the evolution scenario than the OO architecture. For modularity analysis, we focus on a metric related to *concern diffusion* (the degree of scattering of crosscutting concerns):

CDC: concern diffusion over components

Concern diffusion over components. During the development of the digital publishing system, we have manually and rigorously kept track of the traceability mapping of the requirements to the architectural artifacts (components, interfaces, interface operations and interface operation parameters). This mapping indicates for each of these artifacts by which requirement(s) it is affected. As a result, finding out the effects of the crosscutting concerns in architecture is merely a matter consulting this traceability mapping for the crosscutting concerns.

Figures 10 and 11 present the result of tracing the crosscutting concerns to the different components of the OO and AO architecture respectively. The X-axis presents the number of artifacts affected by the respective crosscutting concern. This is an indicator of the weight or impact of the aspect in the architecture. When comparing these figures, it becomes clear that in the AO architecture the advicing components (i.e. the components that are composed by an AO-connector) exclusively contribute to the realization of the crosscutting requirements, while there is a much larger degree of *concern diffusion* (component-level scattering and tangling) in the OO architecture, and this, obviously, in the base components (the components to which the AO-connectors are applied).

The only exception is the `User Management System` component that itself was extended in a non-modular manner to include "aspect-supporting" functionalities: in this case the storage of (1) the user view history (for *user tracking*), (2) user preferences (for *personalization*), (3) the user invoice (for *accounting*), and (4) user name and password credentials (for *authentication and authorization*). This was a side-effect of a pragmatic decision made during refactoring to focus on optimizing the separation of concerns in the business tier, and not in back-end components (data tier).

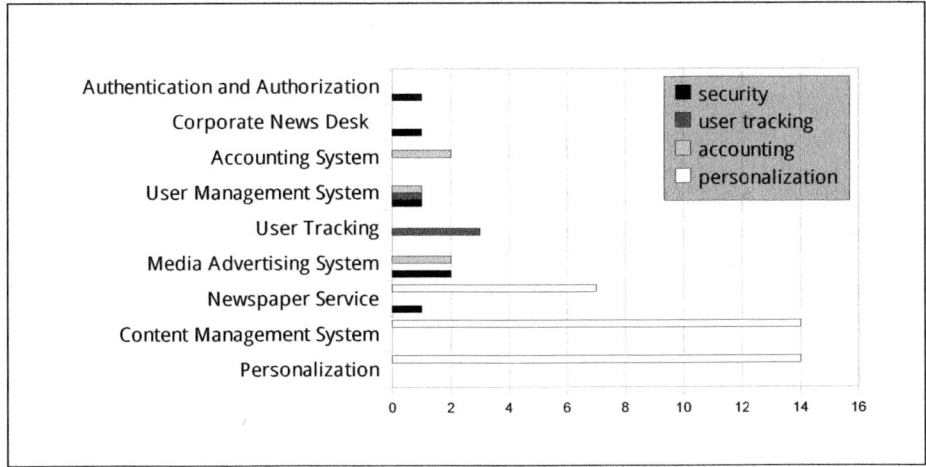

Fig. 10. Concern diffusion to component interfaces in OO architecture

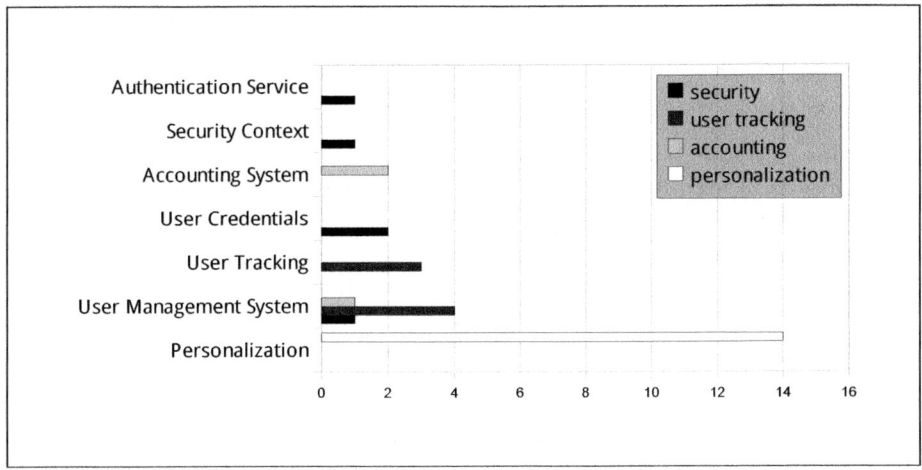

Fig. 11. Concern diffusion to component interfaces in AO architecture

4.2 Performance Evaluation

We evaluate the run-time performance of both application implementations (AO and OO) with respect to the impact of dynamic aspect-oriented composition. Both applications ran on top of the same JBossAS server setup. We measured the performance of both applications in terms of the absolute time it takes for each scenario to execute and return with a result.

Test setup. We selected two key scenarios in the context of the digital publishing application. These scenarios are also affected by crosscutting behavior (i.e. *personalization, user tracking, security*).

Because the goal is to measure the impact of AO composition, we first ensured that the respective implementations of these scenarios were maximally comparable in both versions. This was done by consistently replacing the aspectual connectors of the AO version with explicit calls from the base components to the advice in the OO version. As a result, the only difference between them is the AO composition mechanism itself, and thus, observed differences in performance can only be attributed to the JBoss AOP composition mechanism.

A dedicated testing client was created to execute and time the scenarios, thus entirely avoiding the web-tier. This client is able to directly call the the involved beans. We did this to cut down on external influence as much as possible.

We selected the following scenarios:

- **listNewestArticles:** a scenario that involves a consumer requesting a list showing the fifteen newest articles. This scenario interacts with security, and with personalization, by having the order of the most recent articles modified according to preference.
- **fetchArticle:** a scenario that involves a consumer selecting a specific article from the headlines and requesting to read the article in full. This scenario interacts with security, personalization (direct advertising), and user tracking (registering the interest in this article).

The full scenario is a combination of both. A consumer (the client application) goes through the listNewestArticle scenario, chooses an article, and goes through the fetchArticle scenario. To keep the test fair, the consumer always selects the same article.

We tested both scenarios in a batch of one thousand executions. We ran at least five of these batches to convince ourselves we were indeed getting stable results.

The experiment was carried out on a late-2009 Macbook Pro with 2.26GHz Intel Core 2 Duo processor and 4GB of 1067MHz DDR3 memory, running Mac OS X 10.6.2, Java 1.5.0_19 (32 bit), and JBossAS version 4.2.2.GA loaded with JBoss-AOP 2.0.0.CR1.

Results. The results of the measurements are shown in table 5 and in a set of box-plots in figure 12.

The numbers show that neither implementation has a clear advantage over the other, in terms of run-time performance timings. AO has an advantage in the listNewestArticles scenario (11.8%), while OO has the advantage in the fetchArticle scenario (5.2%). The scenario where the AO solution is slower (fetchArticle) is also the one that involves the most aspect interactions. However, while investigating these results, it became apparent that the aspect interception overhead of our application is very small compared to the overall framework overhead that JBoss brings. Furthermore, we have not been able to exactly pinpoint the disadvantage the OO case shows in the listNewestArticles scenario.

A more clear performance-wise disadvantage of AO was apparent at deploy-time. Deploying our AO implementation takes three times longer (AO takes 92 sec., while OO only needs 28 sec.) than deploying the OO implementation. This is because of all the low-level pre-processing that JBoss has to perform to integrate aspects into the application.

Table 5. Average runtime performance timings of two main scenarios, and the number of aspects in case of AO

	Performance measurements		
Scenario	**OO**	**AO**	**#aspects**
listNewestArticles	873 ms	770 ms	2
fetchArticle	414 ms	437 ms	3
full	1287 ms	1207 ms	2+3

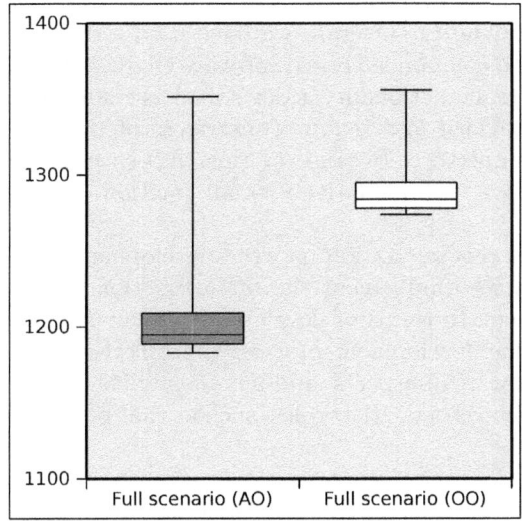

Fig. 12. Performance measure box-plots, showing, from bottom to top: the smallest observation (minimum), lower quartile (25%), median (50%), upper quartile (75%), and largest observation (maximum)

Conclusions. While there is no straightforward winner in our performance test, the AO implementation had an overall 6% advantage over OO, in terms of execution time of the two scenarios that we measured. However, during our investigation of these results, it became apparent that the overall overhead introduced by JBoss had a much bigger impact on the performance than the additional AO interceptions that we introduced. Furthermore, deploying the AO application takes up to 3x longer than deploying the OO version.

5   Lessons Learned

The expressivity, efficiency, and compatibility of a programming paradigm are three important industrial acceptance criteria that indicate a paradigm's potential, some of its costs and ease of integration [8]. Meeting these criteria will certainly promote the acceptance of AOSD in industry. In the construction of the digital publishing system we have used various AOSD development tools and methods. This section evaluates these technologies (with respect to the above criteria) and identifies key challenges in the further adoption of AOSD.

5.1   Integration with Development Methods and Tools

To ensure smooth adoption, AOSD should be as compatible as possible with standard development methods and tools. In general, some of these tools and methods had to be adapted to suit the purposes of AOSD, but most of them could be applied generically. This section describes the employed tool chain and our main experiences with these tools and methods.

Development methods. Overall, we have used a development methodology that is very close to component-based software engineering (CBSE). As outlined in Section 3.2, all real functionality is developed as traditional components, while composing the provided and required interfaces of these components involves aspect-oriented connectors. Because of this, AO-specific development activity in the demonstrator was a relatively small fraction of the total development activity.

Also, because of this separation between development activities, the majority of the developers, who implement the main functionalities, do not need to be aware of the aspects. In terms of development roles, AOSD therefore gives rise to a new role in the development process: the *aspect-base composer*; this is the developer that is aware of aspects, and has the ability to write and maintain the aspect-oriented connectors. Other roles, such as that of the component developer remain unchanged.

Development tools. Especially when dealing with the lesser-known aspect-oriented artifacts such as pointcuts, tool support can have a profound effect on development time and effort. This paragraph lists our experiences with development tools for the different stages of the development life-cycle.

Requirements engineering. As already mentioned in Section 3.1, we have documented the requirements in the UML as a set of use cases. To this end we have used a generic UML tool called Poseidon for UML [36]. As already elaborated in Section 3.1, the two key AO-specific activities are the identification of crosscutting concerns in the description of the use cases, and their separation. For the first activity we have not used any specific tool, although we could have used the EA-Miner tool [37] as delivered by the AOSD-Europe Atelier [38]. Although this is a useful tool for automated identification of crosscutting concerns, a specific lexicon for the digital publishing domain was not readily available, and it would have been too time- and resource-intensive to create one from scratch. For the second activity we have exploited the standard UML mechanisms of use case refinement and extension points.

Architecture and design. To specify the software architecture, we started by using the Poseidon for UML tool [36] as well to graphically design the individual architectural perspectives. As discussed earlier in Section 3.2, we wanted to adhere to the AO-ADL standard representation [17]. This representation introduces new syntactical elements, for the aspectual connectors, the base roles, and the crosscutting roles. As these element types are not part of the default UML 2.0 language, and the Poseidon tool does not offer a way to easily extend the standard UML profile, we resorted to post-processing of the resulting images using a vector drawing application. This was evidently a cumbersome task.

As we felt the lack of a real modeling tool for AO architecture, we switched to modeling with the AO-ADL Specification Tool [39], which is developed in the scope of the AOSD-Europe project. While this is definitely a more principled approach to modeling the architecture, this as well has some downsides such as the lack of graphical representation of the architecture. However, as this is still a tool under active development, it is expected to improve in the next years. One of the major advantages of this tool is the possibility to generate aspectual bindings directly from the tool.

Implementation.   As most of the implementation effort was not specific for AOSD, we were mostly able to use well-known non-AOSD tools such as the Eclipse IDE [40], the Ant build environment [28], the JUnit tool [41] for unit testing, the JBoss application server [7] which is an EJB 3.0-compliant application server. In the Eclipse IDE, we installed the JBoss Tools extension [42] to enjoy support for specific JBoss technologies. Sadly, at the time of writing, the JBoss IDE support for AOP was not included anymore in the JBoss tools. Section 3.4 describes how we have used the Ant build manager to easily build customized variants of the digital publishing system. In terms of the selected platform, technologies and AOP language, the JBoss framework has definitely been a good choice. The JBoss middleware is industry-grade and JEE-compliant (EJB 3), and it has built-in support for JBoss AOP language which in itself is an extension to Java. As discussed in Section 3.3, the dynamic AOP capabilities of JBoss AOP have been instrumental to realize the variability, evolvability, and flexibility requirements, something that would not have been possible in AspectJ [43] because it only support compile- and load-time weaving.

Summary.   The main conclusions drawn from this are summarized as follows: (1) **no tabula rasa:** an AOSD methodology is *complementary* to existing development methodologies; i.e. selecting AOSD does not necessarily exclude other development methodologies and (2) **tool extension, not tool replacement:** as there is no real paradigm shift, adopting AOSD does not force the developer to learn a full new set of tools, which keep the learning curve gentle.

5.2   Efficiency

Performance-wise, dynamic AOP platforms are known to be less efficient than static AOP. From our experiences with JBoss AOP, it is advisable to avoid using some more advanced pointcut constructs (e.g. a `cflow`) because these still introduce a non-negligible performance overhead. Also the amount of pointcut declarations seem to have had an effect on the aspect interception time in JBoss AOP. As such, a good workaround has been to aggregate multiple related pointcut declarations into one. Other than that, the performance overhead of the aspects proved to be acceptable, as shown in our performance evaluation in Section 4.2.

5.3   Expressiveness

Although the development process of the demonstrator was an iterative process, AOSD has considerably simplified the architecture and code of the system, as shown in the validation in Section 4.1. First of all, the more powerful modularization capabilities of AOSD has considerably improved the variability and evolvability of the system. For example, crosscutting features such as user tracking could be (dynamically) selected for a particular deployment of the system. Secondly, AOSD considerably improves the modularization of infrastructural middleware services such as user authentication and authorization. This fosters the reuse of these services. Thirdly, a particular characteristic of our approach was to define the join points for aspects as much as possible at a semantic level, instead of a syntactic level (e.g. abstract extension points in UML use cases, base roles in AO-ADL, annotations in JBoss). Doing this across the life cycle improves the understandability of the crosscutting compositions and allows adopting a model-driven approach where crosscutting compositions in the later stages can be automatically derived from the earlier stages.

An open challenge with respect to expressiveness is the modularization of crosscutting concerns that become visible during build-time or thereafter. The lack of support for distributed AOP in industry-ready AO platforms is a good example to illustrate this point. Currently all server-side components of the publishing system run on a single node. A real deployment of the system typically executes on top of a distributed system of multiple nodes. However, JBoss AOP's support is limited to specifying aspect-oriented compositions within a single node. As a result, aspect-oriented compositions that crosscut across N different nodes (e.g. suppose the `Accounting` component must be invoked from N nodes) cannot be cleanly captured. A workaround in our current architecture would be to deploy N separate JBoss AOP aspects, one for each node of the system. This considerably complicates the build process, however, and obstructs the kind of feature-oriented variability that we have demonstrated before. The advantage of Distributed AOP platforms such as JAC [44], AWED [45], and DyMAC [46] is that these platforms allow specifying such n-to-1 compositions in a single unit of deployment. As a result, using one of these platforms, the build scripts could be kept oblivious from this particular deployment-time concern.

5.4   Threats to Validity

From an industry perspective, there are some obvious yet valid threats to validity of this work and the lessons learned from it. These are related to (i) the complexity of the demonstrator, (ii) the nature of the evolution scenario, and (iii) the scope of the work. We discuss these below:

1. **Complexity:** despite the fact that we have not implemented a full-fledged publishing platform (as discussed in Section 1), there are a number of arguments in favor of the relevance of this work. The numbers regarding the time spent on the development and the total lines of code mentioned in Section 1, together with the fact that the demonstrator is a result of close collaboration with industry partners, indicate that this was a high-effort case study and not a toy example.

2. **Evolution scenario:** there is the fact that we only *mimicked* real-world evolutions as a lab experiment and did not undergo these evolutions in the real world. Therefore, one could argue that the first version of our system already anticipated some of the evolutions that would be implemented in the second iteration. Our counterargument to this is that the architecture used in the first version is based strongly on the software architecture of the publisher we worked with [6], as discussed in Section 2.1. Nonetheless, we agree that in order to promote adoption of AOSD in industry, it is imperative to collect empirical evidence coming from industry.

   Additionally, the choice of the evolution scenario itself poses another potential threat to validity. One could argue that we have chosen a scenario that is more aspectual in nature and thus benefits the AO version of the publishing platform. As a counterargument to this, we point out that the evolution scenario itself is based highly on real-world challenges in the publishing industry. Furthermore, as the evolvability assessment of Section 4 shows, only around 50% of the lines of code introduced because of evolution are related to crosscutting concerns (compare $\Delta(LoC)$ and $\Delta(LoC_{adv})$).

3. **Scope:** as discussed in Section 3, we have selected one specific instance of AOSD, more specifically one which is complementary to component-based architecture design. As there is a wide variety in decomposition styles (e.g. symmetric vs. asymmetric, subject-oriented, feature-oriented, etc), methodologies, languages, platforms which are all under the wide umbrella of AOSD, we can not claim validity of our findings in this broad scope. However, we do believe that our observations of evolvability benefits are a result of the aspect-oriented philosophy to focus on separating and modularizing crosscutting concerns.

6   Conclusion

This paper has presented the usage of aspect-oriented methods and techniques during the construction of an industry-grade digital publishing platform.

In Section 2, we have shown that the competitive digital publishing landscape evolves rapidly, and that therefore, publishing companies will have a competitive advantage in the long run if their supporting ICT infrastructure can sustain and support such rapid evolutions. Because of their built-in support for run-time and dynamic composition, aspect-oriented composition techniques are an ideal building block for such a publishing infrastructure, and the main goal of this demonstrator is to provide some evidence of this.

Section 3 shows how we tailored our development process to support the desired evolvability. Identifying and separating crosscutting concerns already during requirements engineering, has a positive impact on the later development stages because it leads to components and interfaces that are less affected by such concerns, which makes them easier to build and to maintain. During implementation and more so during deployment, we demonstrated that AOSD also supports a decomposition that is more feature-oriented, enabling the publisher to roll out differentiated service offerings in a limited time frame, either at deployor or at run-time.

The evaluation of the demonstrator, in Section 4, focuses on providing empirical evidence that the AO version of the publishing system was in fact easier to evolve than the OO version. Additionally, it presents a performance evaluation which shows that, at least in our demonstrator, there was no show-stopping performance overhead when adding JBoss AOP to the JBoss middleware stack.

Finally, the in-depth discussion of the results in Section 5 provides our main experiences and lessons learned from building the demonstrator. We have guided this discussion on three important industrial acceptance criteria of a programming paradigm [8]: its expressivity, its efficiency, and compatibility. The main lessons learned from developing the digital publishing demonstrator are: (i) AOSD integrates well with existing standard paradigms such as component-based software engineering, (ii) the resulting software exhibits a good evolvability and variability, and this in turn adds to the overall business value of the digital publishing services.

Despite the threats to validity outlined in Section 5.4, we believe that the real value of this work lies in the fact that it presents a realistic application, which is the result of close collaboration with real-world industrial actors in the news publishing field. Furthermore, it shows how AOSD can be leveraged in an industry-relevant development process to achieve the desired degrees of evolvability and variability of concerns that would otherwise be crosscutting and hard to modularize. For these reasons, we believe that this demonstrator provides a valuable asset to promote adoption of aspect-oriented technology in industry.

Acknowledgements

This research is supported by European Commission FP6 Grant AOSD-Europe: European Network of Excellence on AOSD (IST-2-004349), the Interuniversity Attraction Poles Programme Belgian State, Belgian Science Policy, by the

Research Fund K.U.Leuven, and by an SBO project grant from the Flemish Institute for the advancement of scientific-technological research in industry (IWT).

References

1. AOSD-Europe network of excellence: The aosd-europe project,
   http://www.aosd-europe.net/
2. DistriNet, KULeuven: Diginews project,
   http://distrinet.cs.kuleuven.be/research/projects/DigiNews
3. DistriNet, KULeuven: E-paper project,
   http://distrinet.cs.kuleuven.be/research/projects/E-paper
4. DistriNet, KULeuven: Croslocis project,
   http://distrinet.cs.kuleuven.be/research/projects/CROSLOCiS
5. DistriNet, KULeuven: Cocomedia project,
   http://distrinet.cs.kuleuven.be/research/projects/CoCoMedia
6. Van Landuyt, D., Grégoire, J., Michiels, S., Truyen, E., Joosen, W.: Architectural design of a digital publishing system. CW Reports CW465, Department of Computer Science, K.U.Leuven, Leuven, Belgium (October 2006)
7. JBoss technologies: The jboss middleware stack, http://www.jboss.org
8. Kiczales, G.: The aop report card. Dr. Dobb's (2004),
   http://www.ddj.com/showArticle.jhtml?articleID=184415082
9. Singer, J.B.: Still guarding the gate?: The newspaper journalist's role in an on-line world. Convergence 3(1), 72–89 (1997)
10. Thurman, N.: Forums for citizen journalists? adoption of user generated content initiatives by online news media. New Media Society 10(1), 139–157 (2008)
11. Google corp.: Google news, http://news.google.com
12. Van Landuyt, D., Op de beeck, S., Truyen, E., Joosen, W.: Digital publishing demonstrator: source code, supporting documents and videos (2008),
    http://distrinet.cs.kuleuven.be/software/digitalpublishing/
13. Mahieu, T., Joosen, W., Van Landuyt, D., Grégoire, J., Buyens, K., Truyen, E.: System requirements on digital newspapers. CW Reports CW484, K.U.Leuven, Department of Computer Science (March 2007)
14. Joosen, W., Michiels, S., Truyen, E., Vandebroek, K., Van Landuyt, D.: A comprehensive model for digital publishing. CW Reports CW443, K.U.Leuven, Department of Computer Science (April 2006)
15. Jacobson, I., Ng, P.W.: Object-Oriented Software Engineering: A Use Case Driven Approach. Addison Wesley Longman Publishing Co., Inc., Redwood City (2004)
16. Bass, L., Clements, P., Kazman, R.: Software Architecture in Practice, 2nd edn. Addison-Wesley, Reading (2003)
17. Tekinerdogan, B., Garcia, A., Sant'Anna, C., Figueiredo, E., Pinto, M., Fuentes, L.: Approach for modeling aspects in architectural views. AOSD-Europe Deliverable D77 (2007), http://www.aosd-europe.net/deliverables/d77.pdf
18. Pinto, M., Fuentes, L.: Ao-adl: An adl for describing aspect-oriented architectures, pp. 94–114 (2007)
19. Greenwood, P., et al.: Reference architecture v3.0. AOSD-Europe Deliverable D103 (2008)

20. SpringSource: The spring enterprise platform,
    http://www.springsource.com/products/enterprise
21. Gamma, E., Helm, R., Johnson, R., Vlissides, J.: Design patterns: elements of
    reusable object-oriented software. Addison-Wesley Professional, Reading (1995)
22. Sun inc.: The glassfish application server, https://glassfish.dev.java.net/
23. Apel, S., Leich, T., Saake, G.: Aspectual feature modules. IEEE Transactions on
    Software Engineering 34, 162–180 (2007)
24. Apel, S., Kaestner, C., Lengauer, C.: Research challenges in the tension between
    features and services. In: SDSOA 2008: Proceedings of the 2nd International Work-
    shop on Systems Development in SOA Environments, pp. 53–58. ACM, New York
    (2008)
25. Batory, D., Sarvela, J.N., Rauschmayer, A.: Scaling step-wise refinement. IEEE
    Transactions on Software Engineering 30, 355–371 (2004)
26. Mezini, M., Ostermann, K.: Variability management with feature-oriented pro-
    gramming and aspects. In: SIGSOFT FSE, pp. 127–136 (2004)
27. Apel, S., Leich, T., Rosenmüller, M., Saake, G.: FeatureC++: On the symbiosis of
    feature-oriented and aspect-oriented programming. In: Glück, R., Lowry, M. (eds.)
    GPCE 2005. LNCS, vol. 3676, pp. 125–140. Springer, Heidelberg (2005)
28. Apache: The ant build tool, http://ant.apache.org/
29. Moazami-Goudarzi, K.: Consistency preserving dynamic reconfiguration of dis-
    tributed systems. PhD thesis, Imperial College London (1999)
30. Truyen, E., Janssens, N., Sanen, F., Joosen, W.: Support for distributed adap-
    tations in aspect-oriented middleware. In: Research Track Proceedings of the 7th
    International Conference on Aspect-Oriented Software Development, pp. 120–131.
    ACM Press, New York (2008)
31. Sant'anna, C., Garcia, A., Chavez, C., Lucena, C., von Staa, A.v.: On the reuse
    and maintenance of aspect-oriented software: An assessment framework. In: Pro-
    ceedings XVII Brazilian Symposium on Software Engineering (2003)
32. Figueiredo, E., Cacho, N., Sant'Anna, C., Monteiro, M., Kulesza, U., Garcia, A.,
    Soares, S., Ferrari, F., Khan, S., Filho, F.C., Dantas, F.: Evolving software product
    lines with aspects: An empirical study on design stability. In: ICSE 2008: Proceed-
    ings of the 30th International Conference on Software Engineering, pp. 261–270.
    ACM, New York (2008)
33. Bandi, R.K., Vaishnavi, V.K., Turk, D.E.: Predicting maintenance performance
    using object-oriented design complexity metrics. IEEE Trans. Softw. Eng. 29(1),
    77–87 (2003)
34. Cook, S., Ji, H., Harrison, R.: Software evolution and software evolvability (2000)
35. Belady, L., Lehman, M.: A model of large program development. IBM Sys. Jour-
    nal 15(1), 225–252 (1976)
36. Gentleware inc.: Poseidon for uml,
    http://www.gentleware.com/apollo.html
37. AOSD-Europe Project:: The ea-miner tool,
    http://gateway.comp.lancs.ac.uk/computing/
    aosdeurope//deliverables/d108.pdf
38. AOSD-Europe Project:: Atelier,
    http://gateway.comp.lancs.ac.uk:8080/c/portal/layout?pld=1.12
39. CAOSD Group, t.D.o.L., of the University of Malaga., C.S.: The ao-adl specificia-
    tion tool, http://caosd.lcc.uma.es/aoadl/toolsupport.htm

40. The Eclipse Foundation: the eclipse ide, http://www.eclipse.org
41. JUnit project: Junit tool for unit testing, http://www.junit.org
42. JBoss technologies: The jboss ide tools, http://www.jboss.org/tools
43. Eclipse.org: the aspectj aop language
44. Pawlak, R., Seinturier, L., Duchien, L., Florin, G.: JAC: A flexible solution for aspect-oriented programming in Java. In: Matsuoka, S. (ed.) Reflection 2001. LNCS, vol. 2192, p. 1. Springer, Heidelberg (2001)
45. Navarro, L.D.B., Südholt, M., Vanderperren, W., Fraine, B.D., Suvée, D.: Explicitly distributed aop using awed. In: Proceedings of AOSD 2006 (2006)
46. Lagaisse, B., Joosen, W.: True and Transparent Distributed Composition of Aspect-Components. In: van Steen, M., Henning, M. (eds.) Middleware 2006. LNCS, vol. 4290, pp. 42–61. Springer, Heidelberg (2006)

An Aspect-Oriented Tool Framework for Developing Process-Sensitive Embedded User Assistance Systems

Bedir Tekinerdoğan[1], Serap Bozbey[2], Yavuz Mester[1],
Erdem Turançiftci[1], and Levent Alkışlar[2]

[1] Bilkent University, Department of Computer Engineering, 06800 Bilkent Ankara, Turkey
{bedir,mester,erdem}@cs.bilkent.edu.tr
[2] Aselsan, PO. Box. 1, 06172, Yenimahalle, Ankara, Turkey
{bozbey,alkislar}@aselsan.com.tr

Abstract. Process-sensitive embedded user assistance aims to provide the end-user the necessary guidance based on the state of the process that is being followed. Unfortunately, the development of these systems is not trivial and has to meet several challenges. The main difficulties appear to be related to integration of process-sensitive guidance in the application and the crosscutting behavior of help concerns. To address these issues we developed an aspect-oriented tool framework *Assistant-Pro* that can be used to develop process-sensitive embedded user assistance for multiple applications. The framework provides tools for defining the process model, defining guidance related to process steps, and modularizing and weaving help concerns in the target application for which user guidance needs to be provided. The framework has been developed and validated in the context of Aselsan, a large Turkish defense electronics company.

Keywords: context-sensitive user assistance, aspect-oriented software development, industrial applications.

1 Introduction

User assistance is a broad term which refers to the guided assistance to a user of a software product, to help accomplishing tasks and ensure a successful user experience [12][23][16]. The traditional form of user assistance is an off-line printed user manual that is separate from the system. User assistance has now evolved to *online help* systems [30][31][35] that provide information to the user in an electronic format and which can be opened directly in the application. Until recently, online help systems usually have adopted a topic-oriented approach in which help can be requested based on keywords. The corresponding assistance is presented in different formats such as html, text, or PDF.

Embedded user assistance systems can be defined as a special form of online help in which the documentation of the application resides within the application [26]. The key motivation for embedded user assistance is the fact that traditional, separate user

S. Katz et al. (Eds.): Transactions on AOSD VIII, LNCS 6580, pp. 196–220, 2011.

assistance is inherently reactive. This means that users only consult the documentation when they do not know how to proceed. The result is that they stop what they are doing, open the documentation, find the information they are looking for and then return to the application. Research on user assistance has shown that it is basically because of this separate effort and disruption of the user's flow of work, that users are reluctant to using help [4][9].

An important category of embedded user assistance systems are *context-sensitive user assistance* systems [5][26][36]. In context-sensitive user assistance, help is obtained from a specific point in the state of the software, providing help for the situation that is associated with that state. In contrast to general online user assistance, context-sensitive assistance does not need to be accessible for reading as a whole. In general the system is defined as a set of states to which a topic is related that extensively describes the corresponding state, situation, or feature of the software. Context-sensitive help can be provided in different ways including automatic tooltips over controls, notifications in the status bar, or by new panes which are opened after explicitly clicking a button. Context-sensitive help systems, such as Microsoft's WinHelp and Sun's JavaHelp [23] have been applied to various kind of software systems. The advantage of embedded, contextual help is that it can provide immediate assistance to users without having to leave the context in which they are working. This is important because, as noted above, users seem to be very often reluctant to use help that is not integrated [4][9].

One category of context-sensitive user assistance systems focuses on defining help based on the process state, and we define these as *process-sensitive user assistance systems*. In this paper, 'process' implies the steps that need to be followed while using a particular application. The offered help content depends on the steps that have been processed. An example of such applications is a safety-critical system in which a strict process needs to be followed in order to avoid faulty behavior.

Unfortunately, developing embedded context-sensitive user assistance systems in general and process-sensitive systems in particular, is not trivial and has to meet several challenges. First of all, it appears that user-assistance concerns usually cannot be easily localized in single modules and as such tend to crosscut multiple modules. A common problem of crosscutting concerns is that they reduce the modularity of the system and as such impede maintenance. User assistance design can benefit from aspect-oriented software development (AOSD) approaches [8] to modularize the crosscutting concern and support maintenance. Another important problem is the reuse of user assistance tools for different applications. In general, the need for modularizing crosscutting concerns is motivated in case of change of crosscutting concerns for the *same* application. However, in this paper we will also show that this might be required for multiple applications at the same time ('change in time vs. change in space'). Rather than developing custom-based help assistance for each separate application, it is required to support reuse of a help concern and as such reduce the time of development.

To tackle these problems we developed an application framework and the related tools for modularly extending applications with context-sensitive help. The framework has been developed within the industrial context of Aselsan [1], Turkey, which is a leading high technology, multi-product defense electronics company introducing state-of-the-art equipment and software intensive systems solutions for both sophisticated military and professional applications.

The remainder of the paper is organized as follows: In Section 2 we describe the problem statement in more detail using the industrial cases of Aselsan. In Section 3, we define the conceptual model that represent and integrates concepts of process modeling and guidance modeling. In Section 4, we present the architecture of the tool and the required flow of control for using the tools. Section 5 discusses the implementation of the guidance aspect and the weaving process. In Section 6, we present the evaluation of the framework and finally in Section 7 we conclude the paper.

2   Case Description and Problem Statement

Since context-sensitive user assistance add-ons enhance the support for guidance of systems, they have gained importance in recent years. Unfortunately, the development of such context-sensitive user assistance systems also introduces new challenges that have not yet been explicitly considered in the user assistance domain. As stated before, our main target is the *development* of embedded user assistance systems that provide guidance with respect to the state of the process. To clarify the problems, in the following Section 2.1 we will first describe two pilot project applications that have been developed at Aselsan [1], and which also require guidance to the flow of actions. In Section 2.2 we explain the approach that was used at Aselsan to define user assistance. In Section 2.3 we will list the problems of context-sensitive embedded user assistance systems using the two applications.

2.1   Case Description

Example Case Application 1 – Message Management System
Message Management System (MMS) is a kind of e-mail application that helps two or more connected peers to asynchronously send and receive messages among each other and manage messages inside its own mailbox. A screenshot of the application is shown in Fig. 1. By using this application, each peer can view its incoming messages and can reply, forward, or delete them. Also the peer can create a new message, send it to the other peer and if required save this as a template. Messages are listed in the user interface according to their status. All the information about messages are stored in a database.

Example Case Application 2 - Listing and Listening of Voice Records
The *Listing and Listening of Voice Records Application (LLVR)* is used to organize and play the voice records which are stored in different audio formats. By using this application, users can query stored voice records from the database, review all the results as a list or get the print of the list. The selected records can be played, paused, stopped, or replayed from the list. By defining the start and finish times, any part of a record can be replayed. The operator can also attach a text note about the

record to the database. The records can be imported from and exported to a database. Again, this application has no guidance to users. The user needs explicit guidance to operate the application effectively and to reduce the potential faults due to misuse.

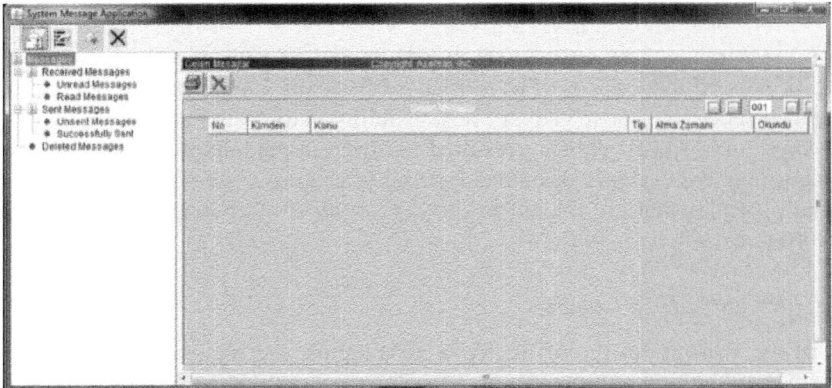

Fig. 1. Screenshot of Message Management System (MMS)

2.2 Current Approach

The above mentioned goals of user assistance and the need for embedded user assistance have also been encountered for the commercial applications that are developed by Aselsan [1]. In many of these applications, it is required that the end user follows a certain sequence of steps in order to complete the corresponding scenario successfully. For defining help, Aselsan adopted both external manuals and electronic help in its products depending on the nature of the application.

To define user assistance for the applications in Aselsan, the earlier conventional approach includes three steps. First, a senior system engineering team develops a scenario in a textual format to fulfill the requirements of the user to achieve a certain task. The textual format includes the control flow of the scenario including alternative flows and unexpected terminations or transitions to other scenarios. In the second step the development team implements the scenarios in the code and UI including the selection of graphical elements and the implementation of the transitions that are defined in the scenarios. In the third step, user assistance specialists write the user manuals for the application in both electronic and hardcopy format. A link is defined in the application to the electronic user manuals. The format of this help is basically defined as PDF documents or wiki pages. It is implicitly required that the users know the scenario as defined in these documents when operating the system. In case the user requires help they need to open the PDF documents and search for the information that solves their problem. To support the definition of help also third party tools, such as *Fast-Help* [11] is used. *Fast-Help* is a Windows Help File Generator that produces online and offline documentation in electronic formats such as HTML, PDF or .HLP. Although these third party products help to better organize the help files and provide better presentation and query mechanisms, the provided help is still not embedded in the application. As such, the earlier mentioned problems of external help still remain. Due to this problem, users very often demand further training to operate the system effectively. This also brings additional undesired costs to the company.

2.3   Problem Statement

Several researchers have focused on the challenges of embedded user assistance systems. In general these seem to have focused basically on the perspective of the user assistance specialist whose primary responsibility is to design and improve the layout of the system [34][12]. This has resulted in different guidelines and design checklists for improving the usability of embedded user assistance systems. In the following we list the obstacles that are related to the *development* of context-sensitive user assistance systems.

1.   Crosscutting Help Concern

One of the reasons for the difficulty of developing and maintaining embedded user assistance is the crosscutting nature of help concerns. User assistance might be required for different places in the code. Very often the need for user assistance is triggered by some widget event, such as clicking a button, selecting a checkbox or radio button. A close analysis of the applications shows that the widget events and as such the need for user assistance places, is not localized but is scattered over multiple modules. Consider some example code snippets in the application as given in Fig. 2.

```
...
ApplicationFrame appFrame = new ApplicationFrame();
...
public boolean replyMessageButtonClicked() {…}
...
new SaveTemplateWindow();
public boolean sendButtonClicked() {…}
public void windowClosing(WindowEvent arg0) { …}
....
public void closeButtonClicked() {…}
....
```

Fig. 2. Example of the code snippets of the MMS application indicating events that need to be monitored and for which help needs to be provided

   To provide process-sensitive help, we need to track all such events in the code that can lead to a state behavior. In fact these events can be anywhere in the code and often cannot be put in a single module. Moreover, since both the application code and the provided help might need to change regularly, the maintenance of the code and the provided help might become cumbersome and too costly.

   The problems of crosscutting concerns have been widely addressed in the aspect-oriented software development (AOSD) community [8]. AOSD provides explicit abstractions to localize and model crosscutting concerns and as such support maintenance and reuse of these concerns. In this context it is beneficial to implement help concerns as aspects and provide a way to compose these with the application tools.

2. Reuse across multiple application tools

Different applications are used in Aselsan that require embedded user assistance based on process context. Typically, we can identify the following categories of applications (1) legacy applications with help implemented, (2) legacy applications without help implemented, and (3) new applications that require integrated help. In general, while implementing help concerns, the same kind of constructs need to be implemented for the different types of applications. For example for both the small applications MMS and LLVR that have been explained in the previous section we need to provide guidance which is typically implemented as status bar descriptions and textual explanations in separate windows. To optimize the effort for implementing help concerns across multiple applications, it is necessary to adopt the right modularization and reuse approaches.

Also in this case AOSD seems to be invaluable to model the crosscutting concerns not only for a single application but across applications. Typically this will require defining an abstract guidance aspect for monitoring the process and providing appropriate help. The abstract aspect might need to be extended for the different applications to provide the required help.

3. Implicit Process

Although embedded user assistance can provide the user with help at the right moment, the related process is still implicit. In general, the required process is not explicitly modeled but is implicitly defined by the applications. This complicates tracking and monitoring the user when realizing the tasks. We can observe this problem in both the MMS and LLVR applications. Although a specific process needs to be followed to complete the task, the process is not defined within the application but resides in external documents.

To improve the understandability, reuse, and management of the adopted process we need to explicitly model the process steps that need to be followed in order to complete the task successfully

4. Tool Support and Presentation Issues

One of the key problems in defining embedded user assistance systems is the lack of tools and standard techniques. To the best of our knowledge there is no framework or tool available to support the development of embedded user assistance systems in a modular way. These tools need to support the implementation of user assistance but also take care of the space problem while displaying help in the application window. Traditional user assistance systems which provide off-line documentation do not have space restrictions. However, since help needs to be integrated in embedded user assistance systems, the space for displaying the help becomes inevitably a problem [34]. In general, user assistance specialists are involved in the design of the user interface from the very start to properly design the layout of the user assistance, and as such avoid having to retrofit assistance to an interface later on. Unfortunately, this does not seem to be sufficient and too static to cope with the requirements for changing user assistance later.

To provide systematic support for integration of different help concerns across applications, we aim to provide a framework-based approach. A framework is a reusable, "semi-complete" application that can be specialized to produce custom applications [10]. In our case, it will need to include the abstractions of context-sensitive embedded user assistance which will include modeling the process and the required help.

3   Process-Sensitive User Assistance Model

To provide context-sensitive help based on process state, it is necessary that we model the process first. Process modeling has been addressed in different domains including method engineering and meta-modeling [33]. One of the important process modeling approaches is the OMG Software Process Engineering Meta model (SPEM) [32]. This meta-model is used to describe a concrete software development process or a family of related software development processes. The SPEM specification is deliberately limited for defining the minimal set of process modeling elements necessary to describe any software development process, without adding specific models or constraints for any specific area or discipline. As such it does not include explicit and

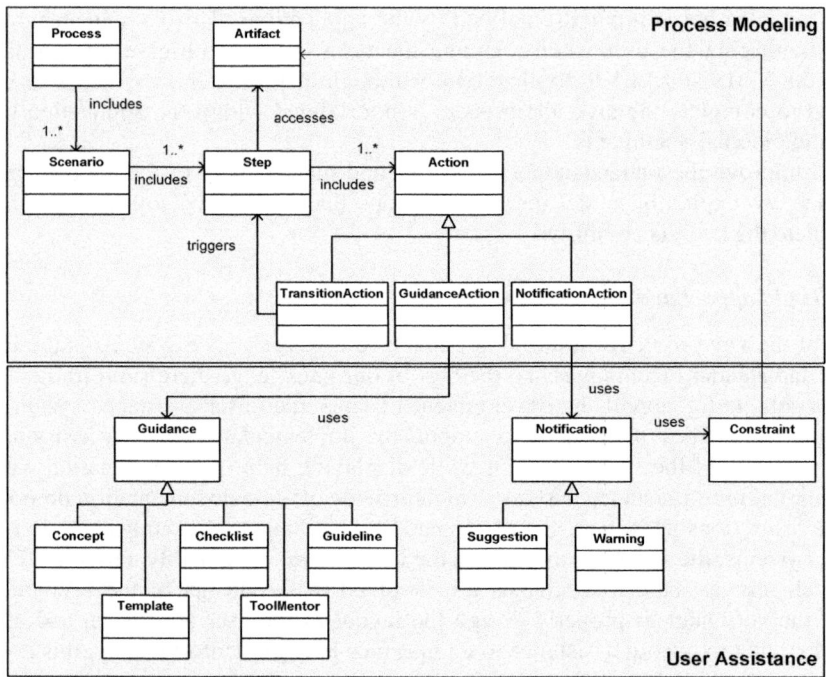

Fig. 3. Process-Sensitive Embedded User Assistance Model

elaborate notions for user assistance concepts. Inspired from SPEM, we have defined a model for process-sensitive user assistance. The model as depicted in Fig. 3 consists of two parts *Process Modeling* and *User Assistance.*

In the *Process Modeling* part, the concept *Process* represents the ordered set of scenarios to accomplish a particular goal in the application. *Scenario* is a particular sequence of steps taken to complete a process. A process may be completed following any of a number of scenarios associated with it. *Step* includes *Actions* that can be triggered through user interface components. There are three types of actions. *Guidance Action* triggers guidance for the current step. *Transition Action* facilitates transition between steps. *Notification Action* defines the notification.

The part *User Assistance* of the model in Fig. 3 defines the concepts necessary for user assistance modeling that can be provided either through *Guidance* or by giving *Notification. Guidance* represents the type of guidance that is provided to the user and defines the types *Concept, Checklist, Template, ToolMentor* and *Guideline. Concept* defines the textual explanation about the step. *Template* defines a predefined document that provides a standardized format for a particular process. *Checklist* is a list of steps that need to be performed to complete a particular scenario. *ToolMentor* shows how to use a specific tool to accomplish a process. *Guideline* is a set of rules and recommendations. *Notification* defines the notification to the user about the validity of the artifacts and can be either *Suggestion* or *Warning. Constraints* are checked when subjected to artifacts to determine if a notification is needed.

4   Tool Architecture and Adopted Approach

We have developed the tool framework *Assistant-Pro* that aims to support the development of process-sensitive embedded user assistance. The tool architecture and the workflow of *Assistant-Pro* are given in Fig. 4. The flow of control is indicated through numbered circles in the figure. The figure shows both, the part of the *Framework* and *Application*. The framework includes the tools, *Process Definition Tool* and *Help Definition Tool* and largely builds on the model as defined in Fig. 3. The tool framework supports four key stakeholders including *Code Analyzer, Process Definer, User Assistance Specialist* and *End-User. Code Analyzer* analyzes the code of the application and annotates this to support the aspect that is generated later on. The *Process Definer* uses the tool *Process Definition Tool* to model the process that need to be followed. Subsequently, the *User Assistance Specialist* uses the *Help Definition* Tool to define the help for the corresponding process steps. The *End-User* will use the application that is extended with help. In the following subsections, we describe the important processes in detail. In Section 4.1, we first explain the process of annotating the application code. In Section 4.2, we explain the modeling of the process using the *Process Definition Tool.* In Section 4.3, we describe the description and association of help to individual steps in the application.

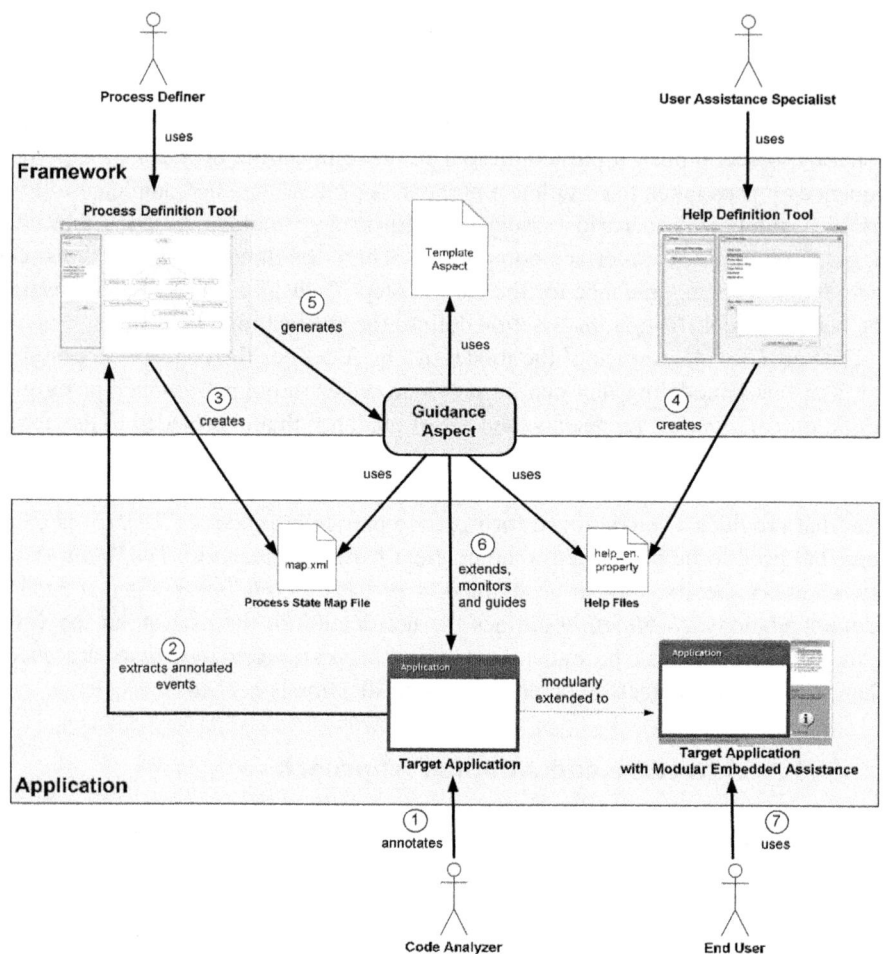

Fig. 4. Tool Architecture and workflow of *Assistant-Pro*

4.1   Analyzing the Code

As depicted in Fig. 4, the first step in the process is the analysis of the application code. Initially, the *Code Analyzer* will annotate the constructor of the main UI component in the application with the annotation *@ApplicationInitialization*. This will be needed later on to initialize the necessary help module and associate a reference of the code with the guidance aspect. Fig. 5 shows an example of the annotated code for the MMS case. Line 2 annotates the method call *mainframe()* with the annotation *@ApplicationInitialization*.

Further, the *Code Analyzer* will analyze the code and determine the different user interface states of the application that correspond to relevant steps in the process to be followed. In parallel, the *Code Analyzer* will determine the method calls (events) in the code that lead to different state transitions. The *Code Analyzer* will annotate these methods with the predefined *@Event()* annotation which has the property *name* to define a unique and relevant name. In Fig. 5 the method call viewMessageButton-Clicked() is annotated with *@Event* and the name "View Message Button Clicked" is given. Note that all the annotation names that we have used here will also appear when defining the process state map in the *Process Definition Tool* in Fig. 6.

```
1.    ....
2.    @ApplicationInitialization
3.    public mainFrame() {
4.    ....
5.    .....
6.    @Event (name = "View Message Button Clicked")
7.    public void viewMessageButtonClicked() {  ...... }
```

Fig. 5. Example of Annotated Application Code

4.2 Modeling the Process Using Process Definition Tool

The *Process Definition Tool* is used by the *Process Definer* to define the required process that needs to be adopted in the application for which help needs to be provided. A snapshot of the tool together with the related steps is depicted in Fig. 6. In the given example the process definition for MMS has been given. To define the process the following actions need to be performed with the tool: (1) extract annotation names from application code, (2) define the state abstractions of the user interface, (3) define the transitions between states, (4) associate transitions with the annotated events of the application, (5) define the processes that represent a set of scenarios.

Extracting annotations from the application is triggered by entering the location of the application when the project is created for the first time (step ② in Fig. 4). *Process Definition Tool* parses the corresponding file, looks for annotated events and describes these in a list that is presented to the *Process Definer*.

Process Definer will define the process by defining the states and the transitions among these states (step ③ in Fig. 4). An example state is *Create Message State* which defines the UI state in which the end-user needs to create a message. The states for the MMS application are shown in the right pane of the tool. The rectangles in the figure represent the states to accomplish the process; the arrows represent the transition between these states. States and transitions can be generated by right clicking the mouse button. Entering a state defines the name of the state. Entering a transition defines the transition between two states, and also associates the transition with the events in the application code. Transitions are associated to the events by referring explicitly to annotations that were derived from the application. By using annotations, a loose coupling with the application code is realized and likewise the *Process Definer* does not need to be bothered about the exact signature of the events in the code that might trigger a state change.

The output of the *Process Definer* is the *Process State Map* file (map.xml in Fig. 4) which defines the total set of states and the transitions. In the given example the process state map starts with *Initial State*, a dummy state to indicate that the application has not started yet. After the MMS application is started, *Menu State* will follow, and from here the user can either go to the *View Message State, Forward Message*

State, Create Message State, and *Reply Message State. Forward Message State* can be followed with *Save Template State, and Select Receiver State. Create Message State* and *Reply Message State* can follow with *Select Receiver State* and *Save Template State.*

In essence, the process state map defines thus the potential number of paths (of state transitions) that the application can traverse. However, not all paths will need to be followed in the end-user application. In the tool we can describe the specific processes that the user has to follow. Each process represents a set of scenarios, thus a specific path traverses through a number of states in the process state map.

An example of such a process as defined in Fig. 6 is *Create Message Process.* For each process we define the name and the final state. For *Create Message Process* typically the final state is defined as *Create Message Save Template State.* The user can be in any state of the program and as such there are usually multiple ways, scenarios, to get to the end state *Create Message Save Template.* While the user will traverse through the states to achieve the final goal, the tool will provide guidance and help as defined in the next section.

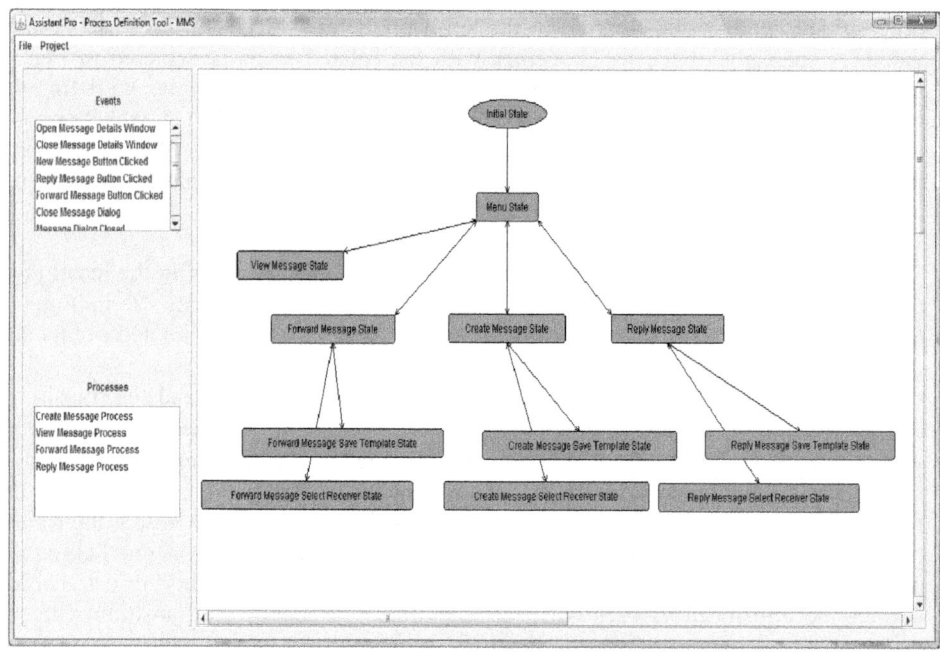

Fig. 6. Snapshot of the Process Definition Tool (for MMS)

4.3   Defining Help Using Help Definition Tool

The role of the *Help Definition Tool* is to define user assistance elements for the states and events (step ④ in Fig. 4). A snapshot of the tool is shown in Fig. 7. In the tool three actions can be performed: *Edit State Hints, Edit Process Names, Edit Event Advices.* By clicking *Edit State Hints,* the textual help description related to a given step can be defined. In Fig. 7, for instance, *Menu State* is selected, and the help description is given in the text field below the menu. *Edit Event Advices* defines the description of the action that the user should do next for each event. *Edit Process Names* is used to describe the process that should be presented to the user. In this way, the user will be provided an explicit description of the process and can follow his/her actions.

The tool also supports the definition of help for multiple languages that are listed in a list box. The *User Assistance Specialist* can create another language and also remove a language by using the tool. For each of the languages in the list the *Help Definition Tool* creates a properties file and saves the *Help Definition*. The help for each Step for each supported language is listed in a tabbed content pane so that it can be viewed, edited, or removed. The *User Assistance Specialist* can select the state from the list, select the language from the supported languages, and enter the help descriptions.

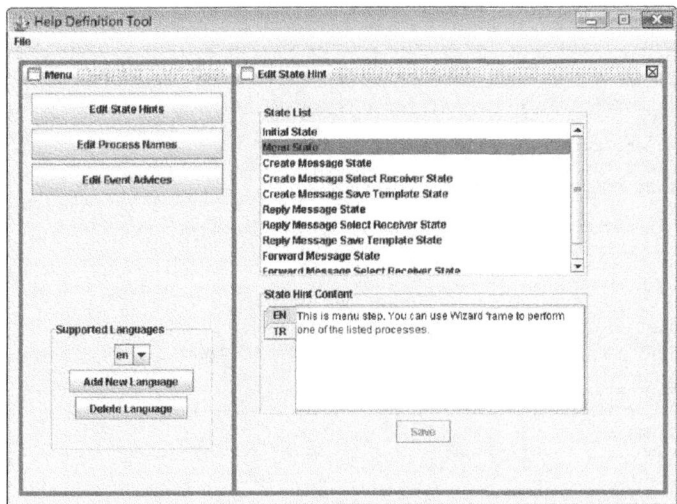

Fig. 7. Snapshot of the Help Definition Tool (for MMS)

5   Implementation and End-User Experience

In this section, we will elaborate on the implementation of the Guidance Aspect in Section 5.1, and in Section 5.2 explain the end-user experience after weaving the aspect.

5.1   Implementation of Guidance Aspect

The guidance of the end-user application is defined by the aspect *Guidance Aspect* as depicted in Fig. 4. In the figure the aspect is located on the border of the framework part with a link to the application in the application part. This is because the aspect is generated (step ⑤ in Fig. 4) within the tool framework, while it will monitor the application at run-time (step ⑥ in Fig. 4).

We have defined an abstract *Guidance Aspect* as given in Fig. 8. The aspect provides abstract methods for reading the process state map file and help file (Line 14-15). Further the aspect defines the abstract pointcuts mainWindow-Initialized() (line 7) and eventTriggered(Event event)(line 17). The pointcut mainWindow-Initialized() is used for capturing the initialization of the application and for initializing the GUI components. The initialization is done using an abstract method initializeMainWindow(mainWindow). The pointcut eventTriggered(Event event) aims to capture the widget events in the application that can cause a transition. It first checks whether the event has resulted in a state change, and if this is the case it will update the help (line 22). The method updateModule() will access the help files and retrieve the help that will need to be presented to the user.

```
1.   package helpmodule;
2.   import java.awt.Component;
3.   import helpmodule.processstatemap.ProcessStateMap;
4.
5.   public abstract aspect GuidanceAspect {
6.   ProcessStateMap map;
7.   abstract pointcut mainWindowInitialized();
8.
9.   after() returning (Window mainWindow): mainWindowInitialized()
10.  { initializeMapInstance();
11.    map.updateState(map.getInitialEvent());
12.    initializeModule(mainWindow);}
13.
14.  abstract void initializeMapInstance();
15.  abstract void initializeModule(Window mainWindow);
16.
17.  abstract pointcut eventTriggered(Event event);
18.  Object around(Event event) : eventTriggered(event)
19.  { Object eventOutput = proceed(event);
20.      boolean stateChanged = map.checkStateChange(event.name(), eventOutput);
21.          if (stateChanged)
22.              updateModule();
23.          return eventOutput; }
24.  abstract void updateModule(); }
```

Fig. 8. Abstract Guidance Aspect

The abstract aspect can be manually specialized by defining a concrete aspect in which the pointcuts, the advices and the necessary code can be implemented. For example, in Fig. 9, *Concrete Manually Defined Guidance Aspect-LLVR* has been defined for the LLVR system as explained in Section 2.1. However, since the points at which help will be provided have been defined earlier on using the *Process Definition Tool* and *Help Definition Tool*, we could implement a generator program that can automatically generate the concrete aspect from the given input. The mechanism for generating the aspect is shown in Fig. 9.

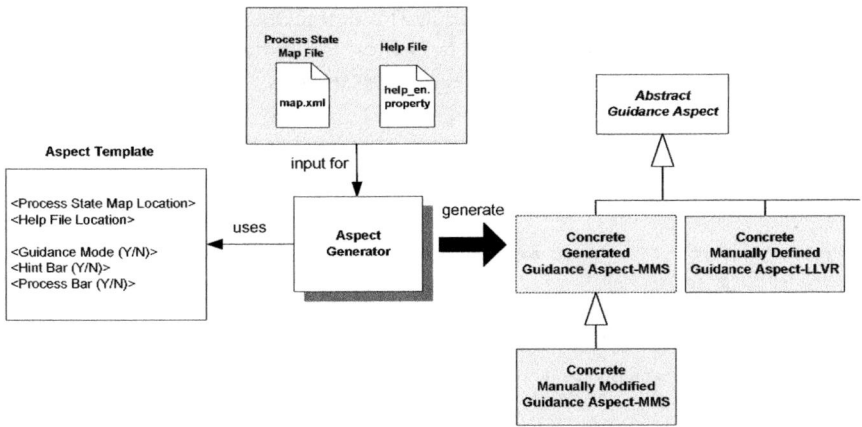

Fig. 9. Generation of Concrete Aspect approach

The input for the generator represents the *Process State Map File* (map.xml) and *Help File* (help_en.property) which have been created before using the *Process Definition Tool* and *Help Definition Tool* as defined in Fig. 4. Further, the generator uses a predefined template in which the aspect codes together with the templates parameters are defined. The actual values for the template parameters are provided when the process definition using the *Process Definition Tool* is finalized.   Thereby, the *Process Definer* can select different configuration options that impact the specific implementation of the *Concrete Guidance Aspect*. By default, these configuration options are the process state map location, help file location, whether an active guidance mode should be applied or not, the decision for visualization of a hint bar, and the decision for visualization of the process bar. Once the parameter values are defined, the *Aspect Generator* generates a concrete aspect that is a specialization of the *Abstract Guidance Aspect*. The dialog menu for generating the concrete guidance aspect is invoked from the File menu in the *Process Definer Tool*. A snapshot of the tool is given in Fig. 10.

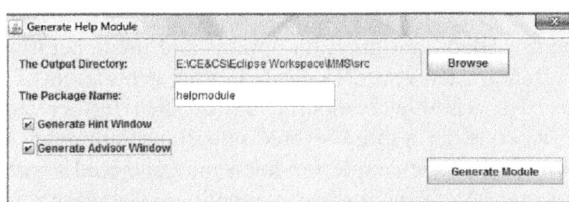

Fig. 10. Dialog for Generating Guidance Aspect

An example of concrete aspect that is generated from the abstract aspect is shown in Fig. 11. Here line 11 defines the concrete pointcut `mainWindowInitialized()` that captures the annotated constructor of the application. In line 14, the concrete pointcut `eventTriggered(Event event)` captures the annotated events that lead to state transitions in the process. The methods `initializeMapInstance()`, initializeModule() and updateModule() define the concrete implementation for accessing the process state map and help files, the initialization of the help modules and the rendering of the help messages, respectively.

```
1.   package helpmodule;
2.   import java.awt.Window;
3.   import helpmodule.processstatemap.ProcessStateMap;
4.   import helpmodule.ui.*;

5.   public aspect MMS-Guidance extends GuidanceAspect{
6.   Window mainWindow;
7.   HelpUIComponent hintUIComponent;
8.   HelpUIComponent advisorUIComponent;
9.   HelpFileAccessor helpAccessor;
10.
11.  pointcut mainWindowInitialized():
12.  call(*.*.new(..)) && @annotation(ApplicationInitialization);
13.
14.  pointcut eventTriggered(Event event) :
         ( execution(*.*.new(..)) || execution(* *(..)) ) && @annotation(event);
15.
16.  public void updateModule()
17.  { hintUIComponent.updateHelpInformation();
        advisorUIComponent.updateHelpInformation();     }
18.
19.  public void initializeMapInstance()
20.  { map =
        ProcessStateMap.readSerializedInstance("src/helpmodule/resources/map.xml");   }
21.
22.  public void initializeModule(Window mainWindow)
23.  { this.mainWindow = mainWindow;
24.
25.  helpAccessor = new HelpFileAccessor("helpmodule.resources");

26.  hintUIComponent = new HintWindow(map, helpAccessor);
27.  hintUIComponent.updateBounds(mainWindow.getBounds());
28.  mainWindow.addComponentListener(new MainWindowListener(hintUIComponent));

29.  advisorUIComponent = new AdvisorWindow(map, helpAccessor);
30.  advisorUIComponent.updateBounds(mainWindow.getBounds());
31.  mainWindow.addComponentListener(new MainWindowListener(advisorUIComponent));

32.  updateModule();     }}
```

Fig. 11. Generated Concrete Guidance Aspect

In general, the provided configuration options and the generation of a concrete aspect might be sufficient. However, if needed, after generation of the concrete guidance aspect, it is also possible to modify and as such further customize the aspect manually. Here, we consider a three layered inheritance approach which is illustrated in Fig. 9. We have given an example in which the generated aspect *Concrete Generated Guidance Aspect-MMS* is further manually extended by *Concrete Manually Modified Guidance Aspect-MMS*.

It should be noted that the abstract *Guidance Aspect* is reusable for all applications in the project that require help. Depending on the nature of each application, the organization might reuse the aspect generator to produce the default help modules or extend either the generated aspect or the abstract aspect to further customize the aspect.

5.2 End-User Experience after Weaving the Aspect

When the application is initialized, the generated aspect weaves the required functionality in the application code. As a result of the weaving process, the application will be monitored for process state changes and the end-user will be guided by the necessary help. As displayed in Fig. 12, by default, the weaving process will add two modular panels to the application: *Hint Bar* on the bottom, and *Process Panel* on the right of the application window. The hint bar provides information about the current context of the application. These are the help descriptions that have been defined for the defined steps using the *Help Definition Tool* in Fig. 7. For each state change, the Guidance Aspect ensures that information is updated whenever the context of the application is changed.

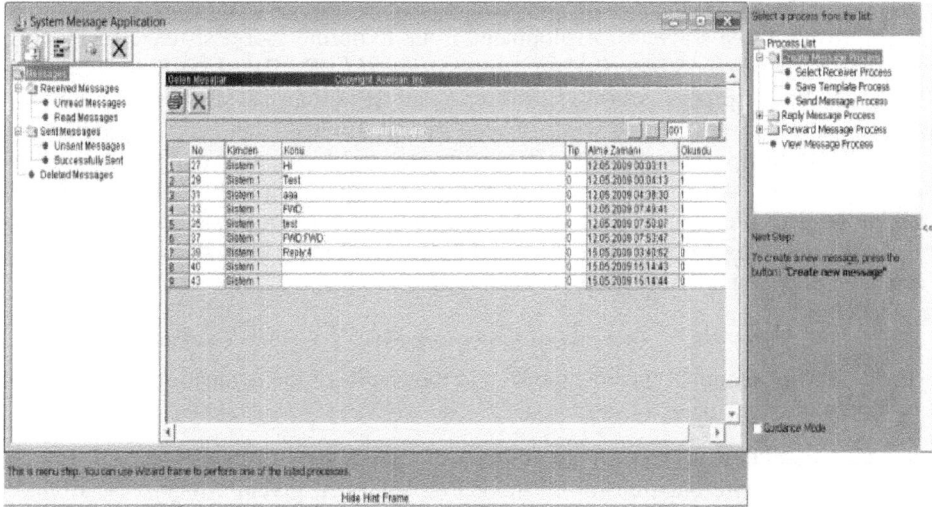

Fig. 12. MMS Application modularly extended with Embedded Help

The *Process Panel* on the right shows the process as defined before using the *Process Definition Tool* in Fig. 6. When the user selects one of the processes on the panel, the instruction for moving to the next step of the process will appear. The message that is presented represents the help description for the transitions that have been defined using the *Help Definition Tool* in Fig. 7. The tool also provides a way to activate a so-called *guidance mode* to ensure that the user can only perform the transitions that are necessary to complete the process. In particular, this guidance mode might be necessary for systems that are safety-critical, when the end-user has to follow the defined process. On the other hand, if guidance mode is not activated, both panels can also be hidden by the user.

Note that the hint bar and process panels are modularly attached to the window of the application. This ensures that no changes need to be made in the original GUI of the application. Likewise the problems of space limitations when integrating context-sensitive help have been eliminated.

The generated aspect provides the default panels which appear to be sufficient for most applications of the Aselsan's applications. However, when a dedicated hint bar or process panel is desired, this can also be relatively easily defined. In this case we have two different options. One possibility is to change the aspect generator resulting in a change of the hint bars and process panels for all the applications for which help was defined. The second option is to refine the Abstract Guidance Aspect manually. The latter option requires manual intervention but the change to the aspect is modular; we do not need to change the existing aspects.

6 Evaluation

One of the key concerns of the developers is to define the process and the related help in a cost-effective manner. To evaluate the cost of using *Assistant-Pro*, the tool has been provided to a software development group to define user assistance for the *Listing and Listening of Voice Records Application (LLVR)*. The LLVR had about the same number of process states (12 in total) and transitions (24 transitions). For each transition, a help description was provided in both English and Turkish and hence 48 help descriptions were provided. The software development group had a standard background in Computer Science and Software Engineering. The time for using the necessary activities of *Assistant-Pro* has been recorded for analysis later on. Based on the following adopted general cost model C for developing embedded user assistance we have provided an evaluation of *Assistant-Pro*:

$$C = C_{Learning} + C_{ProcessAnalysis} + C_{ProcessModeling} + C_{Help} + C_{Implementing\ Aspect}$$

The cost constituents of the cost model and the results of the evaluation are explained below:

- $C_{Learning}$: This is the cost for training the developers in using the tool. For this purpose, a presentation of *Assistant-Pro* has been given, which took around 2 hours together with additional discussions. Before and during the training, the developers were given a 40 page manual of *Assistant-Pro* that they could read in about 4 hours. The tool itself is quite easy to understand since the software developers have in effect to define a kind of state diagram for the possible steps. Since the notion of state diagram was well-known it was not difficult to define the states of the process and the related transitions. Altogether for training costs we can state that it took no more than one working day to train the responsible persons.
- $C_{ProcessAnalysis}$: This is the cost for analyzing the application and defining the potential set of steps and the processes that can be derived from these. In principle this is a domain analysis activity [5] that needs to be carefully done, and actually the time required to complete the activity does not differ with traditional development of embedded user assistance. It should also be stated that the analysis of the application and defining the basic steps is in effect a variable process modeling activity that is dependent on the complexity of the application. The more complex the application is, the more time it will require to define the process steps, transitions and the related help. In any case, although the process modeling

activity needs to be carefully defined it has also an explicit benefit that the developer is forced to think about the process. In fact, the reflection on the process and the modeling supports the reduction of faults that could be integrated in the application if the process is not explicitly defined as is the case in conventional user assistance design. For the process analysis it took around 3 hours to define the steps and the transitions among these steps for the LLVR case.

- $C_{ProcessModeling}$: This is the cost for defining the steps and transitions after the process analysis phase. In fact defining the steps is quite straightforward and consists of adding steps, transitions and processes in the *Process Definition Tool*. As such it took for the developers not more than 2 hours to define the process for the LLVR case.

- C_{Help} : This is the cost for defining the help for the steps and the transitions. This is also a variable cost and depends on the number of steps and transitions in the process that needs guidance. For the LLVR case, it took around 2 and a half hours to define the related help to the steps and transitions. In practice, only simple, one-sentence-based text phrases were defined.

- $C_{Implementing\ Aspect}$: A final cost of the tool is the implementation of the aspect which is dependent on whether the aspect is generated or (manually) extended. In case of generation, the Guidance Aspect is generated in the *Process Definition Tool* and this has a largely negligible cost. In case of extension the cost is related to overriding the abstract pointcuts and methods, and for this it is required that the developer has a basic knowledge of aspect-oriented programming. In our case, the time for defining the pointcut and integrating (weaving) the aspect in the application took about 3 hours (by an AOP programmer).

The cost model and the related reasoning supported the business case for transitioning to an embedded user-assistance approach using *Assistant-Pro*. Aselsan selected the two example applications that we have described in this paper as pilot studies. Based on the evaluation done by Aselsan using the above cost model, evaluation of both case studies was very positive.

7 Discussion and Lessons Learned

The development of embedded user assistance is not trivial and this is even further complicated if context-sensitive assistance is required. One of the key obstacles is certainly the crosscutting nature of the help concerns. The tool *Assistant-Pro* that we have discussed is implemented within the industrial context of Aselsan.

Initially, Aselsan adopted the traditional cycle of developing user assistance (non-embedded) which had several obstacles. The nature of the applications that are developed by Aselsan (process-sensitive, safety-critical) defined the key motivations to develop an improved embedded user assistance system that could track the process, and be reusable for a broad set of applications. The company already had mature knowledge on user assistance systems and experienced maintenance problems in the regeneration and updating of user manuals for multiple applications in case of changes to the process or the application. Although the main cause of the required maintenance activities seemed to be the crosscutting nature of guidance concerns, the decision for an aspect-oriented solution, however, was not straightforward. In fact deciding for a new user assistance development approach would mean that the (user assistance development) processes at Aselsan had to be redefined. On the other hand the topic of aspect-oriented software development was already known to the company because of earlier consultancy and education activities in this domain. Together with the structural maintenance problems and a possible promising solution it was decided to analyze the aspect-oriented design solution and based on this, define two pilot projects as to evaluate the approach as proposed by *Assistant-Pro.*

The results of the two pilot studies were very positively evaluated both by the upper level management and the senior development team. In fact *Assistant-Pro* appeared to have several benefits for the organization that we could categorize as general advantages of embedded user assistance systems, and additional, specific advantages related to the adopted approach in Assistant-Pro.

General Advantages

- *Fewer faults*

The cost for user assistance development is not only reduced due to the integrated help, but also as a result of explicit, context-based guidance. In this way users avoid making faults, and as such the costs related to usage of the tools, and the costs that would be derived from wrong usage are further reduced. Using the active guidance mode in *Assistant-Pro,* the need for repeating tasks several times or moving back and forth over the process to obtain the best results is eliminated.

- *Communication between User Assistance Specialist and Developer*

In conventional user assistance development, the tasks of the user assistance specialist and the developers are strictly separated and there is less communication among both. The lack of communication between the user assistant specialist and the developers lead to problems in defining and aligning the appropriate help for the process states. In embedded user assistance, this problem is eliminated because a close cooperation between the *User Assistance Specialist* and the software developer is required. The *User Assistance Specialist* should normally be the person to design the layout of the user assistance and to write all the content, whereas the software developer will mainly be responsible for the technical implementation. Similarly, *Assistant-Pro* provides a common platform for communication between the *User Assistance Specialist* and *Developer.* One could argue that the introduction of explicit communication channels will also add additional costs to the organization. This is however not a problem of our approach, but of embedded user assistance in general.

Specific Advantages

- *Enhanced support for End-Users*

For the end-users it is important that assistance is given at the right time and right place in the application. With *Assistant-Pro,* help can be relatively easily defined based on the context. We have focused on the process context and as such explicitly modeled the process. Early validation of the tool *Assistant-Pro* shows promising results. In fact the information on the process that was earlier provided in PDF documents or Wiki pages is now defined in the *Assistant-Pro Help Definer Tool,* and later on delivered as modular help as shown in Fig. 12. With the application the end-user can even be strictly guided through the process, where faulty steps are prevented.

- *Modular and Reusable Guidance*

Although we are developing *embedded* user assistance, the help concern is not embedded in the application but modularly integrated. In case of required changes to the help concern this can be easily located and adapted to the new needs by updating the aspects. All the information is stored in XML files and aspects can access these files to define embedded user assistance. Through defining aspects and automating weaving of help concerns in the final application, the complexity of the help concerns is also reduced and maintenance is substantially improved with respect to the earlier process followed. The aspect generator and the generated guidance aspects can be reused for multiple applications.

- *Solving the Space Problem because of Modular UI Extension*

Not only the system is designed in a modular way but also the panes for rendering the help, such as hint bar and process bar, are modularly extended to the original window of the application. Although the user assistance is integrated in the application it does not occupy the space of the original application. Because of this modular UI extension we have solved the space problem that relates to embedded user assistance systems in general. In general this is considered as one of the important problems when developing embedded user assistance systems.

- *Integration with legacy code*

Many applications are not developed from scratch but reside in the project as legacy code that cannot be easily removed. Most of this legacy code however still requires guidance. Since aspects are used to define help, it is now also possible to define help for legacy code. This was very hard if not impossible in earlier approaches.

- *Overall Cost of Help Documentation, Training, and Usage*

In the former approach besides creating the manuals, an additional cost was required for the stakeholders to understand and use the guidance documents. In case the process and the related documentation was not clear or too complex, this soon resulted in the demand for extra training, leading to additional, often unforeseen costs. With *Assistant-Pro* the documentation is not separate but part of the application. Assistance is provided to the user whenever necessary. In fact, because of the active guidance definition, we can state that the training is defined whenever the user starts using the tools. This situation leads to a reduced number of demands for training and as such a reduced overall cost related to user assistance for the application in the organization.

8 Related Work

Two of the main distinguishing characteristics of Aspect-Oriented Programming (AOP) systems is that they allow quantified programmatic assertions over programs written by programmers oblivious to such assertions [12]. In our approach we have used an annotation based approach and as such somehow explicitly declared the points that we would like to give advice to. A key reason for adopting annotation-based AOP is to define expressive and robust pointcuts [17][22][25]. Alternatives to annotation-based pointcut descriptions very often select joinpoints based on the signatures of language elements based on naming conventions or structural patterns. It has been shown that such pointcut descriptions are more fragile and either fail to catch the required joinpoints or catch undesired joinpoints. Annotations can provide semantic information that are attached to the required places in the code and as such can support the definition of robust pointcuts. In our case we have to deal with user assistance for process-sensitive systems, which are very often mission-critical in defense applications. Hereby, the definition of robust pointcuts is a strict requirement and it is not acceptable that either the wrong process element is caught or somehow a process element is missed due to an inappropriate pointcut description.

In our approach, process guidance consists of modeling the process that needs to be adopted and the corresponding help that is defined for the process steps. Process modeling has been addressed in different domains including method engineering [6] [19][29] and meta-modeling [33]. A particular approach for process modeling is *situational method engineering* which is targeted at creating method components rather than complete methodologies and tailoring them to specific situations or context at hand [28]. Several efforts have been made to standardize situational method engineering, which has led to, for example, the OPEN Process Framework (OPF) [26][37], OMG's Software Process Engineering Metamodel (SPEM) [32], and ISO/IEC 24744 [21]. These proposals have been used for modeling methods for different purposes but we do not know of any approach that model the process for providing active user assistance. In our project, the context for the process, or methodology that needs to be followed, was primarily defined by the various command and control applications. In general, situational method engineering and process modeling approaches provide a broader set of method fragment types than that we have defined. But the limitations of the method fragment types was a deliberate design decision since in the project it was neither necessary nor required to define a detailed set of method fragments. The project constraints required that the process modeling had to be as simple as possible to decrease the learning curve and increase its practical use for the average engineer. Nevertheless, we think that the presented approach is general and, if required, the process metamodel could be enhanced with new method fragment types to support the user assistance approach.

For implementing the process guidance we have adopted an AOP approach together with a process modeling approach. The adoption of the techniques that we used was mainly defined by the industrial context of the project. Most projects that needed help were developed in object-oriented languages and there was a mature developer expertise in this context. In fact, for monitoring the process steps we have also analyzed the application of object-oriented design patterns. For example the *Observer* pattern (also known as *Publish-Subscribe*, or *Listener*) is particularly useful for graphical applications. Using this pattern one or more objects (the subscribers) register their interest in being notified of changes to another object (the publisher). In our case we might have defined a *GenericListener* (instead of *GenericAspect)* and register it with each GUI element. Unfortunately, as it has been described in the literature [15][18][24], the invasive nature of pattern implementations and the scattering and tangling of such an implementation with the base code may reduce the modularity of the system, thus affecting its understandability and maintainability. Compared to patterns the AOP solution in our case seemed also to be more powerful. First of all, by using an aspect instead of a pattern we avoided the necessary refactorings that were required to provide guidance functionality to the existing code. For several legacy applications that required guidance, refactoring was very hard or not possible. Moreover, using an aspect we could be more selective in providing guidance to the process actions. Process definers could easily experiment with different pointcut descriptions to define the appropriate guidance. Further, the guidance aspect was only woven into the selected GUI components.

9 Conclusions

In this paper we have presented our experiences in an industrial project for defining an aspect-oriented tool framework for context-sensitive embedded user assistance. The problems were derived directly from the context of the industrial projects of Aselsan in which multiple applications are developed that require guidance for the users with respect to the state of the process. Unfortunately, user assistance so far was largely defined using conventional user assistance techniques that define help separately from the application. The problems related to both, the end-user perspective and developer perspective, have clearly been encountered by Aselsan. In particular we have focused on the problem of the crosscutting nature of help concerns, reuse across multiple applications, lack of explicit process and the necessity for tool support. Existing approaches failed to provide a solution to at least one of these problems. Although existing approaches can be sufficient for defining help when we consider the definition of relatively simple help support such as tool-tips, defining help based on the process-context did not seem trivial. Usually the defined solutions are too static and cannot easily track the changes of the process state and provide the related help at run-time.

To address the problems we have developed the aspect-oriented tool framework *Assistant-Pro* for defining embedded user assistance for guiding the end user with respect to the process state. One of the key problems in defining embedded user assistance is the crosscutting nature of help concerns and to solve this problem, the need for aspect-oriented techniques was necessary. As such in the framework we have modularized and implemented help concerns as aspects. In principle, we did not encounter any difficult problems in doing this. Moreover, we were also able to reuse the aspects for defining different help concerns. For tackling the issue of guidance with respect to a process, we have provided a model that integrates both process modeling and guidance concepts. The conceptual model has been realized in the framework and is used by the tools of *Assistant-Pro*. Modularization of the guidance concern into an aspect here is the driving solution, but it should be noted that the aspect itself is also loosely coupled from the process state and the help definitions. The strength and novelty of our solution is not in the isolated parts but in the integration and the coordination of the different parts.

The tool has been evaluated with respect to a cost model that we have defined and the concerns of the relevant stakeholder. Our analysis shows firstly that the tool can be used by the developers with relatively little effort to develop the process model and the related user assistance systems. For the end users, the key advantage is that the help is now embedded in the system, so that they do not waste time when help is needed. This reduces the cost for additional training about usage of the tools. Further, since end users are explicitly guided by the predefined process, the chance of making faults is substantially reduced.

In fact the framework as such is complete and is tested for different applications. In our future work we will continue the technology transfer activities and apply the framework for a broader set of applications.

Acknowledgments

We would like to thank the anonymous reviewers for their extensive and very useful feedback. Different persons have participated in discussions throughout the Embedded User Assistance project. We would like to thank Alper Bostancı, Baki Demirel, and Özgü Özköse Erdoğan from Aselsan-REHIS group, and Feyyaz Ertugrul and Mert Özkaya from Bilkent University.

References

1. Aselsan, http://www.aselsan.com.tr/default.asp?lang=en (accessed March 2010)
2. AspectJ Development Tools (AJDT), http://www.eclipse.org/ajdt/ (accessed on September 2009)
3. Ames, A.: Just what they need, just when they need it: An introduction to embedded assistance. In: Proceedings of the 19th Annual International Conference on Computer Documentation, pp. 111–115. ACM Press, New York (2001)
4. Andrade, O.D., Novick, D.G.: Expressing help at appropriate levels. In: Proceedings of the 26th Annual ACM International Conference on Design of Communication, Lisbon, Portugal, September 22-24 (2008)
5. Beyer, H., Holtzblatt, K.: Contextual Design: A Customer-Centered Approach to Systems Designs. Morgan Kaufmann, San Francisco (1997)
6. Brinkkemper, S.: Method engineering: engineering of information systems development methods and tools. Information and Software Technology 38(4), 275–280 (1996)
7. Czarnecki, K., Eisenecker, U.: Generative Programming: Methods, Tools, and Applications. Addison-Wesley, Reading (2000)
8. Elrad, T., Fillman, R., Bader, A.: Aspect-Oriented Programming. Communication of the ACM 44(10) (October 2001)
9. Ellison, M.: Embedded user assistance: The future for software help? Interactions 14(1), 30–31 (2007)
10. Fayad, M.E., Schmidt, D.: Object-Oriented Application Frameworks. Communication of the ACM 40(10) (October 1997)
11. Fast-Help, http://www.fast-help.com/ (accessed on September 2009)
12. Filman, R., Friedman, D.: Aspect-oriented programming is quantification and Obliviousness. In: Proc. of the Workshop on Advanced Separation of Concerns, in conjunction with OOPSLA (2000)

13. Galitz, W.O.: The Essential Guide to User Interface Design: An Introduction to GUI Design Principles and Techniques. Wiley, Chichester (2007)
14. Gamma, E., et al.: Design Patterns: Elements of Reusable Object-Oriented Software. Addison-Wesley, Reading (1995)
15. Garcia, A.F., Sant'Anna, C., Figueiredo, E., Kulesza, U., Pereira de Lucena, C.J., von Staa, A.: Modularizing design patterns with aspects: a quantitative study. In: AOSD, pp. 3–14 (2005)
16. Grayling, T.: If we build it, will they come? A usability test of two browser-based embedded help systems. Technical Communication 49(2), 193–209 (2002)
17. Gybels, K., Brichau, J.: Arranging language features for patternbased crosscuts. In: Aksit, M. (ed.) Proc. of 2nd Int' Conf. on Aspect-Oriented Software Development, pp. 60–69 (March 2003)
18. Hannemann, J., Kiczales, G.: Design Patterns Implementation in Java and AspectJ. In: Proc. of Object Oriented Programming Systems Languages and Applications 2002 (OOPSLA 2002), pp. 161–173 (November 2002)
19. Henderson-Sellers, B., France, R., Georg, G., Reddy, R.: A method engineering approach to developing aspect-oriented modeling processes based on the OPEN process framework. Information and Software Technology 49(7), 761–773 (2007)
20. Ter Hofstede, A.H.M., Verhoef, T.F.: On the feasibility of situational method engineering. Information Systems 22, 401–422 (1997)
21. ISO/IEC. ISO/IEC 24744, Software Engineering – Metamodel for Development Methodologies, 1st edn. (2007)
22. Laddad, R.: AOP and metadata: A perfect match. In: AOP@Work Series, IBM Technical Library (March 2005)
23. Miller, M.G.: Writing User Documentation: Hints For Document Writers, 2nd edn., CreateSpace (2009)
24. Monteiro, M.P., Fernandes, J.M.: Towards a catalog of Aspect Oriented Refactorings. In: Proc. of Aspect Oriented Software Developmnet, AOSD 2005 (2005)
25. Nagy, I., Bergmans, L., Havinga, W., Aksit, M.: Utilizing design information in aspect-oriented programming. In: Proceedings of International Conference Net.ObjectDays, NODe2005, Gesellschaft für Informatik, GI. Lecture Notes in Informatics (2005)
26. OPEN Process Framework (OPF) Web Site, http://www.opfro.org/
27. Ray, D.S., Ray, E.J.: Embedded help: Background and applications for technical communicators. Technical Communication 48(1), 105–115 (2001)
28. Ralyté, J., Rolland, C.: An assembly process model for method engineering. In: Dittrich, K.R., Geppert, A., Norrie, M.C. (eds.) CAiSE 2001. LNCS, vol. 2068, pp. 267–283. Springer, Heidelberg (2001)
29. Rolland, C., Prakash, N., Benjamen, A.: A multi-model view of process modelling. Requirements Eng. J. 4(4), 169–187 (1999)
30. Sleeter, M.E.: Online help systems: Technological evolution or revolution? In: Proceedings of the 14th Annual International Conference on Computer Documentation Conference, pp. 87–94. ACM Press, Research Triangle Park (1996)
31. Smith, D.: Developing online application help. Hewlett Packard Journal 45(2), 90–95 (1994)
32. Software Process Engineering Metamodel Specification, Object Management Group Inc. (2006), http://www.omg.org/technology/documents/formal/spem.htm

33. Stahl, T., Voelter, M.: Model-Driven Software Development: Technology, Engineering, Management. Wiley, Chichester (2006)
34. Tidwell, J.: Designing Interfaces: Patterns for Effective Interaction Design. O'Reilly Media, Sebastopol (2007)
35. Turk, K.L., Nichols, M.C.: Online help systems: Technological evolution or revolution? In: Proceedings of the 14th Annual International Conference on Computer Documentation Conference, pp. 239–242. ACM Press, New York (1996)
36. Weber, J.H.: Is the Help Helpful? How to Create Online Help That Meets Your Users' Needs. Hentzenwerke Publishing (2004)
37. Zowghi1, D., Firesmith, D.G., Henderson-Sellers, B.: Using the OPEN Process Framework to Produce a Situation-Specific Requirements Engineering Method. In: Proceedings of SREP 2005, pp. 29–30 (2005)

Author Index

GPSR Compliance

*The European Union's (EU) General Product Safety Regulation (GPSR)
is a set of rules that requires consumer products to be safe and our
obligations to ensure this.*

*If you have any concerns about our products, you can contact us on
ProductSafety@springernature.com*

In case Publisher is established outside the EU, the EU authorized
representative is:

Springer Nature Customer Service Center GmbH
Europaplatz 3
69115 Heidelberg, Germany

Batch number: 09490872

Printed by Printforce, the Netherlands